For decades, the nuclear arms race diverted attention from the immense numbers of civilian casualties caused by indiscriminate antipersonnel weapons, like land mines. This book describes in chilling detail why these 'conventional' weapons have been aptly called 'weapons of mass destruction in slow motion'.

Patrick Leahy, United States Senator

This admirably documented study will bring home to all military men and students of war the appalling long-term damage wrought by the smallest and most commonplace of weapons.

General Sir Hugh Beach, Vice-Chairman,
Council for Arms Control, London

Thoroughly researched and authoritative, Eric Prokosch's book starkly brings into question what is 'conventional' about a class of weapons which have brought death and destruction to so many millions. A brilliant, informative, and desperately needed study.

Dr Jonathan E. Fine, former Executive Director,
Physicians for Human Rights

A ground-breaking book which will alert those campaigning against land mines to the dangers of a host of other antipersonnel weapons.

Robert O. Muller, Vietnam Veterans of America Foundation

A clearly and persuasively argued insight into the ways in which international agreements on the restriction of excessively injurious and indiscriminate weapons are reached.

Françoise Hampson, Reader in Law, University of Essex

Its treatment of Vietnam discloses some of the most savage tactics used there by the US military.

George McT. Kahin, Professor of International Relations Emeritus,
Cornell University

In his timely and valuable book, Eric Prokosch has accomplished an impressive feat. He has turned a subject which is shocking and depressing into an engrossing account of the modern technology of killing.

His exposé of the vast arsenal of killing machines called 'antipersonnel weapons' is written in clear, lively language, backed up by a comprehensive record of historical and technical references. This gives the book great professional value to researchers as well as providing new information and insights for readers concerned about the growing inhumanity of modern warfare.

As an aviator in the US Navy for 35 years, I necessarily had first-hand knowledge of the evolution of antipersonnel weapons. Nevertheless, Mr Prokosch's book greatly expands my understanding, and horror, of these infernal devices and reinforces my support for international sanctions against their use.

Perhaps the most gripping element of this book is the detailed description of the weapons themselves. It is undeniably clear that immense effort and human ingenuity have gone into the design and testing of these weapons, but absolutely no thought or concern has been given to the indiscriminate nature of their effects. In truth, these are anti-human being weapons, military and civilian alike, and it is deeply distressing that so much effort and treasure has been devoted to creating this threat to humankind.

Admiral Eugene J. Carroll Jr (Ret),
Center for Defense Information, Washington

Eric Prokosch holds a Ph.D. in anthropology from Stanford University, and has taught at the University of Wisconsin. He began doing research on antipersonnel weapons in 1966 as part of the US antiwar movement, and has become one of the foremost experts on the subject outside defense circles. He has worked for National Action/Research on the Military Industrial Complex, a project of the American Friends Service Committee, and is now working at the International Secretariat of Amnesty International. He attended the two Government Experts' Conferences on Certain Conventional weapons on behalf of the Friends World Committee for Consultation (Quakers). His articles on antipersonnel weapons have appeared in many newspapers and magazines, including *The New Republic, U.S. Catholic, International Social Science Journal,* and *International Review of the Red Cross.*

THE TECHNOLOGY OF KILLING

*A Military and Political History of
Antipersonnel Weapons*

ERIC PROKOSCH

ZED BOOKS
London & New Jersey

The Technology of Killing:
A Military and Political History of Antipersonnel Weapons
was first published by Zed Books Ltd,
7 Cynthia Street, London N1 9JF, UK, and 165 First Avenue,
Atlantic Highlands, New Jersey 07716, USA, in 1995

Cover photograph: BLU-26 'guava' bomblet casings. Each of these
spherical, one-pound antipersonnel bomblets is embedded with three
hundred $7/32$-inch steel balls. The bomblets are designed to spin so
that they will disperse over a wide area when released from an
airborne dispenser. Some bomblets have delay fuzes to prolong the
effect of the attack. Nearly 285 million 'guava' bomblets are believed
to have been dropped on Vietnam, Laos, and Cambodia in the
course of the US–Indochina war. (North Vietnamese photo.)
Cover designed by Andrew Corbett

Typeset in Monotype Garamond by Lucy Morton, London SE12
Printed and bound in the United Kingdom
by Biddles Ltd, Guildford and King's Lynn

A catalogue record for this book is available from the British Library
US CIP data is available from the Library of Congress

ISBN 1 85649 357 1 Hb
ISBN 1 85649 358 x Pb

CONTENTS

Foreword
by Robert O. Muller   ix

Preface
by Yves Sandoz   xi

Introduction   1

1 The Science of Wound Ballistics   10

Early Research: The Study of the 'Explosive Wound' 11
World War II: Research in Great Britain 15
The Princeton Group: Origins and Experimental Setup 17
The Princeton Findings: Temporary Cavity, Permanent Cavity,
    and Effects on Different Parts of the Body 18
The Mathematics of Wounding 20
Battle Casualty Surveys 22
The Study of Accidents 25
Wound Ballistics at the End of World War II 26

2 Korea: The Redesign of Antipersonnel Weapons   30

Fragmentation, Source of 'Kill Mechanisms' 33
World War II: Criteria for 'Fatal or Severe Wounding' 33
Korea: Criteria for 'Rapid Incapacitation' 35
Controlled Fragmentation: The M26 Grenade 37
Pre-Fragmentation: The Claymore Mine 38
Natural Fragmentation: Cast-Iron Shells 39
Rifle Fire: The ORO Study 41
Mr Barr's Deadly Dart 44

3 Vietnam: Weapons for Counterinsurgency   53

Controlled Fragmentation: The 40mm Grenade 56
Natural Fragmentation: The 2.75-inch Rocket 58
Lighter Bullets: The M16 Rifle 60

Artillery in Vietnam: 'Firing on a Vill' 61
New Directions in Natural Fragmentation:
    The Development of High Fragmentation Steels 63
Canisters and Beehives: The Story of a 'Nasty Thing' 67
Fuzes, Brains of Munitions 71

4   Clusters of Guavas   81

Cluster Bombs against North Vietnam: Early Reports 83
'Guava' Bombs as Seen from the Other Side:
    Allegations and Denials 87
A War against Civilians? 93
A Profusion of Clusters 98
'Improved Conventional Munitions' for Artillery 105
Aerial Mines 107
The Munitions of Vietnam: Implications for Future Wars 111

5   Tackling the Merchants of Death   126

Notes from a Napalm Scrapbook 126
The Corporate Image 131
A Company with Human Feelings 135

6   Banning Antipersonnel Weapons through International Law   148

Lucerne, 1974: Taming the Rash Swedes 149
Lugano, 1976: An Emerging Consensus 155
The 1980 Conventional Weapons Convention 160
Grounds for Weapons Bans: Humanitarian Protection
    versus 'Military Necessity' 163
The Role of the Public Conscience 168

7   The Future of Antipersonnel Weapons: Control or Chaos?   176

The Proliferation of Antipersonnel Technologies 176
New Weapons Used in New Wars 178
A New Humanitarian Response: The Landmines Campaign 181
New Moves for International Bans: The 1995 Review Conference
    of the Conventional Weapons Convention 185
Bringing the 1899 Dum-Dum Ban up to Date 190
The Future of Antipersonnel Weapons 193

Bibliography   202

Conversion Table   210

Index   211

ACKNOWLEDGEMENTS

The author wishes to acknowledge the assistance and advice of Dennis Aftergut, Molly Babize, Eric M. Bergerud, Gérald Cauderay, William Coleman, Thomas Cook, Robin M. Coupland, Marv Davidov, Leroy L. Doig III, Louise Doswald-Beck, Philippe Eberlin, Bert Fowler, David Goodman, Christopher J. Greenwood, Françoise Hampson, Peter Herby, Bo Janzon, George McT. Kahin, Arthur Kanegis, Sergei Kapitza, Michael T. Klare, Frank Knemeyer, Beat P. Kneubuehl, Fay Knopp, Lê Anh Tú, Adam Lloyd, Malvern Lumsden, Marilyn McNabb, Julian Perry-Robinson, Neil Pilfold, Andy and Michael Prokosch, David Ransom, Diana Roose, Bo Rybeck, Nicholas A. Sims, Dan Smith, Gladys Taylor, Carl Vohs, and the many ordnance engineers and military officers who explained their craft to him. The conclusions presented are the author's own.

The research and production of the book were supported in part by a grant from the Joseph Rowntree Charitable Trust.

'Antipersonnel: Designed to destroy or obstruct personnel.'
The United States Air Force Dictionary (1956)

FOREWORD

Those of us who have become involved in the problem over the past fifteen years have come to realize that land mines are atrocious killers. These insidious weapons lie scattered in staggering numbers across the countryside and over former battlefields in scores of countries. Those who fall victim to them are the most vulnerable in society: the innocents, the poorest of the poor. They are the ones who forage in the countryside, knowing that there are mines out there, because they are driven to do so by economic necessity.

The proliferation of land mines shows that the very nature of warfare has been changing. Whereas in World War I, 5 per cent of the casualties were civilians, in World War II it was 50 per cent; in the latter part of the 1980s, 90 per cent of the casualties were civilians.

In Cambodia I have seen villages that stand within minefields, where there are mines literally within meters of houses in which people are living. I have seen the laudable efforts of nongovernmental organizations carrying out de-mining. I gone through the hospitals and heard the screaming of the people who have been blown up by land mines. The emotional connection to the issue is what drives me and many others to work for a complete ban on the use, production, trade and stockpiling of antipersonnel mines.

The campaign against land mines has seen remarkable successes in the few years since it began. When the one-year moratorium on the trafficking of antipersonnel mines enacted by the United States Congress in 1992 came up for renewal in 1993, a three-year extension of the moratorium was approved by the Senate in a roll-call vote of 100 to 0. This extraordinary demonstration of strength resonated in the White House and was reflected later in the year in the adoption by the United Nations General Assembly of a US-sponsored resolution calling for an international moratorium on the export and trafficking of antipersonnel mines. Many other countries have enacted similar moratoria. One of Sweden's major weapons manufacturers has said it will quit the production of antipersonnel mines and will even stop exporting fuzes and detonators to those who might use them for the production of land mines.

Despite the achievements, we are still losing ground. In Cambodia today there are still more mines being laid than there are being cleared. The same can be said of many other areas around the world. More mines laid, more money spent, more casualties, more frustration to peacekeeping and humanitarian efforts.

Eric Prokosch's book gives new insight into the problem of land mines by showing where these weapons came from and how they were developed. It demonstrates that today's antipersonnel weapons are a legacy of the wars in Korea and Vietnam – a legacy with which we are still coming to terms. Those of us working to end the scourge of land mines will learn from this book that the problem is much wider. There is a host of modern antipersonnel weapons whose legality, desirability, and effects on soldiers and civilians need to be reconsidered.

This eloquent book offers a great challenge to today's activists. I commend it to all who are concerned about the devastation wrought by modern warfare.

Robert O. Muller, Executive Director,
Vietnam Veterans of America Foundation

PREFACE

In writing this military and political history of antipersonnel weapons, Eric Prokosch has rendered a signal service, for today there is a crucial need to recapitulate the origins, development, and present state of thinking on a subject that has become more topical than ever. Diplomats are currently engaged in reviewing the 1980 Convention on Prohibitions or Restrictions on Certain Conventional Weapons, and at the same time large-scale campaigns are being launched to increase public awareness of the persistent problem of antipersonnel mines – that veritable scourge, in human and ecological terms, which every day kills and maims countless innocent people, devastates vast regions and prevents the return of those who have fled from combat zones.

In doing so, Eric Prokosch comes up against the stumbling-block that always arises when attempts are made to propose humanitarian standards applicable to armed conflicts: the stumbling-block of public incomprehension. Why seek to humanize war rather than work for its prohibition? The International Committee of the Red Cross, which has been the initiator of modern international humanitarian law from its very origin – the Geneva Convention of 1864 – has constantly been obliged to explain itself on this score.

Even though in the last century war was theoretically accepted in the international system as a continuation of politics by other means (according to von Clausewitz's famous formula), the Committee made it clear from the very beginning that its commitment to 'humanizing' armed conflict was in no way an argument in favor of war. Indeed, had not one of its members, Louis Appia, stated during the very year of the adoption of the 1864 Convention: 'Let us loudly proclaim our grief, our pain at being unable to do more, let us protest against the great collective iniquity that goes by the name of war'? But the success of the Red Cross and its ideas lies in the fact that it has been able to propose a modest but effective step toward resolving a specific and clear-cut humanitarian issue, by standing apart from rather than at the heart of that fundamental political debate on peace which has persisted through-out our century: from the Hague Conferences of 1899 and 1907 to the Covenant of the League of Nations in 1919; from this covenant to the United Nations Charter of 1945; and from this charter to our day.

Alas, it is only too evident that this debate, revived at the end of the Cold War and appropriately relaunched in the 'Agenda for Peace' proposed in 1993 by the United Nations Secretary-General, Boutros Boutros-Ghali, failed to prevent the holocaust and other appalling massacres.

The initiator of the Red Cross and the very first Geneva Convention, Henry Dunant, derived his convictions from the horrifying sight of thousands of wounded soldiers left to die without care on the battlefield of Solferino in 1859, the evening after a bloody encounter between French and Austrian troops. His immediate reaction was to come to the aid of those hapless men and to improvise assistance for them. But his indignation, expressed in his book *A Memory of Solferino*, which created a great stir throughout Europe, did not prompt him to make any grandiloquent proposals for eternal peace, which would probably have gone up in smoke. His incisive and clear-cut message was the following: how can you neglect the young men whom you use to defend your cause, if not your country, to the point of failing to care for them when they lie wounded on the battlefield? The message was heard, and it led to the adoption in 1864 of the initial Geneva Convention, which served as the fountainhead of modern international humanitarian law and of the whole history of the Red Cross. According to the concept already advocated by Jean-Jacques Rousseau, a soldier should be regarded as an enemy only while he constitutes a threat. Once wounded, he becomes nothing but a victim who is entitled to assistance. It must then be possible to render him such assistance – whence the basic idea of the 'neutralization' of medical field personnel. These 'neutralized' soldiers must be duly recognized to enable them to carry out their duties, and the protective emblem of the red cross was instituted to that end. Therein lies the whole simple but ingenious structure of the initial Geneva Convention.

The reason why I have dwelt at some length on the original purpose of international humanitarian law is that these explanations remain as necessary today as they were in the past, the more so since the prodigious technical developments which this century has both initiated and witnessed, and the emergence of nuclear weapons that could annihilate humankind, have made it more vital than ever to build a world in which there will be no place for war. This has now become a question of mankind's very survival.

We know, however, that building this new world will take time, and that the need for it will not prevent the proliferation of particularly disastrous conflicts. It is therefore essential to pursue that goal while at the same time continuing to seek ways of limiting the suffering caused by war, to develop humanitarian standards applicable in armed conflict, and, above all, to make these standards known, accepted and respected.

In this difficult debate on humanitarian standards, the question of prohibitions or restrictions on certain weapons or means of warfare is particularly complex, and in tackling it Eric Prokosch has not chosen an easy path. International humanitarian law is indeed primarily focused on the protection of people who are at the mercy or in the hands of the enemy – the wounded on the battlefield, prisoners or internees, and – after the Second World War – the civilian inhabitants of occupied territories. Yet the use of increasingly murderous means of warfare have led the international community to return to the problem of prohibitions or restrictions on certain weapons. The issue is by no means a new one: did not the Catholic Church censure the 'homicidal and heinous use of catapults' as early as its Council of 1139? Moreover, the use of poison has long been censured or prohibited. But it is the use of weapons of mass destruction that has marked our century, particularly of chemical weapons during the First World War and of nuclear weapons at the end of the Second.

When the overall question of humanitarian law was taken up again in 1949, the shock of the systematic massacre of civilians, particularly Jews, during the Second World War was still imprinted on everyone's minds, and stress was therefore laid on drawing up a convention to protect civilians in enemy hands. A debate on methods of warfare was avoided, although it would have been timely indeed in view of the terrible suffering caused to the civilian population by the mass bombing of cities, both by the Axis forces – London, Rotterdam, Warsaw... – and by the Allied powers towards the end of the war – Hamburg, Hiroshima, Nagasaki... It was during the preparation of the Protocols additional to the Geneva Conventions, finally adopted in 1977, that discussion of these problems resumed. It became necessary to reaffirm rules relating to the conduct of hostilities in order to maintain the global credibility of humanitarian law. For example, how could the protection of a captured pilot be upheld when there were no specific rules on the protection of the population he had bombed?

The establishment of humanitarian rules governing the conduct of hostilities is nevertheless extremely complex. The fact that a prisoner is well or badly treated has no effect on the outcome of the war. It is therefore easier to reach agreement on this subject, because it is in everyone's interests to do so. But this is not necessarily the case when it comes to renouncing the use of a weapon. The debate becomes more heated and is of far greater concern to the military, who would not be inclined to obey rules that would cause them to lose a war. The reason why this debate is particularly difficult is that it involves complex concepts, such as that of proportionality, and calls for a delicate balance between humanitarian requirements on the one hand, and 'military necessity' on the other.

The debate was finally concluded with the adoption of the Additional Protocols of 1977, but only general principles and rules were reaffirmed and developed in those instruments. They did not deal with questions relating to specific weapons. The detailed study of problems of weapons of mass destruction was relegated to the broader context of disarmament, and matters concerning the use of so-called 'conventional' weapons were discussed at an ad hoc conference, which adopted the 1980 Convention currently under review. It is this last issue that Eric Prokosch addresses in his work, to which he brings more than twenty years of research and study.

From both the political standpoint and the media point of view, debates on peace and weapons of mass destruction are of course more basic and more attractive. And, as we have already said, they do need to be addressed as a matter of urgency. Nevertheless, modern warfare kills thousands upon thousands of people with 'conventional' weapons. Every day children are victims of mine explosions, and tomorrow whole contingents of soldiers may be blinded by antipersonnel laser weapons. Yet much could be done and an enormous amount of suffering avoided if states were to consider these problems seriously. There are weapons which kill or maim 'unnecessarily,' even in relation to the ends sought by those waging the war, and other weapons exist which are so cruel that they bring disgrace on those who use them.

We must speak out about all this. We must explain, demonstrate and convince. It is a thankless struggle, often misunderstood and 'set apart' from more fundamental issues, but it has potentially a considerable impact on the humanitarian situation in the short and medium term, saving innumerable lives and preventing an immense amount of suffering. Due tribute must be paid to Eric Prokosch for waging this struggle with such thoroughness, perseverance, intelligence, and conviction.

Yves Sandoz, Director for Principles, Law and Relations with the
Movement, International Committee of the Red Cross

INTRODUCTION

Antipersonnel weapons? You want to know about antipersonnel weapons? – said the retired colonel, settling himself in his chair and lighting his pipe – Well, now, that's not a word we often use. Oh, yes, it's a correct term, but it's cumbersome, and besides, we don't want people to get the wrong idea. But I'll tell you about them.

You see, when you're fighting a war, there are various targets you'll want to destroy, or more precisely, to put out of action, or facilities whose use you'll want to deny the enemy. The target can be a bridge, it can be a tank, a fortification, an airfield, or a soldier. And so, we select a term that denotes the target that a munition is meant to destroy. If it's designed to knock out a tank, we call it an 'antitank' munition. If it's meant to damage materiel, and by that I mean automobiles, parked aircraft, radar installations, and the like, then we call it an 'antimateriel' munition. And if it's designed to destroy personnel, we call it 'antipersonnel.'

When I say 'personnel,' by the way, I'm referring to soldiers and their commanders, plus members of any armed militias or volunteer forces. Our job is to destroy the enemy's capacity to wage war, and so we have to go after his armed personnel, whether or not they are engaged in combat at the time.

There's also the problem of the enemy's rear base, his homeland, so to speak, where he's got his agriculture, his industry, his seat of government, and so on, all of which support his military machine. Now since the aim is to bring pressure on the enemy to induce him to come to terms, one way of doing this is to go after his rear base.

Of course, you can't just go in and kill off the enemy population – the colonel continued – That's forbidden under the laws of war. But if you're flying in to attack a legitimate military target, such as a bridge or a goods yard, and someone fires at your plane, then you have to shoot back; and if you know you're likely to encounter antiaircraft fire over a certain place, then it makes sense to go in just before and lay

I

down a barrage of antipersonnel fire, so that people will keep their heads down when your bombers fly over. That's why it's so useful to saturate parts of the enemy homeland with antipersonnel bombs, or to seed wide areas with antipersonnel mines. If some civilians get hurt in the process, that's just the price you have to pay.

The Americans brought in some useful gadgets along these lines during the Vietnam war. One of them was called the 'Sadeye' – picturesque name, don't you think? Well, this is a long, cigar-shaped device the size of a conventional bomb that is dropped from an airplane and opens in midair, releasing hundreds of little round explosive 'bomblets' embedded with steel balls. The bomblets are aerodynamically designed to scatter in the air so that when they reach the ground, they will be evenly distributed over a large area. The whole thing is called a 'cluster bomb,' referring to the fact that you've got a cluster of little munitions that you eject from a dispenser or container.

Let's take a look at what's happening on the ground. With bomblets going off all over the place, many more exposed personnel are likely to be hit than if you had a single ordinary high explosive bomb that went off at some single point within the same area. And some of the bomblets are set to explode later, when people have come out from under cover to tend to the damage. Moreover, any one fragment from an antipersonnel bomblet is capable of inflicting a serious wound. This comes from the knowledge we've accumulated from our wartime experience and laboratory studies. When a high-velocity steel ball strikes the body, it sets up a motion that destroys tissues far from the actual path of the fragment. The entrance and exit holes may be small, giving little clue to the extent of destruction inside.

You can appreciate the fact that an injury of this sort is hard to diagnose and hard to treat. The patient spends a long time recovering, and you've tied up a lot of enemy medical personnel in the meantime. The wound can easily be infected by bits of clothing or skin which the bomb fragment carries inside. And the effect of such a hail of fragments is terrifying. A weapon can affect enemy morale, you know, in addition to the physical damage.

Let's look at the whole thing from a mathematical point of view – the colonel continued, marking imaginary points in the air with his pipe – You've got six or seven hundred bomblets on the ground, each of them exploding and projecting several hundred steel balls in all directions. A portion of the steel balls will shoot up uselessly in the air or bury themselves in the ground; but because there are so many of them, and because they are distributed uniformly, the probability of hitting exposed personnel is high; and this, combined with the wounding effect of the steel balls, gives what we call a good 'lethal area' for the cluster bomb as a whole. It's an effective way to put a platoon out of action without committing ground troops or lingering over the target.

Now, when these weapons were first used in Vietnam, a lot of well-intentioned but misguided people said that they were 'inhumane,' that they were designed by a superpower to kill off peasants in an under-developed country, that they were useless against steel and concrete.

That's a lot of nonsense, of course. In any war, innocent people are bound to be killed. History bears this out. It's an unfortunate necessity, and no one deplores it more than the military. Anyway, the little fragments from an antipersonnel bomblet don't just injure people; they can also damage light materiel, such as the fuel tank or tires of a truck. It's true that they're too small to perforate armor or concrete; that's how they're designed. By making them small, you get more of them per bomblet, and in that way you increase your lethal area. I often wonder: if people don't want to be hit by an antipersonnel bomb, why do they choose to live near an antiaircraft site?

Most people wouldn't think of it, but an antipersonnel cluster bomb is actually more humane than an ordinary bomb. This is what the lawyers and the diplomats don't realize when they say that certain weapons should be banned. Let's say that preparatory to flying over a city to bomb a target on the other side, you send a fighter plane to drop some cluster bombs. The bomblets explode, antiaircraft crews are forced to take cover, and the bomber can fly over safely. Now suppose you weren't allowed to use cluster bombs. Your fighter planes might drop a regular high explosive bomb, inadvertently hitting a school or a hospital, and that would crush the walls and kill a lot of people, wouldn't it?

And don't think an antipersonnel cluster bomb wouldn't be effective in Baghdad or Tokyo, if it happened to fall without warning on a rush-hour crowd. Imagine the panic that would create.

You know, the Americans were pioneers in trying out new weapons in Vietnam, and the experiences of that war have had a lasting effect on the defense programs of other countries. Look at the Afghanistan war, where the Soviets introduced their own versions of the new American weapons with such deadly effect. Their new small-caliber AK-74 rifle is more lethal than anything the Americans had in Vietnam.

I feel sorry for the Americans. They came in for a lot of grief over Vietnam. It wasn't their fault; they went in to protect an ally and they had to think of the safety of their own men. They were given a job to do and then they couldn't do it; certain targets were out of bounds; Washington kept the Air Force's hands tied. But that's nothing new; you'll always have civilians interfering in military operations. The US armed forces performed honorably under the circumstances.

Now how did I get off on all that? – the colonel demanded – I was telling you that we use different munitions to defeat different targets; and it doesn't take much imagination to realize that a tank is a different target from a human being. What we do is to study the target – what happens when a missile of a certain shape and velocity enters the flesh, for example; what are the chances of hitting a vital organ, and so on. Then we design our munition so that it will produce the level of damage that we require. We might use a bullet of a special shape, for instance, or we might try other designs in order to maximize the effect.

The flechette is one of the more interesting developments along these lines. French for 'dart,' you know. It's like a small finishing nail, with fins at the blunt end. I have one in my desk; here, have a look at it.

The beauty of the flechette is that it flies through the air with very little wind resistance, so that it's still traveling fast when it hits the target. The problem is that it can easily keep right on through the target and out the other side without causing much damage. One solution is to cause it to tumble or deform within the body, by making the tip out of soft metal or weakening the fins so that they will separate from the shaft and slip off in different directions inside the body. Another solution would be to coat it with a chemical agent, but of course that's prohibited under the laws of war.

The Swedes were interested in flechettes at one point, and they manufactured thousands of them for test purposes. Then they gave up the project, and after that you could see them at the intergovernmental conferences, pushing for a ban on flechettes – for humanitarian reasons, so they said.

Odd chaps, the Swedes. They would come up to you at a conference, reach in their pocket, pull out one of those little things, and ask: 'Would you like a flechette?' Then they looked you in the eye, with that proud look of theirs, and said: 'Swedish steel!'

I attended one of the conferences as a military representative of my country, and it was all I could do to restrain myself. Now I hear there is talk of banning antipersonnel mines – clearly an essential weapon for military purposes. A fine lot of humanitarians, the Swedes are, with their socialist traditions and high suicide rate. They had plenty of bloody battles in their day, if you look at Swedish history.

The Americans tried for years to develop a rifle that would shoot flechettes. They finally had to give it up. Made a nasty wound, but they couldn't get the damn thing to shoot straight, although I've heard talk of starting the project again recently.

They had better luck with their Beehive – another of those poignant names. It's a shell that is fired pointblank or downrange from an artillery piece and breaks open, releasing thousands of flechettes. It'll cut a man to bits, and it's been known literally to nail soldiers to trees.

The Americans used Beehives in Vietnam, and they were used in the Middle East in 1973. A mean weapon, no question of it. It's a pity the production costs are so high.

Why are you looking at me like that? – exclaimed the retired colonel, and he squirmed ever so slightly, while his voice took on a harder tone – War is hell. You don't think we like to fight wars, do you?

We've been entrusted with the task of defending our country. We adhere scrupulously to the laws of war. But once the civilian government has given us the order to fight, it is up to us to use whatever means are necessary to bring the conflict to a speedy end.

The greatest humanitarian in the world is a soldier. I could tell you some memorable stories of the courage and compassion of soldiers who rescued civilians pinned down by enemy fire. And the greatest pacifist is a soldier. He doesn't want war: he knows he'll be the first to suffer, the first to put his life on the line.

Men are greedy, men are vicious, men are cruel. As long as you have human beings on earth, you're going to have wars. History bears this out. And as long as you have wars, you're going to have armies and soldiers and weapons. How can you deny it?

The colonel's vision is of a battlefield where his forces can enjoy the advantages of technology without limit. Yet the logical outcome of never-ending advances in killing power is ever more devastation, ever worse injury to soldiers, ever more destruction to civilian life.

War is a supremely irrational and destructive enterprise. Unable to settle their disputes peacefully, or bent on conquest and control, nation strikes at nation and nations and opposition groups strike at each other, destroying the land and the human works of centuries, killing and maiming great numbers of people, displacing many more and consigning them to a miserable future. Yet the conduct and the preparation of warfare are highly organized; the weapons used are based on the best national technologies; and the people engaged in each component of this vast operation are surrounded by an ethos which values their contribution, and a jargon which allows them to communicate comfortably without focusing on the dreadful effects of their work.

Some people have searched for ways to stop particular wars, to limit the damage caused, or to prevent wars breaking out. These efforts have often been viewed as naive, if not treacherous, since they undermine official attempts to present a war as a noble cause and thereby win support. Efforts by war critics to prevent the use of specific weapons arouse antagonism among members of the armed forces, who see these efforts as attempts to deprive them of the tools needed to carry out the job with which their country has entrusted them.

One of the reactions to war has been the progressive attempt to create a body of international law that would limit the suffering inflicted in armed conflict. Two general rules of special relevance are the prohibition of use of weapons causing unnecessary suffering or super-fluous injury, which is aimed at avoiding unnecessary harm to soldiers, and the prohibition of use of indiscriminate weapons – weapons which are of a nature to strike military objectives and civilians or civilian objects without distinction.

From these general rules, the community of nations has been able to adopt a few agreements banning or restricting the use of specific weapons: the 1899 Hague Declaration on dum-dum bullets, the 1899 and 1907 Hague Regulations banning the use of poisoned weapons, the Geneva Protocol of 1925 banning the use of poisonous gas and bacteriological methods of warfare, and – most recently – the 1980 Convention on Prohibitions or Restrictions on the Use of Certain Conventional Weapons Which May be Deemed to be Excessively Injurious or to have Indiscriminate Effects, known as the 'Conventional Weapons Convention,' whose three protocols respectively ban the use of nonmetallic fragmentation weapons and impose restrictions on the use of land mines and incendiary weapons. Yet these achievements, few and far between, can scarcely keep pace with advances in the technology of antipersonnel weapons.

From the early days of human existence, people have used their ingenuity and the technological skills passed down through the generations to devise ever more effective means of attacking their enemies. The dagger, the club, and the spear were weapons for combat close at hand, or as far as a warrior could throw. The bow and arrow took advantage of the elastic properties of bow and string to project a missile further than it could be thrown. The discovery of explosives extended the range still further. Explosives could also be packed in a metal shell and detonated, shattering the shell into fast-moving fragments to kill soldiers and destroy materiel.

In the course of the nineteenth century, with the advent of more powerful rifles, a new and terrible type of wound began appearing on the battlefield. Entrance and exit holes were often small, but the damage inside was as extensive as if it had been caused by a small explosion. The study of the 'explosive wound' gave rise to a new branch of military science, the science of 'wound ballistics,' whose findings would have implications for both defense and offense. World War II gave rise to a new series of laboratory experiments and field studies which placed the new science on a solid empirical footing (Chapter 1).

In the Korean war, US commanders confronted the nightmare of seeing their forces overrun by hordes of enemy soldiers. Rising to the challenge, US weapons laboratories reexamined the design of the army's munitions to see if their casualty-producing efficiency could be improved. The result was a revolution in antipersonnel weapons design (Chapter 2).

Vietnam was a proving ground for the new weapons; they were used profusely, and other new munitions were devised as 'quick-fix' responses to meet the needs of an anti-guerrilla campaign. In the ground war, massive firepower carried the risk of hitting civilians indiscriminately. In the air war, the extensive use of new 'cluster bombs' gave the North Vietnamese public the sense that the war was directed against them. When US forces withdrew from Indochina in 1975, they left a legacy of destruction and unexploded munitions that would affect the population for many years to come (Chapters 3–4).

While the war was going on, the secrecy, compartmentalization, and specialization of weapons design and production meant that few Americans could have a clear picture of what was being done in Vietnam in their country's name. The growing antiwar movement encompassed new research to discover the causes and consequences of the war, and to combat the official deceptions. One part of this research was aimed at revealing the true nature of the war by studying the weapons used, and showing the links between local arms plants and the effects of their products in Vietnam. Chapter 5 explores the multifaceted antipersonnel weapons makers, and tells of attempts by parts of the antiwar movement to stop the production of napalm (in California) and cluster bombs (in Minnesota). The arms production continued, but the innovations of these and other protestors introduced a range of tactics and concerns about corporate responsibility which have had a lasting impact on the conduct of public policy.

Moved by concerns over the Vietnam war, Sweden and other governments proposed introducing bans on the use of antipersonnel cluster bombs, aerially delivered antipersonnel mines, and other types of new antipersonnel weapons. Chapter 6 is an eyewitness account of the two Conferences of Government Experts where – in the formal sessions and in the corridors – the US and its NATO allies successfully blocked the Swedish proposals. It assesses the meager scope of the 1980 convention which resulted from the process, and draws attention to the important role which public opinion must play if tougher weapons bans are to be achieved.

The most striking consequence of the failure to impose tighter controls in 1980 is the problem of land mines. Among the new munitions developed since the Korean war are small antipersonnel mines, often made of plastic or other undetectable materials, which can be sown in huge numbers by hand or from aircraft, artillery, or vehicular dispensers. Today eighty-five and possibly over one hundred million unexploded land mines are believed to lie scattered in over sixty countries. Hundreds of thousands – possibly millions – of civilians have been killed or injured. Productive land is rendered unusable, and

precious resources must be expended on mine clearance and the rehabilitation of victims. The problem grows worse each day as armed
forces and armed opposition movements continue to sow vast quantities
of mines with wanton disregard for their short-term and long-term
effects on civilians.

One response to the problem has been the birth of an international
campaign to ban the use, production, stockpiling, and export of antipersonnel mines. With its direct and powerful humanitarian appeal, the
campaign has already achieved remarkable results. Eighteen countries
have enacted comprehensive or partial moratoria on the export of antipersonnel mines, and a United Nations conference is due to be convened
in 1995 to review the 1980 convention and consider how it might be
strengthened. But the natural reluctance of armed forces to give up the
possibility of using any particular type of weapon makes a total ban
unlikely, and other munitions which are less in the limelight – wide-area
cluster bombs, fuel-air explosives, or bullets that tumble in the body –
risk being forgotten in the discussions (Chapter 7).

This book is about an area of weaponry which has received scant
attention in the literature of arms control.[1] The weapons in question
include many of the most common, yet most of them are unknown to
the public. They account for by far the most casualties in warfare, but
little has been done to control them. These weapons depend for their
effect on the mechanical destruction of body tissues caused by the
impact of a projectile or the force of a blast wave. Their designation as
'conventional' distinguishes them from nuclear, chemical, and biological
weapons. They are 'antipersonnel' weapons; weapons (in the words of
The United States Air Force Dictionary) 'designed to destroy or obstruct
personnel.'[2]

The years since World War II have seen a terrific growth in the
killing power of antipersonnel weapons. Military commanders now have
at their disposal an unprecedented capacity to inflict awesome casualties
with a range of weapons that will kill outright or maim for life. Those
in charge of military operations can put large numbers of enemy soldiers
out of action through the use of remote-control weapons covering large
tracts of land with fast-flying lethal fragments. Wishing to avoid casualties among their own forces, they will be tempted to use weapons that
can kill thousands of people against targets where only a few soldiers
may be present. By doing so, they increase the risk of hitting civilians
and exacerbate the problem of unexploded munitions which remain on
the surface or buried after an attack.

This book is aimed at bringing antipersonnel weapons into the
domain of public discussion so that decision-makers and concerned
citizens can find new solutions to the problems these weapons pose. It

seeks to convey an understanding of the fundamentals of antipersonnel weapons design and of the human environment from which these weapons come, in the interest of promoting an informed debate.

It appeals to weapons designers and those who direct their efforts to halt the technological rush to produce an ever-increasing severity of effects on an ever-increasing number of people hit. It appeals to military commanders to impose restrictions on combat which will avoid the widespread injury and loss of life that have characterized recent wars.

It appeals to governments to continue the work of the 1980 Conventional Weapons Convention by adopting progressively stricter bans on weapons which cause unnecessary suffering or have indiscriminate effects.

It appeals to people of good will throughout the world, moved by the horrors of modern warfare, to press the political authorities to prevent wars and to find political solutions to the problems that lead to war. Such solutions will benefit both the civilian populations and the armed forces who, offering their lives in defense of their countries, are increasingly at risk from the new armaments being devised.

Notes

1. The only comprehensive work on the subject is the study by the Stockholm International Peace Research Institute (SIPRI), *Anti-personnel Weapons* (1978).

2. Heflin, ed., 1956.

CHAPTER I

THE SCIENCE OF
WOUND BALLISTICS

Thus, a new field of inquiry has arisen, that of wound ballistics, a study of the mechanics of wounding and related subjects. The field has two aspects. One is a determination of the factors involved in injury and the relation between the severity of the wound and such characteristics of the missile as its mass, velocity, shape, momentum, energy, and power. The attempt is made to relate the ability to wound or to kill with some physical property of the projectile. Such inquiry gives an answer to the question, whether an antipersonnel bomb is more effective if it breaks into a large number of small fragments or a smaller number of relatively large fragments.

The second aspect of wound ballistics involves a study of the nature of the damage to tissues, whether it results from stretching and displacement or from pressure changes accompanying the shot. Of particular interest is the commonly observed injury of organs far away from the bullet path. Such knowledge greatly aids the surgeon in his treatment of the wound and is necessary for the establishment of rules for removal of dead tissue and the amount of debridement necessary for proper recovery. The knowledge of wound ballistics is, therefore, important not only in offense but also in defense.[1]

These words from the Princeton University wound ballistics study, published in the US Army history *Wound Ballistics*, summed up the scope of the new science at the end of World War II. Earlier researchers had used imagination and skill in trying to unlock the secrets of what happened inside the body when it was struck by a missile, but their efforts had been frustrated by the opacity of the body, the rapidity of the process, and the lack of suitable instruments for observation and recording. Building on their work, the World War II researchers were able to reach a new level of understanding backed by empirical data.

The 'mechanics of wounding' was conceived of as a physical process, explainable by application of the laws of physics. Experimental shots into 'flesh simulants' such as gelatin and water would be used to test the explanations, and to show that the process was regular and reproducible under laboratory conditions. The aim was to develop formulas relating salient characteristics of a missile to the severity of the wound produced; this, in turn, would be related to the military goal of putting enemy soldiers out of action. By applying the formulas, ordnance engineers could then design antipersonnel weapons of maximum efficiency.

Wound ballistics draws heavily from the medical sciences. Like them, it has a humanitarian element – to heal and relieve the sufferings of wounded soldiers. But the knowledge obtained through the research is intended also for a purpose diametrically opposed to the first, although ineluctably bound up with it in the logic of war: to inflict more suffering, more efficiently.

This duality of helping and harming characterizes warfare in general, but it is especially acute in the field of wound ballistics. The fearsome knowledge obtained through research is be used not only to heal but to destroy, and to destroy more effectively than before. This knowledge is not something which exists in the abstract, ready for the taking. Like all scientific knowledge, it has to be obtained, tested, and elaborated through hard, careful work, an effort requiring dedication and resources – an adjunct to the effort of making war. It can be inspired by individual ideas, individual initiatives, but the necessary resources are unlikely to be allocated unless it is seen to be relevant to a clear military need – often a need that has appeared through some recent combat experience.

Early Research: The Study of the 'Explosive Wound'

In the middle of the nineteenth century, as advances in small arms technology made for faster and more powerful bullets,[2] wounds of a devastating sort began appearing on the battlefield. In the words of the Princeton group, such wounds

> appeared as though they had been caused by an actual explosion within the body. External signs of injury were often slight, the entrance and exit holes small, but an unbelievable amo unt of damage occurred within… Not only is the tissue pulped within a large region about the bullet path but intact nerves lose their ability to conduct impulses and bones are found to be broken that have not suffered a direct hit.[3]

This 'explosive effect,' with damage to parts of the body that were not directly hit, was the object of much speculation. Early students of the so-called 'explosive wound' sought to explain how it was caused, and tried to corroborate their explanations by reproducing similar effects experimentally.

One of the first was Huguier, who had seen such wounds in the fighting in Paris in 1848. He made 'observations on certain dead organs, *e.g.* lung, liver, etc.,' Victor Horsley later wrote, 'and suggested that the reason why there was so much lateral disturbance was that the tissues contained water in large quantity and that the energy of the moving projectile being imparted to the particles of water, caused the dispersion of these in a hydrodynamic fashion.'[4]

Elaborating on Huguier's ideas, Professor Horsley, in a lecture at the Royal Institution in 1894, demonstrated by ingenious experiments the fallacy of some current theories of 'explosive' wounding, and offered in their place the explanation that 'the particles of the substance are hurried forward ... in front of the bullet...'. His idea was that bits of flesh, suddenly forced aside to make room for the bullet, would themselves act as 'secondary missiles,' pushing aside other bits of flesh next to them. The tissues near the path of the bullet were violently stretched aside before the elastic character of the tissues forced them further away to return to their original position. It was in this stretching that the tissues were damaged.[5]

As the tissues moved out from the sides of the bullet path, a vacuum or 'cavity' was formed for a very brief moment. This idea was suggested by the American researcher Charles Woodruff, working at the end of the nineteenth century. Like Huguier, Woodruff drew from hydro-dynamics; the connection to this science was apt, because human flesh is fluid and has a density similar to that of water. In seeking to describe the motion within the body which could account for the 'explosive' displacement of tissues, Woodruff borrowed from marine engineering the notion of 'cavitation,' a term denoting a partial vacuum produced in water by a high-speed screw propeller.

> The particles of fluid making way for the bullet are given a tremendous centrifugal velocity, which they impart to all surrounding particles, even to the extreme outer layers.... The fluid being incompressible, the particles [adjacent to the nose of the bullet] cannot move until surrounding ones make room for them. Consequently there is an instantaneous outward or centrifugal motion of all the fluid [flesh] surrounding the point of the bullet. As soon as they make room the bullet enters.... The particles of fluid moving away from the bullet track, even after the bullet has passed, must then form a vacuum or cavity. This *cavitation* is at the basis of the explosive effects in fluids, for it enables the whole mass to expand... (original emphasis)[6]

In describing what seemed to be happening – a process which they themselves could not observe – nineteenth-century writers used abstractions and metaphors, such as Horsley's image of 'particles' of flesh 'hurried forward,' much as a Christmas shopping crowd might be 'hurried forward' to clear the store at closing time. Thus Woodruff wrote of particles of fluid 'making way' for a bullet; and Arthur Keith and Hugh Rigby, two British researchers whose experiments involved shooting dum-dum bullets into specially prepared cadavers, used a picturesque seaside scene as an image for 'explosive' wounding in the head, whose 'contents' could be driven apart so forcefully as to rupture the hard wall of the skull:

> In the summertime, when the harbours of the northeast coast are crowded with fishing craft, one can see the explosive effect exemplified. If a little tug enter the shoal of boats gradually it can push its way through them, disturbing only the boats that touch its bows; but were it to steam wildly through them it would scatter them right and left, transferring the shock straight to the harbour wall. A bullet entering the brain at a low velocity drives the contents against the walls of the cranial cavity, but it has not momentum enough to drive them with a rupturing force. A flat-nosed bullet, like the dum-dum, is able to transfer its momentum more rapidly and more effectually than a fully mantled bullet – hence its greater explosive effect.[7]

Some early experimenters shot into cadavers or animal carcasses. Others used various materials or combinations of materials to represent combinations of body substances. Woodruff, for instance, fired bullets into tomato cans and cattle bladders, and examined the entrance and exit 'wounds.' Horsley (and, later, Callender and French) used modeling clay; Keith and Rigby (and, later, various twentieth-century researchers) used soap – substances which later became known as 'flesh simulants.' In the words of the Princeton group, materials such as these 'served as models to explain what must happen in the body.'[8] Because these materials could be cheaply prepared in uniform lots, an experimenter could afford to conduct a series of trial shots, varying such factors as the missile shape, size, or velocity.

Thus Louis B. Wilson, a US Army doctor working in 1916 and 1917, fired into gelatin, a flesh simulant favored by later US researchers because of its translucence. Wilson was interested in 'explosive' wounding effects on various parts of the body. Simulating the connective tissues, he embedded black threads in gelatin and fired into it: the tearing of connective tissues, he considered, was 'well illustrated ... by the ripping out and tangling up of the enmeshed fibers of cotton and silk' in the gelatin. To represent body materials of varying degrees of softness, he prepared gelatin solutions of 5, 10, and 20 per cent, and concluded from trial shots that

> the softer the organ or tissue the further away from the track of the missile will serious secondary results of injuries occur. The pulped tissue not only is almost certain to become the nidus for the growth of pathogenic bacteria which had been disseminated through it on fragments of dirt and clothing carried into the wound by the missile, but certainly the pulped muscle and

probably also other shredded organs break down quickly and give out toxic products which according to Cannon's experiments are one of the causes of so-called secondary traumatic shock.

Soft glandular organs, such as the kidney, spleen, and liver and the nerve trunks, which have not been even touched by high velocity bullets may be seriously affected by the transmission of energy to them through intervening soft parts.[9]

Wilson's knowledge gained through experiments was in advance of the common understanding in US Army circles of the time. Called to active service in 1918, he had occasion to observe many battle wounds. Military surgeons, Wilson found, were generally unaware of the extent of tissue damage surrounding the bullet track in 'explosive' wounds. 'Failure to appreciate this by any of the warring nations early in the war and by many American surgeons even as late as the summer of 1918, no doubt resulted in many instances in insufficient cleaning out of pulped and infected tissues with resulting gangrene and death,' he told the Association of Military Surgeons in Boston in 1921.[10]

In the period between the two world wars, two US Army officers, George R. Callender and Ralph W. French, carried on Wilson's work in a series of experiments in the US Army Ordnance and Medical Departments, initially under Wilson's supervision. Some of their work involved shooting into anesthetized pigs and goats, preferable to cadavers and animal carcasses as, in live targets, physiological effects could be studied, and there was no *rigor mortis* to distort the effect.

Like Wilson, Callender and French were interested in the ways in which different tissues responded to missile impact. Observing that liquid-filled cavities were more readily damaged than the lungs, they drew attention, as Wilson had done, to the different densities of the materials through which a missile passes. 'Air with a density of one presents a very different resistance to the moving bullet from water with its density of 800,' they wrote. 'The lung, the viscus nearest approaching air in density, at the highest velocities used [in the experiments] shows relatively slight destruction by the bullet alone, though if secondary missiles of bone strike or penetrate it, extensive destruction may occur.' In contrast: 'If the bladder is full of urine this viscus will be torn asunder as will the rectum if struck when filled with fecal masses.'

One of Callender and French's innovations was to place sets of electrically wired metal screens in front of targets and behind them in order to measure the velocities of bullets when they entered and emerged from the targets. Such measurements enabled them to calculate the loss of velocity and rapidity of loss of velocity in the target, and to compare these figures to target damage (shown by X-rays and other means) much more closely than had previously been possible. Touching on a topic that would greatly interest later weapons designers, they drew attention to the importance of velocity in missile wounding and suggested that there was a threshold of about 2,500 feet per second, above which 'the character of the wound begins to change radically.' They drew attention to the wounding potential of high explosive shell fragments moving at speeds above this threshold: 'Experiments,' they wrote, 'indicate that shell fragments may have velocities well in excess of 3,000 feet per second to which is added their great irregularity in shape.'[11]

Over the decades, students of the 'explosive wound' had accomplished a great deal by the time of World War II. They had drawn a connection to hydrodynamics and introduced the notion of cavitation in describing the wounding process. They had pointed to the importance of such factors as velocity, momentum, rapidity of energy transfer to the tissues, and shape of projectile, as factors affecting the severity of the wound produced. They had looked into the effects of missile impact on different parts of the body. Their experimental techniques had become increasingly accurate and sophisticated.

World War II: Research in Great Britain

Wound ballistics took a new direction in World War II as a reaction to the German bombardment of Great Britain. Bullet wounds had hitherto been the main focus, but the experience of bombardment led to an interest in the effects of high explosive bombs.

At the outset of the war, a newly established Research and Experiments Department of the British Ministry of Home Security was asked by the Air Staff to make a census of bombs dropped over Great Britain and 'quantitative studies of the total effects of air raids,' according to an official history.[12] Working in a branch of the organization, a team of scientists from Oxford University's anatomy department complemented the bomb survey with a series of experiments on wounding. One of the team was Solly (later Lord) Zuckerman, a man whose long and distinguished career exemplified the importance of putting scientific knowledge to public use.[13]

The first published reference to the work of the Oxford group was in a letter from Zuckerman to the *British Medical Journal*, published in reply to another letter which had appeared in July 1940. The previous writer, describing severe wounds from bomb fragments 'of about the diameter of a halfpenny and less,' attributed their wounding effect partly to rotation. In reply, Zuckerman confirmed that wounds from small fragments were being inflicted in the air raids on England, and were common in casualties in Flanders and France, but he discounted the effect of rotation and emphasized instead the importance of velocity. Citing earlier studies, he described the 'explosive' effect, and wrote:

> diminution of mass, as in small splinters [fragments], is more than compensated, from the point of view of destructive power, by increase in velocity.... As a basis for work on measures of counteraction, it is hoped to have definite information about the frequency and distribution of these wounds and about the circumstances attending their infliction as soon as a survey which is at present being conducted for the Research and Experiments Branch of the Ministry of Home Security is completed.[14]

In December of the next year, Zuckerman, A.N. Black, and B.D. Burns published some of their findings in the *British Medical Journal* under the title 'An Experimental Study of the Wounding Mechanism of High-Velocity Missiles.'[15] They had fired $3/32$-inch steel balls (corresponding in weight to 'a very large proportion of the splinters which are shot off from any bomb or shell') into blocks of gelatin (whose 20 per cent dilution 'corresponds to the dilution of protein in the body') and into the hind legs of anesthetized animals. Borrowing from exterior ballistics the technique of 'spark shadowgraphy,' in which a sparking device casts a brief shadow of the target on to photographic paper at different moments over a series of shots, they were able for the first time to photograph the external changes in targets being struck by missiles.

Immediately after perforation at high velocity by a steel ball, the photographs showed, 'the block of gelatin undergoes considerable expansion, until it becomes some three to four times its original volume.' It then regained its original shape, leaving only 'the small threadlike track made by the passage of the ball.' These changes, the researchers wrote, could 'only be explained as being due to the formation of a cavity within the blocks with explosive violence.' When animal limbs were photographed while being shot, they too were found to swell momentarily; leading the researchers to conclude that

> precisely the same changes occur in human or animal tissues that are traversed by high-velocity missiles. The distortion to which they are subjected can only be likened to that of an internal explosion, and at the height of the deformation, which occurs after the missile has left the part, the tissues must be stretched around a central cavity of relatively large dimensions. Under such conditions it is obvious that structures at great distances from the track of the projectile can suffer damage.

A US Army specialist wrote later: 'The modern era in wound ballistics can be considered to have begun with the work of Black, Burns and Zuckerman.'[16] Among their achievements, one of the most important was the photography of external changes in targets during wounding – changes which earlier researchers could infer only after the fact. Once photographed, the temporary bulges in gelatin blocks and animal limbs could be measured and their size compared with missile characteristics such as velocity, so as to obtain formulas for the destruction which a given missile could be expected to cause. This knowledge, in turn, could be applied to weapons design.

The ethical dilemma inherent in wound ballistics was that the knowledge needed for defensive and humanitarian purposes to relieve suffering could also be used to increase it; yet it was only natural that scientists seeking to defend their country should also want to improve their country's means for counterattack. Many years later, I wrote to Lord Zuckerman raising this ethical dilemma. He replied: 'I can assure you that the question of ethics was not one which posed itself at any time during the Second World War ... to people like myself who were engaged, directly or indirectly, in military operations.'

The Princeton Group: Origins and Experimental Setup

In the United States, a project established during the war continued with what the British group had done. Using new experimental techniques, they documented the wounding process with unprecedented thoroughness and precision.

The origins of the project were described by Major James C. Beyer of the US Army Medical Corps in his preface to the Army Medical Department history *Wound Ballistics* (1962). In September 1943, Beyer wrote, R.H. Kent, an Army physicist who had been connected with Callender and French's wound ballistics work in the 1930s, approached the chairman of a division of the National Research Council

> regarding the establishment of a research project designed to test the casualty-producing effectiveness of US weapons. As a result of this request, a meeting of the newly created Conference on Wound Ballistics, later called the Conference on Missile Casualties, was held on 25 September 1943. [Colonel] Callender presided.... After accepting the general tenets of Mr. Kent's proposal, the Conference granted contracts for research projects to several groups of nvestigators.

One of these contracts led to what Major Beyer referred to as the 'monumental' work of E. Newton Harvey and his colleagues at Princeton University, a work many of whose 'original conclusions ... have been the basis for continuing ballistic research after World War II.'[17]

In their experiments, the Wound Ballistics Research Group at

Princeton used mostly $1/16$- to $1/4$-inch steel balls; some bullets, wire nails, and other fragments were also used. The balls and fragments were fired from a .30 caliber smoothbore rifle, using a wooden sleeve, or 'sabot,' which separated from the missile after it left the gun. Different propellant charges were used to obtain different velocities. The balls and fragments were fired into blocks of gelatin and tanks of water, representing human flesh.[18] The researchers also used deeply anesthetized cats and dogs, reducing the size of the missiles proportionately so that the firings would be scaled-down versions of actual rifle fire into human beings.

To record the changes in the targets as the missiles passed through them, the researchers used spark shadowgraphs (as the British group had done), as well as high-speed motion pictures made with cameras capable of taking several thousand frames a second, and instruments for recording pressure changes. For opaque targets such as muscle, high-speed X-rays with exposures of a millionth of a second were taken at very brief intervals. The photographs revealed what Woodruff and other early researchers had long imagined to be at the heart of 'explosive' wounding: a cavity, formed momentarily.

The Princeton Findings: Temporary Cavity, Permanent Cavity, and Effects on Different Parts of the Body

As a steel ball hits a target at high velocity and passes through, a cone-shaped cavity is formed behind it, the photographs showed. This 'temporary cavity' expands and contracts several times before collapsing altogether, the substance coming to rest around the 'permanent cavity' or wound track left behind as a record of the missile's passage. This all happens very quickly, the temporary cavity reaching its maximum size in less than a thousandth of a second and vanishing after a few thousandths of a second.

With a non-spherical fragment, twisting as it passes through a target, the temporary cavity is irregular. It is widest in those places where the fragment travels broadside and narrowest where the fragment travels head-on. In similar fashion, a bullet entering a target nose-on produces a cone-shaped temporary cavity similar to that formed by a steel ball, but if it wobbles or changes its orientation, the temporary cavity becomes broader.

After the temporary cavity collapses, a smaller, 'permanent' cavity remains. Its shape is basically fusiform – thicker in the middle and thinner at the ends. This shape could be seen in a gelatin block, the researchers found; similarly, 'Dissection of the wound track in the thigh reveals that the permanent cavity is largest near the center of the thigh and smallest at the points of entrance and exit of the [ball].'[19] The formation of the temporary cavity 'results in a stretching and tearing of the tissues for a considerable distance away from the missile track,' the researchers wrote. This violent movement accounts for what earlier researchers had noted: the destruction of various parts of the body at considerable distances from the actual path of the missile. In a series of experiments, the Princeton group studied the damage inflicted on various body materials:

- Muscle fibers near the center of a temporary cavity are badly swollen. Those further away exhibit 'muscle clots' accompanied by other phenomena of cellular disorganization. Individual muscles 'are often widely separated and stripped from their surrounding connective tissues.'

- There are multiple ruptures of the capillaries, and 'the muscle fibers are widely separated by accumulations of extravasated blood.' (The larger blood vessels, which are very elastic, can be thrust aside by the formation of a temporary cavity and return to their original place, apparently undamaged, when the cavity collapses.)

- Nerves can be pushed aside by the temporary cavity and then return to their original positions without being broken, but the stretching and compression damage them, and they can lose the ability to conduct impulses if a high velocity missile passes within a centimeter, even though there is no externally detectable break in continuity. Histological examination showed that the fibers of such nerves have been severed, kinked, or separated.

- A bone struck directly by a high velocity missile can shatter or apparently explode, as if a temporary cavity had been formed in it. But bones can also suffer 'indirect fractures' if a high velocity missile passes nearby, at distances up to 3 centimeters. The Princeton researchers wrote: 'The explanation of the indirect type of fracture is found in the rapidly expanding temporary cavity. As this cavity expands, high pressures are brought to bear against the rigid bone. The situation is similar to that of striking the bone a hard blow with a hammer.'

- Gas-filled pockets in the intestines can rupture if a high velocity missile passes nearby. The momentary drop in pressure in the temporary cavity around the intestine causes the gas to expand, exploding the intestine.[20]

- The human head offers a special illustration of the effect of temporary cavity formation on materials nearby. In the words of the

Princeton group, the head consists of a 'liquid medium' (the brain) enclosed in the skull. Penetration by a high velocity missile creates a temporary cavity with the substance being violently pushed outwards, although

> The cavity formed by a missile in the brain of an intact cranium is of finite size, partly because brain tissue is forced through regions of less resistance (such as the frontal sinuses and the various foramina of the skull) and partly because of the stretching of the cranium itself. When the energy delivered is very great, skull bones are actually torn apart along suture lines.[21]

The Mathematics of Wounding

With the formation of the temporary cavity so closely linked to the destruction of various body materials, it was clear that the size of the temporary cavity would be one measure of the seriousness of the wound produced by a missile striking the body. What factors led to the production of temporary cavities of different sizes?

The Princeton group wrote: 'Study and measurement of a large number of temporary cavities show that the total volume of the cavity is proportional to the energy delivered by the missile.' In other words, there was a direct relation between the size of a temporary cavity and the amount of energy transferred to the tissues by a missile penetrating the body.[22] This finding served to emphasize, as earlier researchers had done, the importance of velocity in missile wounding.

In physics, the kinetic energy (energy of motion) of an object is proportional to its mass (M) multiplied by the square of its velocity (v), according to the formula

$$K.E. = \frac{Mv^2}{2}$$

From this it follows – with tremendous implications for weapons design – that, as Zuckerman wrote in 1940, 'diminution of mass, as in small splinters, is more than compensated, from the point of view of destructive power, by increase in velocity.' If the mass (or weight) of a missile in motion is doubled, its kinetic energy also doubles; but if the velocity is doubled, its kinetic energy, available for wound production, is quadrupled. If mass is halved and velocity doubled, the energy also doubles, according to the formula. Thus, a wounding missile can be made smaller and still be as effective – or more so – if its velocity is increased.

These considerations refer to the *capacity* of a missile striking the body to form a large temporary cavity; but will it actually do so? If a high velocity fragment hits the body and is stopped inside, all its kinetic energy will have been transferred to the tissues, and the destruction is likely to be extensive. But if a bullet passes through the body and emerges from the other side at nearly the same speed, it will not have lost much kinetic energy, and the wound may not be very serious if the bullet has not punctured a vital organ.

Here more formulas came in. For spheres, the Princeton researchers found that the maximum displacement of the temporary cavity at any point is proportional to the square root of the kinetic energy of the missile at that level. As a sphere penetrates further, it slows down, and its kinetic energy, and the energy which it transfers to the target medium, decrease accordingly. Hence the cone-shaped temporary cavity formed by a sphere: the cavity is widest at the point of impact, where the velocity and kinetic energy of the sphere are at their greatest, and tapers off as the velocity and kinetic energy decline.

The *retardation* of a missile is thus of great importance in its wounding effect. Retardation is brought about by *drag*, the force which a medium, such as air or water, exerts on a moving projectile, slowing it down. The Princeton researchers found that the retardation of a sphere 'is proportional to the square of the velocity of the sphere, a general law for liquids expressed as a *retardation coefficient,* α.' The sphere is slowed down fastest when it is moving fastest. If the material or size of spheres differ, the various quantities are related in the following way:

$$\alpha = \frac{\rho A C_D}{2M}$$

where ρ is the density of the target medium, A is the projected cross-sectional area of the sphere, M is the mass of the sphere, and C_D is the 'coefficient of drag' for the target medium in question.

The notion of *projected area* is very important here: it is the area of the projectile which is pushing against the target medium. With a nonspherical fragment or a wobbling bullet, the projected area will change as the missile turns. Where such a missile is traveling most nearly broadside, its projected area is greatest and so are – consequently – its retardation coefficient, the rate at which it slows down, and the rate at which it transfers energy to the target. It is at this point that the temporary cavity is broadest, as mentioned above. Along with the size of the temporary cavity, another important measure of the wounding capacity of a missile is its *distance of penetration* in a target medium. The further the missile penetrates, the greater the chances of striking a vital organ lying behind the layers of skin, muscle, or other materials.

Following from the formula for retardation cited above, and from experimentally determined retardation coefficients in water, gelatin, and muscle, the Princeton researchers were able to obtain formulas for *how far a steel ball would penetrate* into living soft tissue, and for *energy loss* and *rate of energy loss* in relation to distance of penetration. Another finding was a formula for *retardation by skin*, obtained through experiments in which steel balls were shot through several layers of fresh human skin and the impact and exit velocities recorded.

Taken together, the formulas showed that as the size of a steel ball is decreased, the ball penetrates less deeply into the target, slows down more rapidly, loses energy faster, and forms a wider, shallower temporary cavity; it also loses more of its energy in passing through the skin. As the striking velocity is increased, or as the density is increased by making the ball out of a denser material, the distance of penetration increases.[23] These formulas would make it possible to find the optimum weapons design to produce the desired level of wounding.

The Princeton group regarded their work as 'an attempt to place wound ballistics on a sound quantitative basis.' It was possible to do this because, as they found, the laws of physics can be applied to wounding. In the science of exterior ballistics, the flight of a bullet can be predicted from the force of the air slowing it down as well as the effect of extraneous forces, such as crosswinds blowing it off course. Similar forces are at work on projectiles moving through denser media such as water, gelatin, or the tissues of the body.

Comparisons between the observed behavior of missiles moving through water, which was governed by known laws, and the behavior in tissues revealed a 'remarkable similarity' between the two phenomena, the researchers wrote. In their view, 'Wound ballistics is actually a special branch of underwater ballistics.'[24]

Battle Casualty Surveys

While gelatin blocks and anesthetized cats were being perforated by high-velocity steel balls, soldiers and civilians around the world were being killed and injured by bullets and fragments from high explosive munitions. If information on their wounds could be systematically gathered, it might complement the ballistic formulas being worked out in the Princeton experiments.

Doctors and others had long been interested in war wounds. Huguier's ideas on 'explosive' wounding had come from his observation of injuries in the fighting in 1848. La Garde, a US Army doctor, had done wound ballistics experiments and later made observations on casualties in the Spanish–American war. Wilson had gone on from his experiments to observe World War I battle casualties. Wound specimens had been collected and placed in medical museums for study. 'Such specimens are original documents, they constitute an original and reliable source of knowledge for all time, and supply the most valuable basis possible for present and future medical and surgical treatment of the diseases and injuries of war,' the Director-General of the British Army Medical Service had stated in 1917.[25]

In Great Britain in World War II, the surveys of civilian air raid victims yielded detailed information on the wounding power of bombs. Later in the war, in 1943, Solly Zuckerman was sent to northern Africa in the wake of the German retreat to study the damage done by Allied bombing. His approach, he later wrote, was 'to treat each operation as one might an experiment of a very crude kind' in which results were compared to the plans for attack.[26] In the course of this work, a survey was made of 3,919 missile casualties, showing, among other things, which parts of the body were most often hit.[27]

In the United States in October 1943, Colonel Callender's Conference on Missile Casualties recommended the creation of a casualty survey unit to be trained by the Oxford group and comprising specialists drawn from a variety of fields. The Army Surgeon General turned down the proposal for lack of trained personnel but recommended that theater commanders be advised of the need for data on battle wounds and that they assign medical officers to collect such information for transmittal back to the conference.[28] In an article sent to all theaters, Colonel Callender outlined what was in effect a method for the collection of battle casualty information, and listed the purposes for which it was needed:

> Study of the character and distribution of injuries by type of weapon on all battle casualties or on sufficient numbers to make possible conclusions of value will not only indicate to the surgeon his problem in a given battle, but will be a guide to the commander. It will also be of value in indicating the areas for which the use of body armor should be considered. Similar information obtained from enemy casualties would be of assistance in determining the effect of our own weapons and of value to our commanders...
>
> Such information is often difficult to obtain, but if personnel are made aware of its usefulness they will find opportunities. Medical officers assigned to examine the bodies of the dead before burial may be able to record the location of wounds and determine with some degree of accuracy those responsible for death. Under certain conditions autopsies can be performed and the character of tissue damage determined...
>
> Information on the kind of action in which casualties occur, including terrain, weather, range and type of weapon, can often be obtained from wounded or other personnel of the units engaged. This, plus the actual findings in the casualties, gives a more complete and valuable picture of the effectiveness of the weapons concerned.

Callender listed the 'information desired,' including the following:

Location of the wounds. Note: Diagrams, even roughly drawn diagrams, are of great value.

Wound description. Describe all wounds, using measurements when possible, and state the shape and the character, such as punctured, lacerated, etc. An opinion as to whether wounds are entrance or exit wounds may be of considerable value.

Description of the wound track. This is rarely possible in those killed in action, but occasionally opportunities will present themselves for a thorough postmortem examination. In the living, X-ray findings and data from the operation should be included. Where multiple wounds exist, describe all of them and give an opinion as to the probable missiles responsible.[29]

The first person to investigate battle casualties along the lines now being recommended was Major Allan Palmer of the US Army Medical Corps. In November 1943 Major Palmer was sent to study casualty survey methods with Solly Zuckerman. In January 1944, with the help of a medical officer from Zuckerman's unit, Palmer made a sample survey of one hundred US Army casualties sustained in a week's fighting near Cassino, Italy. They noted such factors as the weapons responsible for wounds, the effect of posture on wounds, and the number of casualties suffering injuries from blast. Later in the year, Palmer made a detailed study of casualties among US bomber crews returning to England. He examined the bodies of eighty-nine dead flyers, interviewed wounded crew members, and analyzed the explosive characteristics of German antiaircraft shells in relation to which parts of the aircraft were most often hit and which hits caused the most casualties. This study enabled Palmer to draw conclusions about the body armor needed to give crew members better protection.

Two further studies were done in Italy, where Brigadier General Joseph I. Martin, Surgeon of the Fifth US Army, had requested complete records on all battle casualties dying in army hospitals from the beginning of 1944. One, initiated by General Martin, was a six-volume study of the bodies of one thousand soldiers received for burial at US military cemeteries; it dealt with the location of missile wounds in the body. The other was a three-volume study of hospital reports on wounded soldiers who died in hospital or were dead on arrival. This study considered immediate causes of death, such as neural trauma, bleeding, and shock, in relation to the location of wounds; its main purpose was to learn how hospital treatment could be improved.

In the Pacific, as a result of Colonel Callender's article, a team organized by order of the US Army Surgeon General studied 2,335 American casualties in the fighting on Bougainville Island in 1944. The purpose of the study was 'to obtain information on the relative effectiveness of different weapons as casualty-producing agents.' Elsewhere in the Pacific, a young US Army doctor, Captain James E.T. Hopkins, 'deeply impressed by the many casualties among US troops which apparently resulted from carelessness,' began collecting records of his own 'in order to demonstrate how combat losses could be reduced.' Later, Hopkins came in contact with Colonel Callender, and with Callender's help he analyzed his data along the lines of the other casualty studies then being made. His surveys yielded unusual insights into the infliction of casualties in jungle warfare.

The battle casualty studies, profusely illustrated, were published along with the Princeton study in the US Army volume *Wound Ballistics*. In this thick book, printed on shiny paper, pictures of swollen gelatin blocks and bulging animal limbs from the Princeton experiments are followed by photos of naked dead soldiers with parts of their bodies blown away and captions marked 'Wound of entrance' and 'Wound of exit.' These young men had made a double contribution to their country. They fought, and gave their lives; now, in death, their bodies could yield secrets to improve the efficacy of future wars.

The Study of Accidents

A further source of wound information was to be found in incidents where weapons went off by mistake. 'Unfortunate as these accidents are, they can still serve as a source of some valuable information concerning the potential and possible lethal effects of our own weapons,' Major Beyer wrote in the preface to *Wound Ballistics*. Under the 'semi-controlled circumstances' in which they occurred, 'These unfortunate accidents can ... be utilized as biological indicators of the effectiveness of our weapons.'[30]

On 12 June 1944, a 20-lb fragmentation bomb being loaded on an American B-17 bomber at an airfield in England was inadvertently dropped onto the concrete pavement six feet below, and exploded. Major Allan Palmer, then involved in a study of battle casualties among bomber crews, set to work to reconstruct the accident. Observing the bomb crater in the concrete and the pattern of fragment hits on the underside of the bomber, he plotted the location and orientation of the bomb at the moment of explosion. He studied the casualties medically, and worked out the positions of exposed men in relation to the bomb. Using figures compiled by Burns and Zuckerman for the 'mean projected area' of soldiers, Palmer compared the accident with previous estimates of the likely effects of the 20-lb bomb, and found that there had been 'a desirable distribution of fragments for anti-personnel effect.'[31]

Wound Ballistics at the End of World War II

The findings of the World War II experiments and casualty surveys were relevant to subjects ranging from weaponry to the design of body armor and the treatment of the wounded. As the Princeton group had written, the knowledge of wound ballistics was important 'not only in offense but also in defense.' From a military point of view, offense and defense are but two sides of the same coin. Whether by improving the means of attack, or better protecting soldiers so that they can continue fighting, or healing the wounded so that they can return to battle, the military commander is ultimately enhancing the effectiveness of his fighting machine.

Within this logic, warfare is an activity not to be prevented or stopped, but to be improved. As the US Army Surgeon General wrote in the foreword to *Wound Ballistics*:

> War, which has been a bane to man since his earliest days, has always been characterized by the presence of those who attempt to devise more and more effective ways to maim and destroy the enemy, of others who strive to develop the means to protect their comrades from the implements of the foe, and of still others on both sides who devote themselves to improving techniques for the care and repair of the unfortunates who are the casualties of war. These three facets of war are interdependent, and one group cannot achieve the best results without the advice and assistance of the others. The thread which binds and correlates their activities is the science and application of the principles of wound ballistics.[32]

For the first group, those attempting 'to devise more and more effective ways to maim and destroy the enemy,' the World War II studies offered a wealth of information. The laboratory experiments had yielded well-documented physical explanations of the mechanism of wounding, along with formulas which a weapons designer could use to achieve the desired effect. The casualty surveys showed the circumstances in which wounds were actually inflicted: by what weapons, at what range, on what parts of the body and with what degree of damage or disablement. The two lines of inquiry informed and reinforced each other, resulting in an unprecedented understanding of how soldiers were injured.

Wound ballistics research in World War II had laid the basis for the revolution in munitions design that was to come about during the next decade. Its most important finding, borne out in the Princeton formulas, was summed up in Zuckerman's statement that for antipersonnel effectiveness, smallness in a wounding missile is 'more than compensated ... by increase in velocity.' As World War II-era munitions tended to explode into a relatively small number of fragments that were much larger than what was needed to cause injury, it would seem to follow that there must be an enormous potential for injuring more soldiers if the same munitions could be redesigned to produce a larger number of smaller fragments moving at a higher velocity.[33]

All that was needed to turn this vision into a reality was the recognition of a clear military need to make antipersonnel weapons effective against more people. That impetus was to come just a few years later, in the horribly destructive form of the Korean war.

Notes

1. E. Harvey *et al.*, 1962, p. 144.
2. At the beginning of the nineteenth century, most armies were using smoothbore muskets firing round lead balls. Major innovations in the course of the century were the introduction of cylindrical pointed bullets fired from barrels with rifled grooves; smokeless powder, which was far more energy-efficient than the black powder previously used; and changes in the firing system (breech loading with metal cartridge cases) and bullet construction (Sellier and Kneubuehl, 1994, pp. 47–52).
3. E. Harvey *et al.*, 1962, p. 144.
4. Horsley, 1894, pp. 233–4.
5. *Ibid.*, p. 232.
6. Woodruff, 1898, pp. 594–5. Something of the same sort, Woodruff wrote, could be seen 'by merely moving the hand rapidly through the water in a bath tub.'.
7. Keith and Rigby, 1899, p. 1505. Other early wound ballistics investigations were conducted by researchers on the European continent including Busch, Bircher, Delorme and Chevasse, and Kocher (E. Harvey *et al.*, 1962, p. 145; Sellier and Kneubuehl, 1994, pp. 62–7). According to Sellier and Kneubuehl, Kocher was the first investigator to use soap and gelatin as model substances in experiments. Kocher may also have been the first to apply the findings of wound ballistics to reduce rather than to increase the level of suffering inflicted by projectiles. Having determined that the mushrooming of the lead bullets then in use was responsible for greater injuries, 'Kocher demanded the production of harder non-deformable projectiles.... As a result, in 1880 the Federal Ammunition Factory of Thun ... produced a full-jacketed bullet with a newly patented bottleneck-case, joined together into a cartridge.... The direct result was that all important armies introduced this type of projectile around the turn of the century' (*ibid.*, p. 64). As in military rifle ammunition used today by the armies of the world, the effect of surrounding the core of a bullet fully with a hard metal jacket is to prevent the core from mushrooming when the bullet hits the body.
8. E. Harvey *et al.*, 1962, pp. 144–5.
9. Wilson, 1921, pp. 248–9.
10. *Ibid.*, p. 246.
11. Callender and French, 1935. Wilson, too, had emphasized the importance of velocity in wounding. 'The chief interest centers around missiles of high velocity,' he told the Association of Military Surgeons in 1921. 'Comparatively

speaking, it is not the push of the elephant's shoulder with which we are concerned, but rather the kick of the mule. Though the former may be the more ponderable force, the latter creates the more disastrous results' (Wilson, 1921, p. 241).

12. UK Air Ministry, 1963, pp. 41–2.

13. The urgency with which British scientists of the time felt impelled to contribute to the war effort can be gauged from a Penguin Special, *Science in War*, written in great haste by Zuckerman together with twenty-four other scientists and published in August 1940. 'The tragic events which have led to the danger- ous pass in which we now stand have run their course not so much for lack of will or action, as for lack of thought, and particularly for lack of scientific thought and foresight,' they wrote. 'There is ... a greater need for science in the present situation than there ever has been in the quiet days of the past' (*Science in War*, p. 7).

14. Zuckerman, 1940.

15. Black, Burns, and Zuckerman, 1941.

16. Krauss, 1957, p. 221.

17. Beyer, ed., 1962, pp. xii–xiii.

18. The Princeton group followed earlier researchers in using flesh simulants in wound ballistics experiments. They explained: 'To supplement the direct ex- periments on animals, it is highly instructive to study nonliving models. These models simplify the physical conditions and serve to illustrate what can happen in a homogeneous medium.... The tank of water, particularly, allows high-speed photography and a complete analysis of all that happens' (E. Harvey *et al.*, 1962, p. 147). 'Most soft tissues contain about 80 per cent water, and it has been found that many of the important events in wounding can be reproduced by shooting into a tank of water' (*ibid.*, p. 153).

19. Noting that the question of what happens to the tissues displaced by the permanent cavity was 'a significant one,' the researchers showed from firings into water, gelatin, and animals that such 'materials' are thrown out in a 'splash' where the missile enters, and swept out at the other end. In a spark shadowgram of the thigh of a cat, taken immediately after perforation by a steel ball and published in their report, the thigh is seen to bulge at the points of entrance and exit, and a cloud of hair and tissues seems to be flying out from the fur at both sides. 'A definite splash has occurred at the point of entrance of the missile, and materials are flying out at a high velocity,' the researchers remarked. 'Large amounts of material are also being swept out by the missile as it emerges at the left.'

20. Pressure changes and the effects on gas-filled pockets were studied through firings into tanks of water in which balloons, excised frog hearts, and the intes- tine of a cat were suspended.

21. The fact that the shattering of the skull is due to the formation of a temporary cavity in the brain was demonstrated by an experiment in which 'the brain of a cat was removed through the foramen magnum and the air-filled head was then shot with a ⅛-inch steel sphere moving 3,800 feet per second.... It will be noted that no shattering has occurred, the only damage being rather neat entrance and exit holes. Without a liquid medium, the high pressure necessary to blow skull bones apart cannot be built up.'

22. The researchers expressed this relation as 'an expansion coefficient which gives the volume of cavity formed for each unit of energy and is equal to 8.92 × 10⁻⁷ cubic centimeters per erg for water.' Their study also established an 'excavation coefficient' giving the volume of permanent cavity formed for each unit of missile energy.

23. According to the Princeton formulas, the distance of penetration of a sphere is proportional to the impact velocity and inversely proportional to the retardation coefficient. As the retardation coefficient (as mentioned earlier) is proportional to the projected area of the sphere divided by its mass, A/M, a decrease in the radius of the sphere, R, results in a proportional decrease in penetration (A/M is inversely proportional to R, as area is proportional to the square of the radius while mass is proportional to volume, which in turn is proportional to the cube of the radius). From the same formulas, an increase in density brings about a proportional increase in penetration, as the mass of an object is proportional to its density.

To investigate the results of using missiles of different densities, the Princeton researchers fired a steel ball and an aluminum ball of the same size and at the same velocity into tanks of water. The aluminum ball formed a 'short, wide cavity ... indicating that it lost energy at a more rapid rate than the steel sphere.'

24. *Ibid.*, pp. 146, 158.

25. Beyer, ed., 1962, pp. xi–xii.

26. Zuckerman, 1966, pp. 115–16.

27. Beyer, ed., 1962, p. 847.

28. *Ibid.*, p. xiii.

29. Callender's article was published in the *Bulletin of the US Army Medical Department*, March 1944, pp. 19–22, under the title 'Need for Data on the Distribution of Missile Wounds.'

30. Beyer, ed., 1962, pp. xv–xvi, 827.

31. *Ibid.*, pp. 827–41. Four of the loading crew had been killed outright in the accident, two died later, and eleven others were injured. Major Beyer considered that Palmer's inquiry could 'serve as a model for future studies of accidental discharges of weapons during wartime or during training procedures' (*ibid.*, p. xv).

32. *Ibid.*, p. ix.

33. These points were shown most clearly in Palmer's study of the accident involving the detonation of an M41 20-lb. fragmentation bomb at an airfield in England. Palmer found that 'M41 bomb fragments of less than 1 gm. in weight are relatively incapable of producing fatal injuries but are definitely incapacitating in their effect.' Yet explosive tests of the bomb had shown 75 per cent of the recovered fragments to be over 2.25 grams in weight and 25 per cent to be over 7 grams – a considerable overkill if the purpose of the bomb was to knock personnel out of action (Beyer, ed., 1962, pp. 836, 841).

CHAPTER 2

KOREA: THE REDESIGN OF ANTIPERSONNEL WEAPONS

Early in the 1950s, the Department of Army embarked on a program to develop special antipersonnel munitions for a variety of weapon systems. These munitions were characterized by a design philosophy which considered the efficient distribution of the smallest effective fragment. The definition of effectiveness was the fallout of a considerable wound ballistics program which evolved the lethal potential of small fragments at high velocity. By small is meant one- or two-grain fragments at velocities of 3,000 to over 6,000 feet per second.

US Army Project Manager for Selected Ammunition, 1973[1]

On 25 June 1950, North Korean forces crossed the 38th parallel, the line which had divided the two Koreas since 1945, and moved south on a broad front. By 28 June they had taken Seoul, and by August they were in possession of most of the South. Then General Douglas MacArthur, commander of the United Nations forces, made his famous amphibian landing at Inchon; Seoul was recaptured; and the North Korean forces, largely broken, fled north. General MacArthur's forces regained the 38th parallel, but instead of stopping where the war had begun, they crossed over and continued northwards. In June, the US Secretary of State had said the UN action in Korea should be 'solely for the purpose of restoring the Republic of Korea [South Korea] to its status prior to the invasion from the north'; now the idea was to liberate the communist North and reunite the country, with elections under UN auspices.[2]

Reginald Thompson, correspondent for the London *Daily Telegraph*, observed the technique of massive firepower which characterized the advance of the mainly US troops fighting under the United Nations flag. In one instance, an armored column moving through a valley was halted for over an hour by a few North Koreans firing from a hillside. The response was to unleash 'a deluge of fire' from the tanks, causing so much noise that it was impossible to detect the enemy or assess his fire:

At the first slight lull in this tempest of din the stutter of the enemy machine gun came again from the hills, and an odd shot or two, calling forth again an immense reply.... Within 15 minutes the fighters had joined in, diving down upon the hillside with their rockets.... In terms of money the American reply to every short enemy burst of .50 caliber was equal to about one thousand dollars to a dime.

Thompson considered the operation wasteful of time and ammunition: 'In ten minutes a section could have outflanked the enemy post on its feet. A patrol could have gone through immediately ahead of the advance and swept the whole thing out of the way...' At last a platoon was dispatched, and in ten minutes they had flushed out the enemy soldiers and killed them.

Thompson, a veteran journalist, commented:

I have described this in some detail because it was typical of the whole advance and the whole method. Every enemy shot released a deluge of destruction. Every village and township in the path of war was blotted out. Civilians died in the rubble and ashes of their homes. Soldiers usually escaped. Time and again a handful of men held up a regiment, forcing a few of them at last — but never at first — to get on their feet off the road and deploy.[3]

Advancing on the North Korean town of Namchonjon, the Americans were fired on, so they pulled back. When they moved in the next morning:

...it was the usual slow business. They knew no other way. The odd bursts of fire. The halt. The air strike. The artillery. Tanks forward....

Namchonjon was an appalling ruin, a scene of almost absolute desolation. There was nothing left of it. It had been a considerable town of at least 10,000 souls, perhaps more, in Korea. None now.[4]

After Seoul was recaptured, with perhaps 50,000 people killed, Thompson had sent his newspaper a dispatch which ended with this judgment:

It is inescapable that the terrible fate of the South Korean capital and many villages is the outcome of a new technique of machine warfare. The slightest resistance brought down a deluge of destruction, blotting out the area. Dive bombers, tanks and artillery blasted strong points, large or small, in town and hamlet, while the troops waited at the roadside as spectators until the way was cleared for them. Few people can have suffered so terrible a liberation.[5]

The United Nations forces advanced rapidly through the north, toward the Chinese border. Warnings from the Chinese were ignored.[6] Then Chinese troops entered North Korea, and soon the Americans and their allies — ill-equipped for winter, thinly strung out, their lines of communication clogged – were retreating in great confusion, back to the 38th parallel and beyond.

There was talk of using atomic weapons. A young broadcaster asked some scared GIs for their opinion on the bomb. 'Hell, yes, use it,' they replied. 'They're overrunning our CP's [command posts]!'[7]

Had it indeed been the 'compleat' miracle weapon, the bomb might have stopped the Chinese advance. Had there been any Hiroshimas or Nagasakis, they could easily have been destroyed. But Chinese infantry in the countryside and rudimentary airbases in Manchuria were hardly the spectacular targets whose destruction would have been so decisive as to outweigh the political cost of using the bomb. Korea was already in ruins from the American 'liberation.' There was nothing left to bomb.

> I would say that the entire, almost the entire Korean peninsula is just a terrible mess [Major General Emmett O'Donnell, Jr., commander of the US Far Eastern Air Force Bomber Command during the first six months of the war, testified in the US Senate 'MacArthur hearings' in 1951]. Everything is destroyed. There is nothing standing worthy of the name.... Just before the Chinese came in we were grounded. *There were no more targets in Korea.*[8] (emphasis added)

Here was the paradox. The mightiest country on earth, using massive firepower and possessing a superweapon believed to be capable of stopping a war, had been routed by 'hordes' of Chinese foot soldiers – lightly clad, lightly armed, short of artillery, lacking airpower, but in hordes. American military might had been challenged by an enemy, technologically inferior but with inexhaustible reserves of manpower. And the lesson drawn from the experience was – not that the decision to invade the North had been a mistake, nor that the 'new technique of machine warfare' could be inferior to conventional infantry tactics, nor that the use of that machine itself might be questioned because of the terrible suffering it brought to the people on whose behalf it was used, but that the answer to the threat must be to improve the machine.

> We cannot hope to match the communist enemy in manpower [US Secretary of the Army Robert T. Stevens wrote in his annual report for the first half of 1953]. If we wish to maintain our present standard of living, or anything approaching it, we cannot hope to match him in sheer weight of reserve materiel. We must, therefore, use our limited manpower far more effectively. And *we must provide our soldiers with the finest weapons and equipment that the talent of our scientists and military experts and the ingenuity of our industrial community can produce.*[9] (emphasis added)

Superior technology must defeat superior manpower. The search for better nonnuclear means of attacking enemy soldiers was to inspire munitions designers for the next decade. World War II studies of wounding had pointed the way to a solution: the massive deployment of small, high velocity wounding missiles. The key to this was fragmentation.

Fragmentation, Source of 'Kill Mechanisms'

Fragmentation. A fragment of a poem, of a flower. The fragmentation of a broken heart, of the tribes of Israel, of the postwar world order. In ordnance:

> Fragmentation is the rupture of a metal container by a high explosive filler. Its purpose is to produce the optimum distribution of a maximum number of high velocity lethal fragments. Due to using high explosive filler, fragmentation is always accompanied by blast.
>
> The fragment acts as a kill mechanism by impacting the target at high velocity with its mass and forcing its way through the target material. The kinetic energy of the fragment at the time it strikes the target is one measure of its lethality. The optimum fragment mass, velocity, and distribution will vary according to the target be it a human, vehicle, airplane, building, missile, satellite, etc.
>
> It is generally desirable to have a shell or bomb body break up into pieces no larger than are required to 'kill' the particular target. This provides the maximum number of effective fragments by avoiding fragment sizes that are larger than necessary.[10]

'The fragment acts as a kill mechanism by impacting the target at high velocity with its mass' – and a target made of flesh and bone is easier to 'kill'[11] than a hard-skinned airplane or a brick-walled edifice. 'Forcing its way through the target material,' the fragment disperses the flesh with explosive rapidity, creating a temporary cavity whose size is a measure of the extent of wounding. But how much of a wound is needed to 'kill' an enemy soldier?

World War II: Criteria for 'Fatal or Severe Wounding'

World War II wound ballistics researchers had devoted considerable thought to the question: what sort of a wound was needed to put a soldier out of action? As in other domains, it was the British who led the way, with Burns and Zuckerman defining a class of what they called 'severe' wounds – damage to the liver, heart, or other vital organs.[12] In the United States, the concept was refined by two members of the Princeton group, J. Howard McMillen and J.R. Gregg, who characterized a 'fatal or severe wound' as damage to certain 'vulnerable regions'

– the organs, including the eyes, nerves and blood vessels with a diameter greater than a quarter of a centimeter, and 'all tissues found in such peritoneal, pleural, pericardial, vertebral canal and cranial cavity.' A missile penetrating any of these regions would, in their definition, cause a fatal or severe wound.

What was the likelihood of this happening? What sorts of missiles were needed? Using drawings from a recently published anatomical textbook showing cross-sections of the human body, McMillen and Gregg measured the thickness of skin, bone, and flesh through which a missile striking various parts of the body would have to pass before hitting a 'vulnerable region.' Once this was done, it was a simple matter to calculate, from the Princeton formulas for penetration, whether or not a steel ball of a given size and velocity striking the body in a particular place would reach a 'vulnerable region' underneath. The areas where this would happen were then added up and compared to the total area of a person exposed as a target to give a figure for the probability that such a steel ball, striking the body at random, would cause a fatal or severe wound.[13]

As this calculation was repeated for missiles of different masses and velocities, two interesting results emerged. First, it was found that once a steel ball had been endowed with a 'threshold energy' such that a fatal or severe wound would result from impact somewhere on the body, the probability of fatal or severe wounding increased rapidly as the energy of the ball was increased – until an 'optimum energy' was reached. Beyond that point, the probability increased more slowly until it reached a maximum. What this suggested was that it would be more efficient, in the design of a bomb or shell, to have it explode into fragments of *optimum* energy than to endow the fragments with the extra energy needed to achieve the *maximum* possibility of fatal or severe wounding.

The second discovery was that, if one averaged together the calculations for $1/16$-, $1/8$-, and $1/4$-inch steel balls (the three sizes considered in the study), the optimum energy for fatal or severe wounding was 15 foot-pounds. This number was barely more than *one fourth* of the figure then used as a basis for weapons design – the widely accepted '58 foot-pound casualty criterion,' established at the turn of the century, which stated that a missile with 58 foot-pounds (80 joules) of energy was capable of inflicting a casualty.[14]

Taken together with the other World War II findings, these two discoveries suggested that there was great scope for improvement in the design of antipersonnel weapons. The size of fragments could be drastically reduced, to the point where they had no more than the 'optimum energy' needed to inflict a fatal or severe wound.

Korea: Criteria for 'Rapid Incapacitation'

Soon after the outbreak of the Korean war, the US Army headquarters in Washington issued 'requirements' for a series of new weapons.[15] Among them was a hand grenade which was to be 'as dangerous as possible to an enemy within 15 feet of its burst and as safe as possible to the thrower.'[16]

Two engineers at the US Army Ballistic Research Laboratories (BRL) in Maryland set to work on the project. They looked at McMillen and Gregg's criteria for fatal or severe wounding, and at similar, later criteria devised by the US Army researchers Gurney and Sterne, and thought these could serve as measures of the 'dangerousness' of a grenade to an enemy soldier. But McMillen and Gregg's calculations had not been 'checked by comparison with experiments against living targets,' and it seemed wise to make sure.

> Aware of the possible inadequacy of all existing wounding criteria, the Ballistic Research Laboratories asked the Biophysics Branch, Medical Laboratories, Army Chemical Center, Edgewood to conduct experiments against live targets to obtain experimental values for the probabilities of incapacitation caused by fragment hits. The Biophysics Branch most graciously cooperated, and the US Army Medical Corps assigned certain medical officers to participate in the experiments by assessing the incapacitating effects of the observed wounds … as though the wounds had been of humans. The first experiments were conducted on 25 July 1951, and early in August it became apparent that while the probabilities of 'fatal or severe' wounding that had been employed up to this time in the grenade design study were substantially correct, the whole notion of fatal or severe wounding was probably not appropriate to the purpose for which hand grenades are normally used in battle.
>
> What had been revealed by the experiments was the critical importance of the 'level,' or type, of incapacitation that was employed in evaluating hand grenades. The McMillen and Gregg, and Sterne, criteria gave the probabilities that random hits by fragments with particular masses, striking velocities, and presented areas would cause fatal or severe wounds. The experiments showed that these probabilities were substantially correct. Yet the experiments also showed that *a moribund animal,*[17] *which had suffered wounds that would eventually lead to its death, was by no means invariably incapacitated soon after wounding*, to anything like the extent that would be necessary to prevent a human soldier from continuing to offer effective resistance for periods of many minutes or hours. (emphasis added)

Although the official requirement had said nothing about rapid incapacitation, the report continued, 'it seemed clear to all who were familiar with the tactical use of hand grenades that in most situations great rapidity of incapacitation was necessary if a hand grenade was to accomplish its purpose.'

Fatal or severe wounding was not enough: how rapidly, then, should enemy soldiers be immobilized? Infantry experts consulted by the researchers asked for 'immediate incapacitation,' but the Edgewood Arsenal experts

> pointed out that 'immediate' incapacitation was either difficult or impossible to obtain. However, incapacitation within five seconds, although difficult to obtain, would not be impossible. Taking into account the practical impossibility of a soldier's effective action within five seconds of a loud and unexpected explosion next to him, that enshrouded him in smoke, almost all of the people who were consulted agreed eventually that incapacitation within about five seconds would be a desirable goal for the designer of a hand grenade to seek to achieve.

Even five-second incapacitation would be 'difficult to obtain.' In the judgment of the medical officers who watched the experiments, it could normally be achieved only by severe injury to parts of the brain or to the spinal cord above the second or third thoracic vertebra – a paralyzing wound. Because these parts of the body occupied much less room than McMillen and Gregg's 'vulnerable regions,' the likelihood of five-second incapacitation would be less than that of 'fatal or severe wounding.'[18]

The BRL researchers went to the drawing boards, and by varying the construction of the grenade body and the amount and type of explosive – and thence the size, mass, and velocity of fragments produced on explosion – they came up with a design for a hand grenade that was one-and-a-half to two times as likely to produce five-second incapacitation at 15 feet from the bursting point as the familiar 'pineapple' grenade of World War II. Taking into account that a soldier could be hit by more than one fragment at once, they calculated that the new grenade would have a probability of five-second incapacitation of 4 per cent at 15 feet from the bursting point – still a low figure, but it would be higher for soldiers closer to the burst.

The BRL study was important because it led to a new way of thinking about how antipersonnel weapons could best be designed to attack soldiers in different tactical situations. The 'five-second incapacitation criterion' which emerged from the experiments was later abandoned because it was deemed too difficult to achieve. Instead, in the early 1950s the US Army adopted two other, classified criteria developed at the Ballistic Research Laboratories: a *30-second incapacitation criterion*, used in the design of small arms, where the enemy is nearby; and a *five-minute criterion*, used for artillery ammunition, where the enemy is further away and does not need to be disabled so quickly. Both criteria have been used in weapons design in other NATO countries as well as the United States.

Controlled Fragmentation: The M26 Grenade

Research and design work continued at the Ballistic Research Laboratories in cooperation with other Army labs and private companies working under Army contracts.[19] The result was the M26, the first of a new postwar generation of hand grenades. It was introduced to readers of the defense industry journal *Ordnance* in the following terms:[20]

> After some 40 years of faithful service, the old cast-iron Mk II grenade has been put aside for a newcomer, the M26 grenade.... Instead of using conventional cast iron for the body, the M26 grenade body is made of notched, $1/8$-inch-square wire, wrapped to shape and enclosed in a thin sheet-metal cover. The wire and the cover break up into more than a thousand fragments at a velocity of over 4,000 feet a second, encouraged by the 6 ounces of Composition B used as the filler.[21]

The M26 embodies the principle toward which World War II wound ballistics research had pointed: a drastic reduction in fragment size. This is accomplished through the use of wire with notches at regular intervals. On explosion, the wire breaks at the notches, producing a spray of fast-moving metal fragments. The fragments are uniform in size, and the size and shape of fragments are predetermined by the dimensions of the wire and the spacing of the notches. This predetermination of fragment characteristics is known as *controlled fragmentation*.[22]

The decrease in fragment size entailed a number of factors which combined to yield a far more effective weapon than the familiar cast-iron 'pineapple' of World War II. The differences between the two designs are shown in the 1952 BRL study, and in descriptions in Army manuals.[23]

- The wire is quite thin. In discussing a grenade design of this type, the BRL study recommended using rectangular wire, approximately $1/8$ inch by $1/12$ inch in cross-section, wound with the flat side toward the center and deeply notched at $1/8$-inch intervals. The wire was to be made of steel with sufficient tensile strength to withstand shattering or chipping of the fragments on explosion. The dimensions of the wire could be varied to achieve the fragment characteristics most appropriate for the type of casualty desired – a larger and heavier fragment, for example, would be needed to penetrate far enough to produce a paralyzing wound amounting to 'rapid incapacitation' than if a merely 'fatal or severe' wound was required.

- The Mk II 'pineapple' grenade, in contrast, is made of cast iron with shallow external grooves in a rectangular pattern. If on explosion it breaks along the grooves, the result will be about 40 fast-flying chunks of metal, about half an inch on each side. Each of these will be large enough to cause a serious wound, but fewer soldiers are likely to be hit.

- The thinness of the wire means that the M26 grenade casing is much lighter than on the thick-walled iron grenade. The M26 casing weighs approximately half a pound, half the weight of Mk II casing. The result is a lighter grenade. Together with the fuze and explosive filler, the M26 has an overall weight of 16 ounces, while the Mk II weighs 21. The lighter grenade can be thrown further and more accurately, and, weight for weight, more of them can be transported to the battlefield and carried by a soldier.[24]

- As the two grenades are of approximately the same size, the thinner wall of the M26 means that there is more room for the explosive. Some 5.8 ounces of explosive are packed inside the M26, as against 2 ounces in the Mk II. As the initial velocity of fragments thrown off by the explosion of a shell depends mainly on the characteristics of the explosive and the 'charge-to-mass ratio' (C/M, the ratio between the mass of the explosive charge and the mass of the metal casing), more explosive and less casing material results in faster fragments. And whereas the 'pineapple' grenade uses TNT as the explosive charge, the M26 is packed with 'Composition B' – a mixture of TNT with the more powerful explosive RDX.[25] Together with the improved charge-to-mass ratio, the use of Composition B results in faster fragments.[26]

These comparisons show what tremendous improvements could be made once munitions were reexamined in light of the wounding discoveries made during World War II. By 1952, the BRL scientists were already able to predict that their redesigned grenade would produce paralyzing wounds within five seconds 50 per cent to 100 per cent more frequently than the Mk II grenade. The five-second incapacitation criterion was later relaxed, but the M26 still has an impressive 'effective casualty radius' of 15 meters. The Army defines 'effective casualty radius' as 'the radius of a circle about the point of detonation in which it may normally be expected that 50 per cent of the exposed personnel will become casualties.'[27]

Pre-Fragmentation: The Claymore Mine

The M26 grenade, with its notched wire, exemplifies the technique of controlled fragmentation. In a form of controlled fragmentation known as *pre-fragmentation*, the fragments are manufactured beforehand and embedded in the case.

The M18A1 Claymore mine is one such weapon. Standardized by the Army in 1960, it was the first modern US high explosive munition in which steel balls were used as fragments. (An earlier version, the M18, used pre-formed rectangular steel fragments and a smaller explosive charge.)[28]

Named after the old Scottish two-edged sword, the Claymore mine is a curved boxlike object made of plastic. It stands on four folding legs and is meant to be installed with the convex side facing the place where the enemy is expected to appear. Seven hundred 10.5-grain steel balls are embedded in the outer face; behind them is a layer of plastic explosive.[29] According to an Army manual, the mine has an 'optimum effective range' of 50 meters; this is defined as the range at which the most desirable balance is achieved between lethality and area coverage. The 'killing zone' is a 60-degree arc extending 50 meters in front of the mine, but the fast-flying fragments remain 'moderately effective' out to 100 meters and dangerous out to 250 meters. Friendly soldiers can stay within 16 meters of the back of the mine, as the concave face has no metal fragments and the plastic enclosure disintegrates on explosion.[30]

The *New York Times* reported on 1 May 1966 that the Claymore had received its 'first test of war' in Vietnam. 'It forms some of the principal defenses of every US camp or position in Vietnam,' the newspaper stated. Typically, Claymore mines were placed around military outposts with electric wires running back to a point where a sentry could watch, ready to detonate the mines if he saw the enemy approaching. But the mine can also be used with a tripwire, as an ambush weapon, or as a booby trap; indeed, in the words of an Army manual, 'The number of ways in which the Claymore may be employed is limited only by the imagination of the user.' The Claymore and other mines based on the same design may be found in the inventories of armed forces throughout the world today.[31]

Like other weapons described in this chapter, the Claymore was developed in response to the experience of the Korean war. 'Claymore was designed specifically to kill the Chinese human-sea charge,' the journalist John S. Tompkins wrote in his book *The Weapons of World War III*. 'A well-placed line of them can reduce a human-sea charge to mincemeat at the touch of a button.'[32]

Natural Fragmentation: Cast-Iron Shells

When an explosion is set off inside a metal shell, gases are produced, causing the shell to expand rapidly until it ruptures. How it ruptures will determine the size of the resulting fragments.

In controlled fragmentation, the size and shape of each fragment is predetermined. The alternative is *natural fragmentation*, the fragmentation of a shell case which has not been subjected to controlled-fragmentation techniques such as grooving or the use of steel balls. Here the size and shape of individual fragments cannot be predicted, but it is still possible to reduce the average fragment size by making the shell wall thinner, using a more powerful explosive, changing the metallic properties of the shell, or making the shell out of a different material.

As with other basic innovations in antipersonnel missile design, the US search for new shell materials was prompted by the Korean war, where the UN forces were bombarded with Chinese mortar shells more lethal than their own. According to a US study of 'enemy ordnance materiel' in Korea:

> the communist use of cruder cast metals in mortar shells seemed greatly to increase the number of fragments per shell and the effectiveness of their antipersonnel mortar fire when compared to conventional steel-walled shells.[33]

At the time, the United States was making virtually all its artillery ammunition out of steel. It was known that cast iron would yield more fragments because it was more brittle, but steel, being stronger, was better able to withstand the launching stresses to which artillery shells are subjected as they are propelled through the barrel of a gun. The Korean war reawakened interest in cast iron, and in the design of mortars and mortar ammunition generally. With its high trajectory, mortar fire had proved ideal for 'the relatively close-in fighting in rugged mountainous terrain which characterized much of the operations in Korea,' according to the same study;[34] and it accounted for many injuries. A US Korean war casualty survey team found, for example, that out of 950 wounds sustained by 286 Turkish members of the UN forces in three days of fighting in late November 1950, 59 per cent were caused by fragments from mortar shells.[35]

The Chinese shells were found on examination to be made of gray cast iron, but the Americans did not consider this material safe enough: there was too great a risk that a shell would break during launching and jam in the gun barrel, causing the gun to blow up and injure the crew.[36] After investigating the strength and fragmentation characteristics of a number of other materials, the Army planners settled on pearlitic malleable iron, a common industrial material used in pistons and automobile transmission parts. Considerable work was done on the manufacturing process, and an ultrasonic inspection device was introduced so that every shell could be examined for the hidden flaws that can occur during casting.

The outcome was reported in *Ordnance* in 1961:

The US Army Ordnance Special Weapons-Ammunition Command, Dover, New Jersey, recently announced that a revolutionary method has been developed for the casting of artillery and mortar shell for the US Army. The new process permits casting shell from malleable iron instead of forged steel.

A contract for the production of 173,800 rounds of 81mm. mortar shell has been awarded to the Albion Malleable Iron Company, developers of the process.

In addition to *more effective fragmentation*, the new process permits production with a noncritical material, thus making more steel available for other defense work.[37] (emphasis added)

In 1963, William C. Truckenmiller, the man responsible for projectile component development at the Albion Malleable Iron Company, told an American Ordnance Association seminar about his company's cast-iron shells. He referred to 'the high level of lethality associated with the cast pearlitic malleable iron,' and described the manufacturing process with its use of a recently developed core material yielding smooth and accurate interior surfaces in the shell castings. The introduction of the cast-iron shell helped to relieve the demand for steel shells, freeing steel forging facilities for other military uses, broadening the base of supply, and reducing the demand for scarce and strategic alloying materials. 'The foregoing advantages are obtainable with no lessening of safety or accuracy and at essentially the same cost per item, resulting in the purchase of substantially more effectiveness per defense dollar,' Truckenmiller said.[38]

Soon the use of cast iron was extended to other munitions, including a shell for the lightweight 60mm mortar, a seemingly obsolete weapon which the US Army revived in Vietnam because of its portability.[39] The demand for cast-iron munitions in Vietnam was to become so great that the Army would be forced to turn back to steel, opening the way for further innovations in antipersonnel lethality (Chapter 3).

Rifle Fire: The ORO Study

A mortar shell is an example of a fragmentation munition which does not have to land exactly on the intended target; the target can still be hit if it is within the area covered by fragments from the explosion. The alternative in precision is a weapon used against a 'point target'[40] in 'direct fire' – 'fire directed at a target which is visible to the aimer,' in the NATO definition. The classic example of such a weapon is the rifle.

In 1952 the Operations Research Office (ORO) of Johns Hopkins University in Maryland sent the US Army a secret report entitled 'Operational Requirements for an Infantry Hand Weapon.'[41] It had been commissioned under Project Balance, an ambitious program aimed at selecting a 'balanced' system of new weapons for the Army. The experience of US soldiers in Korea outnumbered by the enemy had clearly made an impression:

> It appears almost certain that future large-scale ground operations will involve a numerically superior enemy and necessitate, at first, a defensive strategy on our part. Moreover, frequent attempts to overrun infantry positions, with attendant close combat, are to be anticipated. Thus, to increase each infantryman's capability with respect to defensive rifle fire becomes highly desirable.

Defensive fire meant close ranges; but this was not the only reason for thinking that short ranges were important. Battle casualty data from Bougainville and Korea, and interviews with soldiers and officers who had served in World War II and the Korean war, showed that most rifle fire and most hits inflicted were at ranges of 300 yards or less. One reason for this could be unevenness of terrain; to check this point, the ORO researchers made some 18,000 readings of topographical maps from different parts of the world, and concluded that '70 per cent of the ranges at which an erect human target can be seen by a defending prone rifleman are less than 300 yards.' And special tests at Fort Benning, 'designed to simulate some of the conditions of combat,' showed shooting by expert riflemen to be satisfactory only up to 100 yards.

The ORO researchers considered that ranges up to 300 yards were the most important. From this it followed that contemporary military rifles, with ranges of several thousand yards, were overdesigned.

The purpose of antipersonnel rifle fire is to 'kill' an enemy soldier. In ordnance, the probability of 'killing' a target is considered in two parts: the probability of hitting the target and the probability that a hit will result in a kill. The relationship is expressed mathematically in the equation $P_k = P_h \times P_{hk}$, where P_k is the probability of a kill, P_h is the probability of a hit, and P_{hk} is the probability that a hit will result in a kill. Both parts deserved attention in rifle design, the ORO researchers wrote:

> It has been assumed that it is desirable to increase in both *number and rate* the hits which may be inflicted on the enemy by aimed small arms in the hands of the infantry.
>
> It has been further assumed that it is desirable also to increase the mortality of wounds caused by these hits. (original emphasis)

The problem with the hit probability of rifles, the researchers found, was that soldiers often did not hit the targets they were aiming at. Training to improve marksmanship would be costly and impracticable, they thought, but there was still the possibility of 'compensating for man-aiming errors through a weapon design principle.' A weapon could be designed to fire several projectiles at once: not in ordinary automatic fire, where (because of recoil) the second bullet would land far from the first, but in a 'salvo' of little missiles designed to land close to each other in a pattern that 'would tend to maximize hit probability on the human-target shape.' A soldier being fired at would have less chance of escaping four or five bullets, and he might even be hit by more than one. At a range of 200 yards, the researchers calculated, five bullets in a crucifix pattern would have a 41 per cent 'probability of killing an enemy per burst,' some three times the kill probability of the current M1 Army rifle.

These ideas gave rise to Project Salvo, a US Army research and development effort that lasted from the early 1950s to the early 1960s. Among the designs considered in Project Salvo were 'duplex' cartridges with two bullets, one behind the other and pointed slightly to the side, and 'squeezebore' ammunition with several hollow conical projectiles in tandem fired through a tapered gun barrel.

As for the second part of the problem, to increase 'the mortality of wounds' resulting from a hit, the researchers found in their analysis of rifle fire that bullets, although aimed, actually landed on the body in a random way, like the unaimed fragments from a hand grenade. If a rifleman's chances of hitting the heart or the spine were no better than those of hitting an arm or a leg, it was essential that the bullet be capable of incapacitating no matter where it hit.

Here the researchers' thoughts turned to poison. The use of poisoned weapons had been forbidden under the Hague Regulations of 1907, but

> Quite apart from any consideration of or comment upon, the protocols and conventions according to which the rules of land warfare have been codified, it is proper to estimate in a purely physical way the results of the use of toxic missiles in such weapons.

Illegal they might be, but poisoned bullets could have effects that 'would constitute an order of lethality not achieved by any missile projecting ground weapon yet devised.' 'Developmental work in the field of toxic missiles is reasonably complete and shows that up to 90 per cent of hits from agent-loaded bullets at common ranges may be expected to incapacitate in a matter of minutes and bring about death regardless of the region of the body struck,' the researchers wrote. They referred to a promising new chemical agent which could 'be manufactured in large supply at low cost' and which was highly toxic. Moreover, 'death is rapid and the course of the effects is violent. The progress of the physiological symptoms is demoralizing to witness; thus real psychological effects not normally characteristic of weapons design are added.' Enthusiastic about developing such a terrifying weapon, they pointed out that 'Apart from flaming weapons, ordnance development has not taken advantage of possible designs to produce fear in the enemy as well as physical damage.'

Of all the proposals in the ORO report, the most important one was for a reduction in caliber, which would be consistent with the reduced ranges over which they had found rifle fire actually needed to be effective. If bullets were smaller, the researchers pointed out, they would be lighter, and a soldier could carry more; the rifle, also lighter, would be easier to carry, and the lower recoil from firing the lighter bullet would mean that the soldier's aim would be better. Velocity could be increased, so that the kinetic energy of the bullet would remain high; echoing Solly Zuckerman, the ORO researchers wrote that 'the effect of increasing the velocity of a small caliber missile more than compensates for the reduced mass.' And evidence, they wrote, showed that if it hit the target fast enough, a light bullet could even 'produce wounds of measurably *greater* severity' than those caused by a standard bullet at the same speed (original emphasis).

As it turned out, the ORO proposals were ahead of their time. The major US Army rifle project in the 1950s was the development of a successor to the M1 rifle of World War II; introduced as the M14, the new rifle was lighter than the M1 but had the same caliber (7.62mm). It would take the combat experience of Vietnam to bring home the advantages of reducing the bullet size.

In the meantime, research continued on various multiple projectiles under Project Salvo. Toward the end of the decade, attention began to focus on rifle ammunition using another form of missile: a tiny dart, actually a nail with fins at the blunt end, called a 'flechette.' That subject was of great interest to a man outside the Army with a lifelong passion for lethal missiles: Irwin R. Barr of AAI Corporation.

Mr Barr's Deadly Dart

'Death by Darts Is Coming.' So read the headline in the Baltimore *Sun* Sunday supplement. 'Mr. Barr's Deadly Dart' was the subtitle. The article told the story of AAI Corporation of Cockeysville, Maryland; its flechette rifle, then in development; and the father of the rifle, AAI vice-president Irwin R. Barr, his background, his achievements, his attitude toward his work.

> This country is up against a determined opponent [Mr. Barr told the magazine]. My son may be drafted. He's facing the possibility like a lot of other young men. If there's any fighting I'd want them to have the best possible equipment. Even if this gun doesn't make it – it's not that important. The important thing is that the men get the best weapon.

'My ambition as a kid was to design all the small arms of the United States,' Mr Barr told the *Sun*. 'My heroes were inventors and gun designers like John Browning, who invented the US .30 and .50 caliber machine guns used in World War II, the Browning automatic rifle, and the Colt automatic pistol.... When I was 14 my mother used to say all I thought about were guns and bombs. I used to draw pictures of guns and weapons of the future.'

Young Barr managed to blow up the linoleum floor of his mother's kitchen using a mixture of sugar and gargling powder; and, intent on investigating an automatic pistol which his father kept locked up, 'he simply fashioned a key for the lock and experimented with the handgun at will,' the *Sun* reported. But the turning point in Barr's creative play came when his brother presented him with a .22 caliber rifle. 'Not content merely plinking with .22s like other youngsters, the budding inventor took some old-fashioned steel phonograph needles from the family Victrola and fired them from the rifle,' the magazine related. 'The concept of the flechette intrigued him thereafter.'

After military service in World War II, Mr Barr went to work for the Martin Company, where he gained experience in the aerodynamics of rocket design. But:

> He continued to work on flechettes as a hobby. 'I began making them out of sewing machine needles heated on the gas range at home,' he recalls. 'I'd forge half a fin from the needle and use part of a razor blade for the other half. I fired the flechettes from a .22 rifle. Every now and then these would go very well, but it was hard to know without instrumentation why sometimes they didn't work.'

In 1950 Barr and several colleagues formed their own company, Aircraft Armaments, Inc. (later AAI Corporation). There he continued his experiments, and by 1958 AAI had a flechette rifle ready for testing. The Army was skeptical, but when they 'performed certain tests themselves using our ammunition,' they became interested, Mr Barr recalled.

In 1962 the Army decided to sponsor the development of a flechette rifle for possible Army use. It was blandly called 'Special Purpose Individual Weapon,' SPIW for short, and the SPIW program took the place of the ill-fated Project Salvo. Those were the days when 'special' or 'unconventional' warfare was becoming fashionable, with ample funding from President Kennedy's 1961 emergency budget, adopted in the aftermath of the Berlin Wall crisis (see Chapter 4). A lightweight, dart-propelling rifle appealed to the imagination of military planners who, a few years earlier, would have rejected the idea as frivolous.

I asked a young and enterprising engineer in one of the US Army weapons labs to tell me about the SPIW program.

'Around 1962 we awarded the initial contracts for investigations of the sequential launching of flechettes,' he said. 'There were several contenders who were supposed to submit systems that could fire flechettes sequentially – I suppose I'd better not tell you their names.' (In a time-honored government tradition, companies were not supposed to be named, lest it appear that the Army was infringing on the free-enterprise system by promoting the work of one company over another.)

'Well, all right, it doesn't matter,' I said. 'I know who they are anyway. One of them was AAI, and one was Olin...'

'All right, I guess I can tell you,' he said, and named the three companies which had received Army contracts to work on SPIW; a fourth design was submitted by the Springfield Armory. 'We wanted to obtain a high cyclic rate with a controlled burst to increase the hit probability,' he continued.

What he meant was that the SPIW designers wanted to fire several flechettes at once, landing close together, so as to increase the chances of hitting a 'target,' compensating for the poor marksmanship which had been revealed in the ORO study. This was in line with Project Salvo, which had concentrated on multiple-bullet rifles. In SPIW experimental models, the engineer told me, a 'pattern dispersion' of flechettes was obtained by means of a rapid burst of three darts launched in sequence, or by packing several darts side by side in a cartridge and firing them together.

In 1964, word of the flechette rifle reached the public through an article in the *New York Times*. It evoked the casualties that could be inflicted by the experimental weapon:

> The flechettes have a tendency to tumble on impact, or to penetrate the flesh sideways, or end over end, thus inflicting tremendous wounds, most of them lethal.
>
> A recent article in *The Army Times*, unofficial Army newspaper, reported the comment of an officer who was asked about the medical task of healing a man wounded with flechettes.
>
> 'Don't kid yourself,' *The Army Times* reported the answer, 'it is not a job for a surgeon but for graves registration.'
>
> Thus, the flechette could have considerable psychological effect on the battlefield.[42]

However, the casualty-producing effect of flechettes could not be taken for granted. Conceivably, a missile well stabilized to streak through the air would also pass directly through the body, causing relatively little damage. To maximize the weapon's capacity for putting enemy soldiers out of action, the designers would need to pay attention to the wounding effect.

'Studies were made of the point configuration to increase the effects *out there*,' my Army interlocutor said, giving me a significant look. It wasn't polite to mention destroying a human being, but I seemed to be a person savvy enough to understand he meant that the Army had looked at ways of altering the tip of the flechette to cause massive wounds – just what the framers of the Hague Declaration of 1899 had meant to avoid in prohibiting the use of dum-dum bullets whose tips would mushroom on impact with the body.

In 1966, Irwin R. Barr took out a patent on 'a projectile adapted to curl and tumble on impact with a target, and having a long cylindrical shank section with a concave tapered blunt nose and rear stabilizing fins.' The concave tapering of the nose would weaken the flechette just where the strain was greatest on impact; the nose would then deform, and the flechette would tumble. 'The tumbling action transmits much more of the energy of the projectile to the target,' Mr Barr noted in his patent application. 'The tumbling projectile will thereby effect considerably more damage to *a relatively soft and thick target, such as an animal*, than would otherwise be effected by passage of the projectile thereinto or therethrough in the straight elongated form' (emphasis added).[43]

Had the flechette rifle gone into production, Mr Barr could have made a lot of money out of his invention. But 'In December 1973, the decision was made to remove flechette ammunition from immediate consideration within the Future Rifle System Program because of technical problems which may not be correctable in the time frame of the future rifle,' the Army laboratories reported the next year.[44] The accuracy of the rifle was uncertain, according to the Army engineer with whom I spoke, and there were problems with the separation of the flechette from the fiberglass or nylon sleeve ('sabot') that enclosed it while it traveled through the gun barrel.

In the meantime, flechette-filled artillery shells had been used in Vietnam (Chapter 3); but as far as the SPIW program was concerned, 'death by darts' was still a long way off. It was just as well. A rifle sending forth flechettes which deformed in the body would have represented an escalation in the severity of battle casualties, arguably breaching the universally accepted ban on the use of mushrooming bullets in war. And besides the legal objections, moral considerations could come in. Even the most enthusiastic inventor sometimes posed ethical questions about his work. As Mr Barr told the *Sun*: 'What I build does tear up people and sometimes you wonder.'[45]

Notes

1. Chase, 1973, p. L-1.
2. Rees, 1964, pp. 98–104.
3. Thompson, 1951, pp. 142–4.
4. *Ibid.*, pp. 150–51.
5. *Ibid.*, p. 94. Although Thompson saw it as a 'new technique of machine warfare,' massive firepower was not a new invention. The historian R.F. Weigley has written that in World War II, 'The quantity of American weapons ... over-whelmed enemies with sheer weight of firepower.' He described a tactic used by General George S. Patton, Jr: 'Patton liked the power of a "marching fire offen-sive," wherein casualties might be great but results could be too. All the infantry moved forward together in a thick skirmish line, generally with close tank sup-port.... Everybody fired at every possible center of resistance within reach. All the large weapons that could be mustered laid down a supporting fire.... If the method was old-fashioned, automatic weapons, tanks, and modern artillery co-ordination could once again make it effective' (Weigley, 1967, pp. 471–4).

In the Pacific fighting, massive firepower left enemy soldiers riddled with wounds, making subsequent study impossible. This effect was noted by Captain James E.T. Hopkins, whose battle casualty surveys were mentioned in Chapter 2. Although thousands of enemy soldiers were killed, Hopkins wrote: 'Neither the New Georgia–Burma nor the Bougainville [casualty survey] records contain any information concerning the effect of US weapons on enemy dead. It is charac-teristic of US troops to use all firepower available, which means that there was a high incidence of wounds per enemy casualty. This consideration, together with other factors, made it impossible to gather reliable information on this phase of the survey' (Beyer, ed., 1962, pp. 262–4).

6. General Matthew B. Ridgway, who later took over the command from General MacArthur, wrote that there had been almost daily radio broadcasts from China threatening that they would enter the war if North Korea were invaded (Ridgway, 1967, p. 44).
7. Thompson, 1951, p. 252.
8. Quoted in Stone, 1952, p. 312.
9. US Department of Defense, annual report for 1 January–30 June 1953, p. 124.
10. US Military Academy, 1968, p. 19-2.
11. To 'kill' a target means to destroy it or put it out of action. In the official NATO definition, 'kill probability' is 'a measure of the probability of destroying a target.' (Note: all official NATO, US Department of Defense, or US Army definitions quoted in this book are taken from the *Dictionary of United States Army Terms*, US Army, 1972b.)
12. Cited in McMillen and Gregg, 1945.
13. The cross-sectional drawings were taken from the textbook *A Cross-Sectional Anatomy* and represented, in McMillen and Gregg's words, 'the average dimen-sions of 50 Negro subjects.' The total exposed area was known as the 'projection area' and the portion of it which overlaid the 'vulnerable regions' was called the 'vulnerable projection area.' For a standing man, excluding the hands and feet,

McMillen and Gregg found that the projection area was 5.3 square feet and the vulnerable projection area was 43 per cent of this figure. Were a series of missiles to strike a standing man at random, 43 out of a hundred would land over one of the vulnerable regions. This meant that the *maximum probability* of causing a fatal or severe wound was 43 per cent. For most missiles, in practice, the likelihood of causing such a wound would be less, as even if they landed on a 'vulnerable projection area,' they might still be stopped by the intervening tissues before they could reach the vital part underneath. The figures would be different if the man was crouching or lying, but the method of calculation was the same.

14. McMillen and Gregg, 1945. On the historical development of casualty criteria, see Sellier and Kneubuehl, 1994, pp. 303–13.

15. A 'requirement' is a formal document stating that a military service wants to procure an item of equipment. The terms of the requirement serve as goals for those who have to design, build, and buy the item.

16. The description is from Dunn and Sterne, 1952, p. 5.

17. Goats were the animals used as targets in the BRL experiments. It is evident from the description that they were not anesthetized.

18. As mentioned above, McMillen and Gregg had calculated that the 'vulnerable regions' corresponded to 43 per cent of the exposed target area of a soldier, which meant that there was a maximum probability of 43 per cent that a fragment striking the body at random would cause a fatal or severe wound. As the regions described in the BRL study (Dunn and Sterne, 1952) corresponded to only 10 per cent of the body surface, the maximum probability of five-second incapacitation from a random hit was 10 per cent. In practice the figure would be lower, since some fragments striking the body would lack the energy to penetrate to the regions concerned.

19. Many of the companies that helped to develop modern antipersonnel weapons, including the M26 grenade, are mentioned in Prokosch, 1972.

20. *Ordnance* was the journal of the American Ordnance Association. It was later renamed *National Defense*, and the American Ordnance Association became the American Defense Preparedness Association, described in its literature as 'a membership society of American citizens dedicated to peace through industrial preparedness for national defense.'

21. Crossman, 1966.

22. According to a US Army ordnance engineering textbook, a controlled fragmentation missile is 'one in which the configuration, direction of flight, and velocity of each fragment can be predicted' (US Army Materiel Command, 1963, p. 7-12). In somewhat more elaborate terms, the official US Army definition states that controlled fragmentation is 'the technique of design and fabrication of a projectile, mine, grenade or bomb to cause a predetermined size, shape, density, velocity and pattern of the fragments upon detonation.'

23. US Army, 1966b, 1971.

24. The effect of grenade weight on range and throwing accuracy was studied in tests at Aberdeen Proving Ground in which twenty-two soldiers who had returned from Korea were asked to toss grenades at targets from different positions and distances (Dunn and Sterne, 1952, pp. 28–9).

25. Technically, RDX has greater *brisance* – greater shattering effect, which is

linked to a faster rate of detonation. TNT, in contrast, is less sensitive and therefore safer to handle. Composition B has the best qualities of both: it is only slightly more sensitive than TNT, and has nearly as much brisance as RDX. Composition B consists of 60 per cent RDX, 39 per cent TNT, and 1 per cent desensitizer. It is used today in various high explosive munitions where a high degree of fragmentation is desired. Composition B is a type of *cyclotol* – a generic term for mixtures of RDX and TNT (US Army, 1967b, pp. 4-11 to 4-12, 7-75 to 7-76).

26. A casing of approximately half a pound divided into 1,000 fragments would yield fragments weighing about 3 grains each. This size and the velocity reported in the *Ordnance* article are in line with the concept of a 'small' fragment mentioned by the US Army Project Manager for Selected Ammunition, as quoted at the beginning of this chapter. The 15-ounce grenade recommended in the BRL study was not far from these figures; it was to have produced at least 810 2.5-grain fragments moving at an initial velocity of 5,400 feet per second.

One other improvement of the M26 design over the Mk II is that the fragments are distributed in a wider angle around the grenade, giving a better chance of hitting a person nearby no matter how the grenade falls.

27. US Army, 1966b, pp. 142, 169.

28. The development of the Claymore began during the Korean war. The inventor, Norman A. MacLeod, later wrote in a letter to the *New Scientist* ('Genesis of the Claymore,' 5 January 1967, p. 44) that his idea for a weapon to repel mass attacks 'was rejected by US Army Ordnance... In 1952, I received support from the US Marine Corps and finally by 1953 [the year when the war ended], I made 10,000 prototypes for field evaluation.' MacLeod considered that 'Not having used the weapon in Korea where its first use would have been in the favour of the UN troops, it would have been prudent to have kept it in this secret category until such time as its initial use in war would be to our advantage.' But 'An article in the January 1960 issue of *Infantry* magazine (available in any US public library) broke security and destroyed the secrecy of the invention and my patent issued in February 1961 (No. 2,972,949) so that all that had to be done to obtain the results of several years of research and development was to pay something less than a dollar for a copy of the patent and a photostat of the article.' With the publication of the patent in 1961, the new technique of pre-fragmentation entered the public domain.

The ball-studded M18A1 'improved' Claymore mine replaced the M18, which was standardized in 1957. Standardization is a stage in the Army development and acquisition process, involving the adoption of standard technical specifications and a standard model number (M-), replacing the 'experimental' (T- or XM-) designation given to the item earlier in the process. The name of the mine goes back as far as 1953, a year in which the US Army Ballistic Research Laboratories prepared a confidential report entitled 'Effectiveness Study of the Claymore Antipersonnel Weapon.'

29. The explosive, composition C4, contains 91 per cent RDX. It is slightly more brisant than its close relative Composition C3, which itself was found to be 133 per cent as effective as TNT on the basis of fragmentation tests of shell charges (US Army, 1967b, p. 7-82). The steel balls are several times larger than

the M26 grenade fragments, and likewise larger than the ideal fragment size cited by the Army's Project Manager for Selected Ammunition as characteristic of the antipersonnel munitions developed in the 1950s and quoted at the beginning of this chapter. The larger size would allow the steel balls to travel further, giving the Claymore a greater range, desirable for a mine of this type but not for a hand grenade, which needed to be 'as safe as possible to the thrower.'

In his patent application, Norman A. MacLeod wrote that the object of his invention was (among other things) to provide an antipersonnel fragmentation weapon 'which may be used in close proximity to the defending users,' a weapon 'which will project an intense beam of high-velocity fragments substantially parallel to the terrain in the direction of the attacking or advancing enemy infantry,' a weapon 'which may be readily used with great effectiveness and safety by untrained infantrymen,' a weapon 'which despite its very effective intensity against onrushing attackers may be effectively aimed to concentrate its beam to an area where a maximum number of useful hits may be obtained,' a weapon 'which may be very small in proportion to its antipersonnel effectiveness, and which is thereby capable of being readily hidden in tall grass and behind other natural concealing means,' and which overcomes the problems of defending a position by means of machine gun posts (which must themselves be defended and moved periodically to avoid enemy counterattacks) by being 'completely expendable and which involves no heavy capital or non-expendable parts that must be moved from place to place as the defense post is changed.' The weapon was to be one in which, 'at the limit of lethal velocity of the fragments, there will be an average of at least one fragment in every two square feet of target area, lethal velocity being defined as that velocity of the particular fragment involved which will just produce substantially complete penetration of the human body.' It was also to incorporate 'a novel method of propelling a layer of fragments without requiring employment of bulky, heavy, non-expendable enclosing members' ('Antipersonnel Fragmentation Weapon,' US patent 2,972,949, 28 February 1961, filed 18 January 1956).

30. US Army, 1966c.

31. *Ibid.*, p. 2. The manual states, however, that 'The mine should not be used against single personnel targets; rather, it should be used for its intended purpose – massed personnel' (p. 10). For information on countries producing Claymore-type mines today, see Human Rights Watch Arms Project and Physicians for Human Rights, 1993, Appendix 17.

32. Tompkins, 1966, p. 116. As stated by Norman A. MacLeod in his patent application, 'Modern infantry warfare has developed a technique, among certain armies, of sustained mass human attack, with little regard to casualties and of such intensity that traversing fire of defending machine guns cannot cut down all attackers, with the result that sufficient attacking infantry break through the defending lines to overwhelm the defense post. It is an object of this invention to provide a simple, inexpensive, lightweight and easily transportable weapon which can be used to effectively withstand such sustained massive suicidal offensive attacks.'

33. Beyer, ed., 1962, p. 87.

34. *Ibid.* Lighter and more transportable than heavy artillery, 'Mortars are used

where high angles of fire are desired for plunging fire behind hills or into trenches, emplacements, or foxholes' (US Army Ordnance Corps, 1960, p. 11-20).

35. Beyer, ed., 1962, pp. 715–17.

36. 'In munitions design in the United States, safety takes precedence over effectiveness,' an American ordnance engineer told me during an interview. He was referring obliquely to the well-known 'Asian disregard for life,' such that the Chinese would gladly have sacrificed the lives of a few crewmen in the interest of having a more lethal munition. Another engineer disagreed that the Chinese would be so irrational. 'The idea of an Asian disregard for life never made much sense to me,' he said. 'If the gun barrel blows up with every hundred rounds, what's the good of that?'

37. 'Malleable Iron Shell,' *Ordnance*, vol. 46, September–October 1961, p. 266.

38. Truckenmiller, 1964.

39. 'The 60mm. mortar was largely phased out of service after Korea though the Marines have reintroduced it. It was revived in Vietnam because the small Vietnamese found it easy to carry, a virtue that eventually impressed our own troops' (Tompkins, 1966, p. 113). Cast iron was also used in the 2.75-inch air-to-ground rocket warhead and the BLU-24 'orange' bomblet (Chapters 3–4).

40. A point target is 'a target of such small dimension that it requires the accurate placement of ordnance in order to neutralize or destroy it,' according to the official Defense Department definition. The implication seems to be that an 'area target,' the alternative to a point target, can be attacked inaccurately.

41. Hitchman, 1952.

42. Hanson W. Baldwin, 'Army Tests Dart-Throwing, Hand-Held Weapon,' *New York Times*, 15 March 1964.

43. 'Concave-Compound Pointed Finned Projectile,' US patent 3,861,314, 21 January 1975, filed 30 December 1966. On the same day, a colleague at AAI took out a patent (no. 3,851,590) on a 'Multiple Hardness Pointed Finned Projectile' whose nose and tail were softer than the shank; on impact, the nose would bend, causing the flechette to tumble. 'It will be readily apparent that increased effectiveness is obtained with this projectile in a soft, dense type target, such as an animal, due to the tumbling and enlarged effective projected peripheral area of the projectile in the tumbling curled configuration ... as compared to the small piercing configuration of the projectile if it should pass into or through the target in a straight linear fashion,' the inventor wrote in his patent application.

44. US Army Armament Command, 1974, p. 3-60.

45. 'Death by Darts Is Coming,' Baltimore *Sun* Sunday magazine, 15 August 1971.

CHAPTER 3

VIETNAM: WEAPONS FOR COUNTERINSURGENCY

Losing the Great Society was a terrible thought, but not so terrible as the thought of being responsible for America's losing a war to the communists. Nothing could possibly be worse than that.

US President Lyndon B. Johnson[1]

The solution in Vietnam is more bombs, more shells, more napalm ... till the other side cracks and gives up.

Brigadier General William C. De Puy,
Commanding General, US 1st Division, South Vietnam[2]

In March 1965, US ground forces were sent to Vietnam to stave off an impending communist victory. American technology was thrown into the fray, and the innovations introduced in the next years would alter the science of warfare. When the last Americans left Indochina ten years later, Vietnam was firmly in communist hands, along with Laos and Cambodia, two neighboring countries which had become engulfed in the war. There had been more bombs, more shells, more antipersonnel weapons, but the other side never cracked and gave up.

The origins of the Vietnamese communist movement can be traced back to Ho Chi Minh's early days in Paris and Moscow, and to the military training which Vietnam's future communist leaders received in southern China in the 1920s. The communist Vietminh forces fought against Japan during World War II, and after the war they continued fighting for independence from French rule. Under the 1954 Geneva ceasefire agreement ending the French–Indochina war, the country was to be temporarily partitioned between the communist North and the non-communist South pending the outcome of elections to unify the country, but the anti-communist South Vietnamese President Ngo Dinh Diem refused to hold them, and the communists decided to take power by force.[3]

The communist action was a combined political and military effort called 'integrated political and military struggle.'[4] The political side of the effort involved setting up a clandestine organization throughout the country to carry out political propaganda, levy taxes, and perform other administrative functions. The military side involved creating a combination of main forces and local force units, supported by village guerrillas who gathered intelligence, mined roads, protected the political cadres, and served as guides, porters, and extra fighters for the local and main force units.[5]

The cadres of the National Liberation Front (NLF) of South Vietnam relied on promises, threats, and existing ties to win the allegiance or acquiescence of the rural population. In their propaganda, the virtuousness of the self-sacrificing guerrillas was contrasted with the corruption and indifference of the urban ruling class. They believed – correctly, as it turned out – that despite the fierce repression launched by President Diem, they would ultimately prevail because the South Vietnamese government was basically incapable of reforming itself to meet the peasants' needs.[6]

The NLF guerrillas assassinated centrally installed village chiefs who were either especially efficient or especially unpopular.[7] They cut roads and attacked government outposts so that the largely inactive government forces would stay confined in their posts, leaving the guerrillas free to move about the countryside at night. With the assassination of Diem in 1963, the government's situation worsened. The secret assessment of US officials at the time was that had the Americans not intervened, the fall of the South Vietnamese government would have been only a matter of time.

In March 1965 the United States introduced regular ground troops into South Vietnam and began systematically bombing the North. Shortly before, the US position was portrayed in a State Department White Paper as one of helping the South Vietnamese government in response to the fact that 'in Vietnam a totally new brand of aggression has been loosed against an independent people who want to make their own way in peace and freedom.... In Vietnam a communist government has set out deliberately to conquer a sovereign people in a neighboring state.'[8] In the logic of the day, the war was part of the global fight against communism, and the war waged by the 'Vietcong' ('Vietnamese communists') in the 'independent' South was portrayed as the product of aggression from the communist North.

The Americans established their bases and set out from them to fight the enemy. They had helicopters for rapid transit, airpower and artillery to provide supporting fire, medical evacuation teams to care for the wounded, and lavish supplies. Yet the enemy remained elusive. In small forays or large 'search and destroy' operations, the Americans might find caches of arms and rice, they might destroy some of the many tunnels where the guerrillas moved about and hid from bombardment, but the enemy forces almost always slipped away before the Americans could catch them.[9]

Enjoying superior firepower, the Americans used tactics such as 'harassment and interdiction fire' – fire directed not at a known enemy position but at a place where the enemy might be.[10] Areas thought to belong to the enemy were designated 'free fire zones' and subjected to bombardment at will.[11] Chemicals were sprayed from aircraft to defoliate NLF jungle sanctuaries and likely ambush sites and to destroy crops thought to be intended for the enemy.[12] Heavy tractors fitted with special blades were used to obliterate forests and cut down swathes of jungle alongside roads.[13] Villagers in NLF-controlled areas were evacuated and their homes destroyed to deny base areas to the enemy.[14]

This 'new technique of machine warfare' (to borrow the phrase used by Reginald Thompson to describe the American effort in Korea) might knock out some of the guerrillas and disrupt plans, but it would not help in the political war – winning the allegiance of Vietnamese country dwellers, who had seen their carts pushed off the roads by American vehicles, their buffaloes killed in wanton target practice, their homes searched and – sometimes – set on fire by American soldiers who distrusted all villagers, not being able to tell friend from foe.[15] The one thing the Americans might have hoped to give the villagers – security – remained elusive, because the NLF were still politically entrenched and able to move through the country in secret. And the American intervention gave NLF propagandists another element for their cause: hatred of the Americans.[16]

There were few strategic targets for the Americans in South Vietnam. There were no cities, bridges, or railway junctions to be captured. Throughout the war the Americans were unable to locate and destroy the shadowy guerrilla command headquarters, 'COSVN' (Central Office for South Vietnam). Instead, each side had the objective of killing the other's soldiers. For the Americans, the progress of the war was measured in the notoriously inaccurate 'body counts,' often inflated by the inclusion of civilian dead.[17] For the guerrillas, there was a special value in killing Americans because the weekly casualty figures published in the United States would help turn public opinion against the war and weaken the American resolve.

It was in Vietnam that the antipersonnel technologies of the 1950s came into their own. From the World War II wound ballistics studies, it could be inferred that small fragments and small bullets would be effective against guerrillas in exposed locations who lacked body armor. Where the guerrillas tried to overwhelm American positions by massed attack, munitions developed in response to the human-sea charges of

Korea would be used to repel them. More often the guerrillas could not be seen, and their exact location was uncertain. Here the Americans devised new ways of getting fragments into enemy areas, often large areas: rocket warheads, artillery shells, and a whole new generation of 'cluster' weapons and aerially emplaced land mines (Chapter 4).

The war brought heavy demands for the post-Korea munitions. In the fiscal year 1966 (1965–6), the Army ordered 5,985,000 M26 grenades, 493,000 Claymore mines, and 3,001,000 high fragmentation cast-iron 81mm mortar shells – sharp increases over the orders placed in the two previous years.[18] Other weapons developed in the 1950s – the 40mm grenade launcher and 'Beehive' shells, described in this chapter – also saw their first use in the battlefield laboratory of Vietnam. The war, in turn, created many new demands, and the US armaments establishment raced to find 'quick-fix' solutions. New warheads were developed for existing weapons, and ways were found to deploy fragments into new areas, such as the jungles which provided cover for the guerrillas, or to deploy them from new weapon platforms such as helicopters.

They were new ways of cutting down the enemy in new locations, but they were variations on the same theme – the deployment of small wounding missiles *en masse*. In something akin to the notion of adaptive radiation in biological evolution, the new mechanisms for the production of wounding fragments were finding their way into new environmental niches.

Within the specialized world of the ordnance community, the anti-personnel innovations of Vietnam were seen as a triumph. In terms of their ultimate purpose, they failed: America lost the war. The many tons of antipersonnel munitions expended in Indochina left a legacy of destruction and unexploded ordnance with which the people of those countries would have to contend for years to come.

The development and introduction of antipersonnel weapons also brought out an uncomfortable contradiction between the lofty aims in which US leaders cloaked the war effort and the inherently malevolent activity of trying to find better ways to harm human beings. For the communists, antipersonnel weapons were a welcome ingredient in the national and international propaganda to taint the motives of the American imperialists.[19] For antiwar protestors in the United States, antipersonnel weapons were yet another source of anguish over what was being done by their country in the name of freedom and democracy.

Controlled Fragmentation: The 40mm Grenade

As described in Chapter 2, the M26 grenade, developed in the 1950s, was the first US antipersonnel munition producing tiny steel fragments by the principle of controlled fragmentation. A related project in the 1950s would extend the same principle to greater ranges through the development of an infantry weapon 'capable of projecting the lethality of the 60mm mortar cartridge to ranges between those of hand grenades and light mortars,' as an Army official later described it.[20]

That weapon was to be the M79 40mm grenade launcher, a breech-loading, shoulder-fired weapon that looks something like a sawed-off shotgun. It has a maximum range of 400 meters, approximately a quarter of a mile, and with its high trajectory it can be used to get at targets which are behind fortifications or other obstacles, and which the soldier cannot see. As for the ammunition, the basic high explosive cartridge weighs half a pound and looks like an oversized bullet. Inside the cartridge is a spherical grenade made of notched steel wire wrapped around an explosive charge of Composition B. On explosion, the grenade produces a cloud of 2-grain fragments moving at 3,000 to 4,000 feet per second.[21] Each grenade has an effective casualty radius of 5 meters.[22]

With the introduction of US ground forces in South Vietnam, demand for 40mm grenades grew rapidly.[23] Other ammunition rounds and other 40mm weapons were developed to meet the needs of Vietnam. Among the most important adaptations were a high velocity automatic launcher for firing at the ground from helicopters and slow-flying airplanes[24] and a tripod-mounted, low velocity automatic launcher that could be used on the ground or from a boat.[25] Many types of ammunition soon appeared: chemical rounds containing CS gas,[26] signaling cartridges emitting smoke of various colors, high explosive rounds for close-in fighting,[27] a round which hits the ground and pops back up in the air before exploding, enhancing the chances of hitting soldiers nearby, 'high explosive dual purpose' rounds which can attack both armor and personnel, and a shot-filled round to ward off immediate attacks.[28] Other innovations, too, were contemplated. Irwin R. Barr's AAI Corporation worked on the development of 40mm 'scatter ammunition,' and Avco Corporation tried to develop a rocket-propelled round which could be used in the jungles of Vietnam.[29]

The 40mm grenade proved popular among infantrymen in Vietnam. According to an unofficial Army history of the war, 'The weapon was a universal favorite with US troops in all units from infantry to quartermaster.'[30] 'Our people ... love the M79 grenade launcher,' Gordon Baxter wrote in his *13/13; Vietnam: Search and Destroy* (1967). 'It's like brass knuckles in a barroom brawl.'[31]

Natural Fragmentation: The 2.75-inch Rocket

The United States had plenty of airplanes and helicopters in South Vietnam, but they were often shot at. The 2.75-inch rocket gave American fliers a means of creating explosions of fragments at places on the ground while remaining at a safe distance from the target. This new counter-guerrilla weapon was a marriage of two inventions: the 2.75-inch 'Mighty Mouse' air-to-air rocket of the 1950s, now obsolete, of which huge surplus stocks were on hand; and a new warhead made of pearlitic malleable iron, a type of cast iron which was already being used to enhance the antipersonnel lethality of post-Korea mortar shells (Chapter 2).

The adaptation of the 2.75-inch rocket began in 1961, at a time when there was a new interest in counterinsurgency under the Kennedy administration, which took office in January 1961.[32] By 1962 the Army was testing 2.75-inch rockets on its contingent of small fixed-wing aircraft and helicopters which had been sent to Vietnam to assist the South Vietnamese army in its fight against the communist guerrillas.[33]

In 1966, at one of the annual, closed Congressional hearings held to consider the Defense Department budget request, an Army official, General F.J. Chesarek, gave a thumbnail sketch of the conversion of the 2.75-inch rocket into an antipersonnel weapon.

> The Air Force used this rocket for a number of years as an air-to-air weapons system, and the Army experimented with a number of Air Force rockets in 1963. We found that these rockets were not suitable for our purposes. We were looking for an *extremely quick fuze reaction*, rather than a delay type, and *a high degree of warhead fragmentation*, rather than blast. In order to achieve stability in flight when launched from a relatively slow speed platform, greater rotational spin of the rocket had to be built in. We proceeded to modify the Air Force rockets, and by November 1964 we were ready for limited production of the Army-type rockets. As the troops in the field began to utilize these rockets with ever-growing success, their demand increased rapidly. (emphases added)

Testifying at the same hearing, a civilian Army munitions official described the rocket in the following terms.

> MR. MATT [US Army, Picatinny Arsenal]   This is a folding fin rocket. It consists of fuze, warhead, and rocket motor. Upon electrical initiation the rocket is launched, and the fins extend for stabilization. The new fuze has a graze-sensitive feature, so that upon contact the rocket will immediately detonate and spew fragments.
> MR. FLOOD [Democrat, Pennsylvania]   Fragmentation?
> MR. MATT   Yes, sir.

MR. FLOOD   Antipersonnel?

MR. MATT   Yes, sir.

The Congressmen wanted to know more.

MR. ANDREWS [Democrat, Alabama]   That is an air-to-ground rocket?

GENERAL CHESAREK   Air-to-ground.

MR. FLOOD   You get a good shrapnel burst with that warhead[?].

GENERAL CHESAREK   Yes, sir, you have a 10-pound warhead...

MR. FLOOD   If that burst were where that water jug is, what would the area kill in this room be, within reason?

MR. MATT   In this room it should take all of us.[34]

Once introduced, the rockets were in great demand. At a US Senate committee hearing in 1966, testifying on the level of production, General Chesarek said:

> In the case of the 2.75 rocket this is *an all-out national effort. There is well over a billion dollars on this one ammunition item alone.*[35] (emphasis added)

In Vietnam, the rockets amounted to a form of airborne artillery which could be used to attack positions beyond the range of ground-based guns.[36] 'Most of the 2.75-inch rockets used in SEA [Southeast Asia] utilized high explosive warheads and these were primarily fired at personnel targets,' Colonel Frank P. Ragano, project manager for the 2.75-inch rocket, told an Army ammunition manufacturers' conference in 1973. The rockets were cheap (about $40 per basic rocket), and they were used in huge quantities. 'Rocket consumption during the peak of the war exceeded 500,000 per month, of which about two thirds were employed by Army helicopter gunships,' Colonel Ragano said.[37]

Highly popular, the 2.75-inch rocket soon underwent further adaptations to increase its effectiveness and fill new niches. By 1972 a Navy manual could list an antitank warhead, a combined antitank and antipersonnel warhead, and a smoke warhead containing white phosphorus,[38] in addition to the Army's original high explosive warhead.[39] The Air Force introduced a flechette-filled warhead,[40] and the Army introduced a new, larger high explosive warhead which when used with a new proximity fuze (see below) to produce airbursts two to three meters from the ground, gave an 'antipersonnel lethality ... approximately four times that of the standard payload,' according to Colonel Ragano. More fuzes were developed so that the rockets could be used against more types of targets, in more types of terrain, and in what Colonel Ragano called 'a more sophisticated battlefield environment' than Southeast Asia. The Army was starting to look beyond Vietnam.

When I met Mr Matt, years after his presentation at the 1966 hearing,

I found him tired by the paperwork of procurement regulations and annoyed at the intense questioning he had had to undergo over the years in defending the Army's budget requests before members of Congress who were not always so enthusiastic as Mr Flood. But when I mentioned the 2.75-inch rocket, he brightened up. 'It was what armed the helicopter,' he said. 'We had been wanting to arm the helicopter for years but this did it.'

Lighter Bullets: The M16 Rifle

Although the Johns Hopkins Operations Research Office study described in Chapter 2 had cited the advantages of reducing the caliber of military rifles, the idea was not taken up because the Army had decided to develop a new rifle of the standard 7.62mm caliber, the M14. Meanwhile, a private company, Armalite, scaled down its own 7.62mm rifle, adapting it to shoot modified 5.56mm (.22 caliber) hunting ammunition. The new rifle, which the company called the AR-15, was, like the M14, capable of being fired either automatic or semiautomatic; it weighed one fourth less than the M14, and the ammunition also was lighter. In terms of wounding capacity, the reduction in bullet size was partly compensated for by an increase in bullet velocity: the AR-15 had a muzzle velocity (velocity on leaving the gun) of approximately 3,250 feet per second, as against 2,800 feet per second for the M14.[41]

The M14 rifle was adopted for Army use in 1957, and introduced into service. But as interest in counterinsurgency grew under the Kennedy administration, the US military quietly bought 1,000 AR-15s and sent them to Vietnam for testing.[42]

Soon reports began appearing of the lethality of the new rifle, a factor often attributed to its high bullet velocity. 'Unofficial reports say the AR-15's light bullet, travelling at 3,300 feet per second, does cartwheels as it penetrates living flesh, causing a highly lethal wound that looks like anything but a caliber .22 hole,' *Army* magazine reported in August 1963. The AR-15 had been used in South Vietnam for several months, *Army* said, and 'came out smelling like a rose.'

Other reports were in the same vein.

'Don't knock this new gun,' one line sergeant pointed out. 'It is superior in many ways. For instance, anybody getting hit by this weapon will become a casualty almost immediately because of its terrible tearing ability' [a Virginia newspaper reported in 1966].

The M16's muzzle velocity it was explained causes the bullet to tumble when it hits an object and tears or chews away, whereas the M14 hit would produce a clean straight-through hole in most cases.[43]

Two US Army doctors evaluated thirty-eight AR-15 wounds (caused by accidental firings or enemy use of captured weapons) sustained by patients admitted to an Army hospital in South Vietnam during a nine-month period in 1966. While wounds inflicted at close range had small entrance and exit holes, those at longer ranges exhibited small entrance holes, 'whereas the exit wound is a gaping, devastated area of soft tissue and even bone, often with loss of large amounts of tissue,' with dis-integration of the bullet and minute splattering of lead.[44] The gaping exit wounds seen by the doctors strongly suggested that the bullets were tumbling as they passed through the body.

The AR-15 was redesignated by the US Army as the M16 rifle, and in 1967 the Army announced that it would be adopted as the standard infantry weapon for US Forces outside NATO – a stunning reversal of the earlier decision to maintain the standard 7.62mm caliber.[45] By 1978 the rifle had been exported to twenty-one countries and was being produced under license in another three, with various other 5.56mm rifles in production elsewhere.[46] With its tremendous wounding effects, the new reduced-caliber rifle had become a reality.

Artillery in Vietnam: 'Firing on a Vill'

If 40mm grenades and air-to-ground fragmentation rockets helped to support combat soldiers, artillery was the mainstay. Artillery provided devastating firepower which was 'immediately responsive, always avail-able, and totally reliable,' in the words of an Army history. To counter the guerrilla threat, batteries of artillery were placed in the countryside, where they could fire back if friendly troops within their range were attacked. The artillery batteries were dispersed 'to provide the maxi-mum area coverage,' with each battery linked to an infantry battalion which operated within its range. Infantry commanders worked with artillery commanders to ensure that their maneuver plans could be fully supported by artillery. 'Only on rare occasions did maneuver forces in Vietnam operate beyond the range of friendly artillery.'[47]

A former US Marine Corps artilleryman who served in Vietnam in 1966–7 drew for me a schematic map of the countryside divided into 'tactical areas of responsibility,' each with a battery of six 105mm how-itzers at the center. The 'grunts' (infantry), on their forays into the countryside, were always within the range of the guns, and if a sniper fired at them from a village, or if they met any other opposition to their presence, they could radio in for an artillery attack.

'Let's say the grunts are out there snooping around and they get fired on – there's VC ['Vietcong'] or NVA [North Vietnamese Army] activity inside the vill, anywhere from three men to a battalion. Fifty per cent of the time they'll go in there and try to clean it out, that means they'd check it, not necessarily kill everyone. Fifty per cent of the time they'll radio back to the artillery outfit saying they've been fired on, giving the coordinates of the village. If it's a free fire zone you get artillery as soon as you ask for it, otherwise it depends on the area.

'Artillery fire amounts to demolishing the village. We usually did this with HE [high explosive] because it was cheaper than flying over with napalm – [in view of the cost of] aircraft fuel and risk to the aircraft.

'HE shells rip up thatch and matting or cardboard walls. People have family shelters, usually outside the house. We had orders not to molest them when we were searching a vill.

'Our guns were set up so that the projectiles would land in a row, six projectiles, 40 meters apart. Each projectile gave off shrapnel in a radius of 20 meters. We'd fire one round [from the six guns] and then shift the guns up and down or left and right, fire another round and so on, pounding all over the vill. The firing lasted a minute, half an hour, forty-five minutes. We'd fire as much as sixty-five rounds per gun. The average mission lasted five or ten minutes for one sniper let's say.

'They never told us if we were firing at a vill or something else but you could usually tell by the type of firing. One time I was positive we were firing on a vill, you could see the rounds landing there...

'We were supposed to fire the first round from one gun with a white phosphorus [target marking] round, then correct for it. Usually we just used HE for the first round. That's how the villagers knew they were going to be bombarded, when the shells started falling on their heads.'

And the artillerymen fired their volley of six rounds set to land in a pattern, shifted their guns and fired again – all at an unseen, unnamed 'target' miles away... 'The grunts would go out with a map, there'd be a vill marked on it, a few houses – it wasn't there, it had been levelled.' But then, why should the villagers have minded? In the view of this Marine, 'there's nothing to rebuilding a house, they'd just bang it together out of cardboard or whatever they had around.'

Lavish supplies of ammunition were available in Vietnam, and it was used on a lavish scale.[48] As Andrew F. Krepinevich Jr observed in his study *The Army and Vietnam*, the Army had 'built-in incentives' for using artillery. Reportedly, artillery commanders were evaluated by the ammunition expenditure of their units. One commander said: 'The ammo kept coming whether or not we had targets for it, so the batteries fired their allotments every opportunity they had, whether there was actually anything to shoot at or not.'

Artillery fire and aerial bombardment caused many villagers to flee their homes, but it did not kill many guerrillas. In one operation by the US 1st Cavalry Division in 1966, lasting a month and a half, over

132,000 artillery rounds were fired and 1,342 were reported killed – a ratio of 1,000 rounds for every guerrilla killed, in addition to fire from helicopters and tactical aircraft. In another operation conducted by the same division a year later, the ratio was similar.[49] With such a low percentage of enemy dead to shells fired, military planners must have been tempted to ask whether the ratio could not be improved if the shells were redesigned to give a better chance of hitting someone.

New Directions in Natural Fragmentation: The Development of High Fragmentation Steels

Against such flimsy targets as a 'Vietcong village' or guerrillas in the countryside, there was a potential for using artillery shells with smaller fragments than what was needed against harder targets. Smaller fragments meant more fragments and a chance to hit more enemy soldiers with each shell burst.

A decrease in fragment size had been accomplished in mortar ammunition by making shells out of pearlitic malleable iron (Chapter 2), and malleable iron was used in adapting the 2.75-inch rocket to 'spew fragments' against ground targets. For artillery ammunition, an attempt was made to use the same material in 105mm howitzer shells. William C. Truckenmiller of the Albion Malleable Iron Company described the program at an American Ordnance Association seminar in 1963:

> Again, as in the mortar round, initial feasibility studies established the high level of lethality associated with the cast pearlitic malleable iron. This was followed by extensive research and development activity during which nearly 20,000 rounds were tested....
>
> With the available industrial capability, reinforced with the specific experience of several producers ... another milestone will have been realized ... and another and more effective item will have been added to the nation's arsenal.[50]

But in test firings of the new round, there were several premature explosions, and on one such occasion, I was told, several people were killed. Unfortunate as such accidents are, they can still serve as biological indicators of the effectiveness of munitions, but a premature explosion is a bad sign when what is needed is safe and reliable functioning. And when the Army tried making 105mm shells out of the ductile iron which the British were then using for 81mm mortar shells, they found (in the delicate phraseology of one of their reports) that 'the shells produced exhibited pronounced separation of material throughout their length.'[51]

In the meantime, another revolutionary development in antipersonnel ammunition manufacture was on the way. In the late 1950s the Army had been working on a new 152mm tank gun with a high explosive projectile that was meant to yield a maximum number of lethal high velocity fragments on explosion. Cast iron would not have worked – the tremendous acceleration forces in the gun would have caused an iron projectile to deform – but it was found that a commercially available alloy steel, AISI 52100, could, with suitable treatment, be made into a shell that was both strong and optimal as regards fragmentation.[52] Other military agencies made their own investigations along similar lines. Soon there were one, two, three ... many high fragmentation steels with different attractions and different applications.[53]

The Army decided to use 52100 steel, with a carbide network heat treatment, in the smaller of its new, thin-walled 105mm and 155mm Rocket Assisted Projectiles. 'These are the Free World's first operational artillery-launched, zoned RAP's,' an Army official wrote. 'RAP's provide all existing howitzers with one third more range and more than 100 per cent greater area coverage. Because RAP's incorporate in design a new high fragmentation steel, they provide significant increases in lethal effectiveness.'[54]

In 1964–6 the US Naval Weapons Laboratory investigated the 'metallurgical parameters required to provide maximum fragmentation effectiveness against personnel and medium shore targets at the lowest cost,' and found that a mixed structure of ferrite and pearlite made for smaller fragments in a commercial AISI 06 tool steel than a martensitic structure with a small amount of free ferrite. Out of this finding came a Navy patent covering a production process for a 5-inch antipersonnel projectile for use in shelling hostile coastal points from ships offshore.[55]

The Bethlehem Steel Company, on its own initiative (I was told), developed a new manganese–silicon steel, HF-1, 'HF' standing for 'high fragmentation.' ('It's a good name,' an Army metallurgist told me.) As work progressed it became apparent that a 'special grain boundary carbide embrittlement' was necessary to obtain maximum breakup to the 'most effective fragment size distribution.'[56]

At the Army Materials and Mechanics Research Center in the old Watertown Arsenal near Boston, fragmentation tests on scale model shells of over 500 different alloys and heat treatments led 'unexpectedly' (in the words of an AMMRC patent application) to the elaboration of a new high boron carbon–manganese steel, PR-2. 'We ascribe the excellent fragmentation performance of the alloy of Example 6 [one of several varieties of PR-2] to the combined effects of a judicious selection of alloying ingredients within the parameters of our invention and the employment of a tempering step prior to final air cooling of the alloy,' the inventors wrote.[57]

As with so many other modern developments in antipersonnel weaponry, work on the improvement of shell casing materials began shortly after the start of the Korean war. A US Army Ballistic Research Laboratories report of 1952 describes a series of fragmentation tests on experimental shells made of a steel with various heat treatments. The study was concerned with 'the development of a means by which the character of fragmentation, as regards size, distribution, and shape of the fragments, can be predicted.'[58] Years later, that predictive formula, relating fragmentation behavior to the material of the casing, had still not been worked out. The reason was that, like the process of wounding, the process of explosion was so rapid that it was impossible to find out exactly what was going on.

When an explosive charge is detonated inside a shell, gases are produced very rapidly, causing the shell case to swell to about one and one half times its original diameter. At that point, the forces holding the casing material together can no longer withstand the forces of expansion, and the case splits into fragments which continue moving outward at high velocity. That much was known, but just where and how did the cracks form?

'This is how I think it works,' a US Army expert told me, and he drew a sketch of a shell wall. As the shell expands, the inside of the wall will be pushed, while the outside will stretch; and a crack, in his view, began at a place near the outside where the pushing and the stretching met. If the steel was tough and ductile, the crack would extend from this point to form a shear fracture running straight through the shell wall, making for large fragments. If the material was brittle, there would be a radial fracture and two shear fractures; if it was more brittle, a radial fracture with several shear fractures branching off; and one would then be approaching the ideal fragment size for antipersonnel purposes, which this scientist put at one to five grains' weight.

'We don't have an analytical solution' for the formation of cracks, he said – there was no simple formula – but one could use a computer to make a series of approximations to what was going on. One would get the computer to imagine that the shell had expanded ever so slightly, and calculate the stresses this would produce, then expand it ever so slightly again and see what would happen on the basis of what had already taken place, and continue in that way. 'Incremental stress analysis' was the name for this technique of inquiry.

I spoke with another Army scientist, a friendly, affable man. Pure research was his work, an inquiry into the nature of fragmentation; his mind was not on the terminal effects. Wound ballistics hardly touched him – 'I've heard they're even using gelatin; I suppose it has something to do with the density of flesh,' he told me. As for what went on in his institution, the machinations of the ambitious bureaucrats, the hustling for budget dollars – all that he viewed with amused detachment. He was simply a scientist who liked his work; and I had a pleasant chat with him as we considered the enigma of the behavior of metals under impulsive loads.

The way in which a steel fragmented could be greatly affected by heat treatments and mechanical working. This much was known, and the emergence of high fragmentation steels was based on this fact. But why steels broke up as they did, and what could be done to them to get smaller fragments, or fragments of a better shape, was still imperfectly understood. One could measure the mechanical properties of a steel – its tensile strength, its ductility, its brittleness – and in general, it seemed, the more brittle a steel became, the smaller the fragments; but two steels of the same brittleness did not necessarily fragment in the same way.

'In spite of all the empirical studies that have been done, we are not able to state a direct correlation between mechanical properties and fragment size,' he said. Mechanical properties were gross measures of what happened to a metal when stresses were slowly applied to it. They worked well enough when one was designing an airplane or a skyscraper, but the explosion of a shell was different. One could take an electron microscope and look at the faces of a fragment, and try to figure out where, on a microstructural level, the steel had separated, and how this varied in steels of different microstructures; but that was still after the fact.

'Does this mean that you don't have general laws relating fragmentation behavior to the fundamental molecular composition of steels?' I asked.

'That's exactly right,' he said; and he doubted that there would be a general theory of fragmentation in his lifetime.

Despite the absence of a comprehensive theoretical understanding, US munitions engineers succeeded in developing various high fragmentation steels. These new materials extended the antipersonnel capability of artillery shells and opened up new sources of supply for mortar shells at a time when Vietnam war demands were placing cast iron production capacity under a strain.[59] As armies elsewhere became interested in using high fragmentation steels for artillery ammunition, the potential for the deployment of small wounding missiles by artillery spread beyond Vietnam.

Canisters and Beehives: The Story of a 'Nasty Thing'

In 1966 this mysterious interchange appeared in the printed record of one of the annual closed Congressional hearings on the Defense Department budget. (The dashes represent the Army censor's deletions.)

GENERAL CHESAREK We mentioned on Tuesday, Mr. Chairman, our new — . I would like to have Mr. Matt describe these rounds to you. They use a very interesting concept.

MR. MATT I have two models here, one the 105-millimeter howitzer round.

MR. FLOOD How big is a — ?

MR. MATT They are — .

MR. FLOOD Different sizes?

MR. MATT No.

MR. ANDREWS You say the shell has — [?].

MR. MATT Yes.

MR. FLOOD What kind of a wound does this make? Will this kill?

MR. MATT Yes, sir.

GENERAL CHESAREK It is a nasty thing.

MR. FLOOD A guy will pick up — [?].

GENERAL CHESAREK It depends on how close he is to the burst.

MR. MATT — .

MR. FLOOD Is it disabling without any question?

MR. ANDREWS Do the Vietcong troops have any of this type of weapon?

MR. MATT No, sir.

MR. FLOOD That is what we have been talking about for years.[60]

The new rounds which aroused such interest among the Congressmen were derived from two ancient forms of artillery ammunition: canisters and shrapnel shells. Canisters open at the muzzle of the gun, dispersing their contents as from a shotgun shell. Shrapnel shells are similar, but are projected downrange before bursting open. They were named after a lieutenant of the British Infantry who, some two centuries ago, devised a cartridge filled with lead balls or other small missiles and fitted with a time fuze to make it break open over the heads of enemy troops. (Today the word 'shrapnel' is popularly but inaccurately used to refer to the fragments produced by an explosive shell.)

The story of the new projectiles was recounted with pride in *Arsenal for the Brave*, a history of the US Army Materiel Command.

Efforts to improve artillery ammunition are of course as old as artillery. One major representative AMC–MUCOM [Army Materiel Command–Munitions Command] effort concentrated on the use of the canister. The concept of canister-type ammunition is not new. Before our own Revolutionary War the lethal effectiveness of cannon loaded to the muzzle with fragments, usually varying in size and shape from culled stones to colonial barn nails, was recognized...

Canister rounds filled with small steel shot had been used in World War II: according to an official US Army history, 'in jungle warfare canister proved surprisingly effective for stopping massed Japanese attacks and for clearing jungle undergrowth.'[61] But shrapnel shells had been abandoned as a result of another of those unfortunate but revealing accidents, an explosion in which the only damage was a couple of fingers blown off the hand of the man holding the shell. 'The shrapnel balls were well sprayed amongst the group of observers at close range and, yet, only a few black and blue places resulted – without penetration of the clothing,' wrote Army wound ballistics experts Callender and French. 'This total inefficiency of shrapnel was further demonstrated by study of known battlefield occurrences.... Needless to say, the manufacture and use of shrapnel was promptly discontinued.'[62]

The Korean problem of defending US positions against enemy hordes revived the Army's interest in canisters. Taking up the story again in the AMC history:

> Combat experience in Korea stimulated the effort to develop improved canister ammunition in several calibers. In 1951 requirements were established for virtually all major gun, howitzer, and recoilless weapons...

Three new canister rounds filled with steel balls or slugs (little steel rods) were eventually developed in response to the Korean requirements, and entered the Army inventory.[63] But the breakthrough came when someone had the idea of filling the canisters with flechettes – the 'deadly darts' which Mr Barr wanted to shoot from rifles.

> Not until the flechette geometry and the concept of a low drag coefficient were adopted for this munition was the potential for a canister-type projectile realized [the AMC history continued]. The result was a concentrated effort on antipersonnel munitions known as the Beehive Program. Because of its high density and lower velocity decay of the fragments, the flechette or Beehive munition results in a *greater area of coverage* and is *much more effective* than conventional canister munitions. In addition, when this round is fitted with a mechanical time fuze, a downrange capability enables Beehive ammunition to compete with conventional high explosive fire for certain *targets of opportunity*. (emphasis added)

Several companies helped the Army to fill the canisters with as many flechettes as possible – the more flechettes, the greater the number of potential casualties. In the mid-1950s the agricultural machinery maker International Harvester Company was able to fit 6,265 flechettes in a 90mm canister originally designed to hold 1,280 slugs, according to a contractor's report.[64] The kitchen appliance manufacturer Whirlpool

Corporation, which took over the work in 1957, suggested ways of raising the number of flechettes to 9,905. 'It is felt that the increase in number of missiles will improve the lethality of the canisters by increasing the target density,' they wrote in their report. Whirlpool also tackled the problem of preventing the flechettes from all fanning out in a cone, leaving an undamaged patch in the center of the target area.[65]

Another problem was how to manufacture and assemble what the AMC history called the 'astronomical number of flechettes' required for the new munitions. To save space, it was decided to pack the flechettes in alternating directions, the tip of one nestling between the fins of its neighbor; on release from the cartridge, the fins would cause the flechettes to straighten out and head forward.

> The solution of flechette assembly problems resulted in production of a new item of ammunition, which could for the first time be issued for field use. This technological breakthrough occurred at a time when renewed interest was being generated for this item.[66]

The 'renewed interest' came, of course, from the Vietnam war. In Vietnam, the artillery pieces pounding the countryside were attractive targets for the NLF guerrillas. They were often isolated from large defending forces, and their neutralization would have made good propaganda in view of the damage they were causing to homes and villages. Infantry were posted to guard the gun emplacements, but they were not always strong enough to stave off the Korean nightmare of a massed attack. Against this threat appeared the new canisters and Beehives.

> Washington (AP) – The Army has started using what amounts to huge artillery shotgun shells against the communists in South Vietnam sources report.
>
> New artillery rounds fired in regular 105mm. howitzer pieces spray thousands of dart-shaped steel shafts over broad areas of jungle or open territory.
>
> One well-aimed round can kill hundreds of enemy troops massing for an attack.
>
> Military men report the weapon has been used with lethal effectiveness in such actions as communist charges against American artillery positions below the Demilitarized Zone.
>
> 'I've seen reports of enemy soldiers actually being nailed to trees by these things,' one officer commented.
>
> Information on the antipersonnel cartridge has been cleared for publication by the Defense Department's security review office but defense officials decided not to announce its development through the Pentagon. A possible reason was the ugly nature of the weapon...[67]

That Associated Press account appeared in American newspapers in December 1967. Early the next year, this report appeared:

Saigon – US troops killed 344 attacking communists with almost point-blank barrages of tiny steel darts today in a Cambodian border battle that closed out the bloodiest truce of the Vietnam war.

UPI [United Press International] correspondent Robert Kaylor reported from Dau Tieng, 60 miles northwest of Saigon, that about 2000 Vietcong smashed into a US Army 25th Infantry Division artillery fortress before dawn in the final hours of a 36-hour New Year's truce.

Fighting against being overrun, the 500 Americans lowered their artillery barrels and boomed round after round of 'beehive' shells into the human waves of guerrillas.

Each 'beehive' shell exploded into hundreds of half-inch darts that shredded the Vietcong, Kaylor said.

The guerrillas killed 26 Americans and wounded 111, US officers said.

But American commanders said the bodies of 344 enemy soldiers were found on the field at daybreak today.[68]

Some of the early engagements where flechette-filled projectiles were used are described in Army studies and histories of the war. 'Beehive was fired in combat for the first time on 7 November 1966 by Battery A, 2d Battalion, 320th Field Artillery. A single round killed nine attacking enemy and stopped the attack.'[69] On the night of 26 December 1966, two Beehive rounds were used to repel an attack by two North Vietnamese Army companies on Landing Zone Bird, an artillery fire base in central South Vietnam; as the first round landed, 'The arrogant chants of the NVA troops suddenly changed to screams of agony.'[70] The battle resulted in 266 'known enemy dead' as against 30 Americans killed, but 'The most important benefit derived from the action at Bird was recognition that the Beehive round was a tremendously valuable asset to the overall fire base defense program. It had gained the confidence and respect of both artillerymen and infantrymen and would continue to play a vital role in position defense throughout the remainder of the war.'[71] And on the morning of 21 March 1967, during Operation Junction City, a huge search-and-destroy operation in War Zone C northwest of Saigon, a heavy NLF attack on an artillery post was repulsed with the aid of Beehives, tank-fired canisters, and high explosive artillery and aircraft fire, resulting in 647 NLF bodies recovered, nearly 25 per cent of the entire body count of Operation Junction City.[72]

Ultimately, some three flechette-filled canister rounds and five Beehive rounds were accepted for Army use.[73] Among them were a canister round containing 2,400 flechettes for the 90mm recoilless rifle, a weapon used by infantry to defend artillery bases in Vietnam; a Beehive round containing 4,100 8-grain flechettes for the 90mm tank gun, enabling the old M48 Patton tanks used in Vietnam to defend themselves against assaults; a 105mm howitzer Beehive round containing 8,000 8-grain flechettes; and other canisters and Beehives for the 105mm and 152mm tank guns, the 106mm recoilless rifle, and the 155mm howitzer.[74]

Judging from the casualties inflicted in the engagements described above in comparison to the number of rounds fired, flechette ammunition must have been one of the most efficient killers of the Vietnam war.

Fuzes, Brains of Munitions

Most modern weapon systems have as their main mission the delivery of an explosive to the enemy. In order to do this efficiently, the warheads of such systems ... must be detonated at some well defined point in space or time.

The component of the warhead which causes functioning at that optimum point, and thus determines the effectiveness of the total weapon system, is the fuze. Fuzes are aptly called the 'brains of munitions.' They have the unique capability to sense the proper condition for functioning. They determine position relative to the target, and cause warhead function.

Lieutenant Colonel Peter E. Hexner, Commanding Officer,
US Army Harry Diamond Laboratories[75]

A fuze is a device with explosive components designed to initiate a train of fire or detonation in an ammunition item. The main types are the *impact* fuze, set in action by the munition hitting the target or another object such as the ground; the *time* fuze, containing a graduated time element which regulates the time interval after which the fuze will function, usually by means of a clockwork device; and the *proximity* fuze, setting off the munition at a predetermined distance above the ground or from the intended target.[76]

The proximity fuze, although more elaborate than the others, is of special value in enhancing antipersonnel effectiveness. If a high explosive shell bursts in the air, the fragments can hit soldiers sheltering in trenches who would be protected from an explosion at ground level. As Colonel Hexner wrote: 'It turns out that in engaging personnel, or "soft" targets, maximum effectiveness is achieved when the high explosive warhead is detonated above the target.'

A US Army ordnance engineering design handbook states: 'The proximity fuze was one of the spectacular developments of World War II.'[77] According to an official Army history, the development of the proximity fuze, employing a radar device (another World War II invention), 'occupied some of the best scientific brains of America and Britain'; the War Department described the fuzes as 'second in importance to the atomic bomb' in bringing about victory, and the Army history noted that 'their widest and most deadly application was against ground troops.'[78]

According to the US Army technical manual *Bombs and Bomb Components*, 'Proximity fuzes are automatic time fuzes which, without setting or adjustment, detonate the bomb on approach to the target at the most effective point on its trajectory.' An Army ordnance design handbook explains that the fuze 'is actually a combination of radio broadcasting and receiving station. The waves, which are constantly being broadcast by the fuze at a set frequency, are reflected back from the target and picked up by the receiving set in the fuze. This fuze functions when it comes within proper proximity to any target capable of reflecting its waves.' The Army technical manual states that 'Proximity fuzes may profitably be employed in any operation in which air burst at heights between 10 and 250 feet will increase the effectiveness of the bomb in which it is used.'[79]

The World War II proximity fuzes, which used vacuum tubes for their electronic circuits, were bulky and expensive. After the war, the US Army, recognizing that 'proximity fuze technology was in its infancy,' set up a special laboratory in Washington 'to advance the state of fuzing technology, and to apply the knowledge gained to the wide scope of military ordnance problems.'[80] By the time of the Vietnam war, advances in electronics would make it possible to produce proximity fuzes at economical prices, even for relatively small munitions which were used in large quantities, giving the American forces improved means of striking at the seen and unseen guerrillas from above.

Among the fuzing innovations of Vietnam were:

- A proximity fuze for helicopter-launched 40mm grenades, making it possible to produce dozens of airburst explosions in a matter of seconds. Selling for only five dollars apiece, the fuze was described by Colonel Hexner as 'a high volume production item whose low cost depends upon modern industrial facilities capable of automatic assembly.'

- A proximity fuze for the 2.75-inch air-to-ground fragmentation rocket. An Army witness at a 1967 Congressional hearing described it as 'an outstanding example of quick reaction in response to an urgent RVN [Republic of Vietnam] requirement.' He said: 'The airburst proximity fuze is much more effective than the impact fuze, *depending upon the type of target*' (emphasis added).[81]

- A similar fuze for the Zuni 5-inch air-to-ground rocket. *Missiles and Rockets* magazine reported in 1966 that the Zuni 'has been used more extensively than anticipated in Vietnam operations. The rocket has been equipped with a proximity fuze that makes it a more versatile weapon against such targets as trucks, bunkers, and *personnel concentrations*' (emphasis added).[82]

These fuzes were developed for munitions which were fired singly or in bursts. Fuzes would also play an important role in the design of a weapon which was to transform the possibilities for the wide-area deployment of lethal fragments: the cluster bomb.

Notes

1. Interview with Doris Kearns (Kearns, 1976; 1977 edition, p. 272).
2. Interview with Daniel Ellsberg in 1967 (Ellsberg, 1972, p. 234).
3. Kahin and Lewis, 1969, pp. 49, 87.
4. Pike, 1986, pp. 216–17. Pike has evaluated the main elements of the Vietnamese concept of *dau tranh* (struggle) in his book *PAVN: People's Army of Vietnam*, Chapter 9, 'Why the Communists Won: Military Dau Tranh' and Chapter 10, 'Why the Communists Won: Political Dau Tranh.'
5. Bergerud, 1991, pp. 54–5, 93–4.
6. *Ibid.*, pp. 21, 57–68, 326.
7. Pike, 1966, p. 248.
8. Quoted in Kahin and Lewis, 1969, pp. 479–80.
9. See, for example, Bergerud, 1991, pp. 121–7, 137–9.
10. In the official US Army definition, 'harassing fire' is 'fire designed to disturb the rest of the enemy troops, to curtail movement and, by threat of losses, to lower morale,' while 'interdiction fire' is 'fire placed on an area or point to prevent the enemy from using the area or point.' 'Supposedly based on intelligence concerning the movement of enemy troops and supplies, H&I missions were often fired routinely, with no particular purpose in mind other than to keep the enemy on edge. Lieutenant General Frank T. Mildren, deputy commanding general of USARV [US Army, Vietnam], contended that 'purely H&I fires in [a] Vietnam environment have little, if any, value while doing practically no damage to the enemy.' Studies done by the Systems Analysis people at OSD [Office of the Secretary of Defense] concluded that 'our unobserved fire alienates the local peasants in most cases, thus harming our efforts to break down their loyalty to and support for the Viet Cong' (Krepinevich, 1986, p. 201).
11. A Stockholm International Peace Research Institute (SIPRI) analysis of the US rules of engagement for surface weapons in the Vietnam war has noted: 'Few restrictions applied to the use of munitions in SSZs ['special strike zones,' previously referred to as 'free fire zones'], other than a requirement to notify an appropriate "clearance authority"' (SIPRI, 1978, p. 260).
12. Hay, 1974, p. 92; according to this source, defoliation accounted for approximately 90 per cent of the herbicide effort in Vietnam, while the remaining 10 per cent was devoted to crop destruction. The damage caused by the use of chemicals in Vietnam has been analyzed in a study by Professor Arthur H. Westing for SIPRI (SIPRI, 1976, Chapter 3).
13. SIPRI, 1976, Chapter 4. According to this source, some 2 per cent of the entire land area of South Vietnam was cleared in this fashion. Among the deleterious effects of Rome plow clearing noted in the SIPRI study are soil erosion, decimation of the tropical fauna, and alteration of the microclimate.

14. In Operation Cedar Falls in January 1967 in the 'Iron Triangle' near Saigon, 5,987 villagers were evacuated; their homes were bulldozed, tunnels were destroyed, and rice and medical supplies were seized. Operation Cedar Falls also resulted in nearly 750 'confirmed enemy dead,' 280 prisoners, 540 defectors, and hundreds of weapons captured (Rogers, 1974, pp. 39–41, 74–9). Whatever the US claims of success for the operation ('From every aspect, the enemy had suffered a great defeat,' Lieutenant General Rogers later wrote), 'enemy forces returned to the Iron Triangle within weeks of the termination of Cedar Falls' (Bergerud, 1991, p. 126).

15. Cf. Bergerud, 1991, pp. 170–2, on American soldiers' distrust of Vietnamese villagers.

16. *Ibid.*, p. 99.

17. Cf. Krepinevich, 1986, pp. 202–5; Davidson, 1988, pp. 401–2.

18. These figures are taken from unpublished Department of Defense procurement records obtained by SIPRI.

19. By 1964, a decision had evidently been taken to publicize the use of certain weapons in order to show that the US war effort was inhumane. A booklet on the war in South Vietnam, published in Hanoi in July 1964, called attention to tests of such weapons as the AR-15 rifle and to the use of napalm, white phosphorus (a smoke agent which causes severe burns), and defoliants. It protested that 'the US aggressors and their agents are still planning large-scale use of noxious chemicals as a means of warfare in South Viet Nam,' and stated: 'It is imperative to stay their criminal hands and to demand that an end be put to these barbarous acts condemned by the entire progressive mankind' (DRV Ministry of Foreign Affairs, 1964, pp. 31–5). After the sustained bombing of North Vietnam began, there were further statements deploring the destruction and the munitions used (Chapter 4).

20. Chase, 1973, p. L-1. According to an unofficial Army history, development of the M79 40mm grenade system began in 1952, but it was not until 1961 that a substantial quantity was available for issue to units (Hay, 1974, p. 51).

21. Chase, 1973, p. L-2. This size and velocity are in line with the concept of a 'small' fragment cited by the Army's Project Manager for Selected Ammunition as characteristic of the antipersonnel munitions developed in the 1950s and quoted at the beginning of Chapter 2.

22. US Army, 1972a. The effective casualty radius is less than that for the M26 grenade because the grenade itself is smaller.

23. According to unpublished Department of Defense procurement records obtained by SIPRI, the Army ordered 12,144,000 M406 and XM463 40mm high explosive cartridges in the fiscal year 1966 (1965–66), as against 1,152,000 M406 and XM398 cartridges in fiscal 1965 and 1,172,000 M406 and XM398 cartridges in fiscal 1964.

24. In 1963 *Ordnance* described the development of the high velocity airborne automatic launcher as a response to military difficulties in Vietnam: 'Vulnerability of helicopters recently used in operations in Vietnam emphasized the need for a new weapon, and the Army has assigned the Ford Motor Company to develop a 40mm. grenade launcher to be mounted on US Army choppers. Helicopter pilots expect to use the launcher in situations where enemy ground fire

has harassed their operations' ('Grenades for Helicopters,' *Ordnance*, January–February 1963, p. 456). A US Army official, however, traced the development of the airborne launcher back to 'a study in the mid-1950s to define an optimized suppressive fire system for helicopters' (Chase, 1973, p. L-3).

25. Aerojet–General Corporation worked on the development of the low velocity automatic luncher from about 1964 to 1976 under an Army contract. For details of this and other contractors' work on 40mm weapons, see Prokosch, 1972, pp. 21–3.

26. Two such rounds were developed under ENSURE, the Army's rapid development program for Vietnam, according to the SIPRI study *The Problem of Chemical and Biological Warfare* (SIPRI, 1973, vol. 3, pp. 32–3). The SIPRI study also lists a third CS gas round, as well as a round filled with the psychochemical BZ, but states that the development of the latter round was curtailed in 1965.

27. The M381 and M441 high explosive rounds have an arming distance of 2 to 3 meters, as against the M406 and M386 rounds, which do not arm – and therefore cannot detonate – until the grenade has traveled at least 14 meters.

28. The US Army Materiel Command history *Arsenal for the Brave* (1969, p. 155) stated that the XM576E1 40mm shot-filled (or 'multiple projectile') cartridge 'showed tangible results in the saving of lives of our combat soldiers.... This unique munition was placed into the hands of our fighting men within nine months of the assignments of task – less than half the time estimated for the accomplishment of this urgent mission.'

A friendly, cheerful engineer who developed the shotgun round at one of the US Army weapons laboratories told me with pleasure of his contribution to the war effort. Bypassing cumbersome Army procurement procedures, he bought shotgun shot from a local sporting goods store to use in test models in order to speed up the process. In a shoot-off with a competing model from another Army weapons laboratory, his design won out.

'We ultimately produced more than ten million rounds,' he said, showing me a scrapbook of newspaper clippings. He was named Federal Civil Servant of the Year for his work on the cartridge, and his name was mentioned in local newspapers.

'I was afraid my house would be picketed – at that time!' he said.

29. Avco's new 'Avroc' ammunition, noted *Ordnance* in January–February 1968, had 'greater range and accuracy than conventional ammunition of the same size.' Another advantage was that 'Present grenade weapons are handicapped when used in dense foliage similar to that found in the rain forests of Vietnam, because of the need to use a high trajectory. With the new ammunition the flat trajectory makes it possible for a man to fire under foliage of this type to reach the target' (which, however, would not be very easy to see with so much foliage in the way!). This seems to have been an example of private enterprise on the part of one of the leading American developers of antipersonnel munitions. Two years earlier, another defense industry magazine had reported that Avco had been working on Avroc ammunition for several years, 'with a minimum of help from government sources' (*Missiles and Rockets*, 28 March 1966, p. 125).

30. Hay, 1974, p. 52. This was one of the 'unofficial' histories of the Vietnam war, in the series *Vietnam Studies*, written by senior officers and issued by the

Army in the interim while the official histories (written by Army historians) were being prepared.

31. Baxter, 1967.

32. In 1961, as shown by the Army Research Office task summary for that year, the Army was studying possible warheads for the 2.75-inch rocket for use in 'arming Army aircraft in the air-to-ground role.' The work on the 2.75-inch rocket warhead was done under an Army project entitled 'Aerial Delivery of Improved Area Weapon.'

33. Hay, 1974, p. 14; Guilmartin and O'Leary, 1988, p. 31.

34. US House of Representatives, Committee on Appropriations, *Department of Defense Appropriations for 1967*, hearings, vol. 4, pp. 89–91. 'Fuze' is the standard spelling in US military usage for an explosive component of an ammunition round which is used to detonate the round.

35. US Senate, Committee on Armed Services, *Status of Ammunition and Air Munitions*, hearings, 1966, pp. 8, 43.

36. Hay, 1974, p. 33. According to Hay (*ibid.*, p. 17), 'the AH-1G [helicopter] with its twin pods of 2.75-inch rockets was comparable to a 105mm. howitzer.'

37. US Army Munitions Command, 1973, vol. 1, pp. E-3, E-25.

38. Although this warhead 'is used primarily to provide smoke for target marking,' according to the Navy manual, white phosphorus also 'has a mild incendiary effect and will set fire to materials having a low kindling point, such as clothing, dry brush, paper, canvas, etc.' (US Army, 1966a, p. 2-56). White phosphorus is hard to extinguish; burns are especially severe, and may be subject to poisoning (SIPRI, 1975, pp. 155–60, 199–200). Journalist Frank Harvey reported from South Vietnam: 'White phosphorus bombs were another incendiary that the VC feared greatly. This stuff is even more vicious than napalm. In the civilian hospital in Can Tho, I saw a man who had a piece of white phosphorus in his flesh. It was still burning' (Harvey, 1967, pp. 56–7).

39. US Navy, 1972b, section IV.

40. The WDU-4/A warhead is derived from the flechette-filled Beehive projectile (see below). It contains 6,000 6-grain flechettes. When the rocket has reached its maximum range and the motor has burned out, the fuze detonates and the flechettes are expelled from the warhead by a small explosive charge. 'They're excellent against troops in the open,' a 31-year-old Air Force major told a *New York Times* reporter (10 May 1972). 'Nails 'em right to the ground.' The flechettes were also better than high explosive warhead fragments for penetrating protective foliage, a perennial problem in Vietnam. A US captain told CBS News (29 April 1971): 'we … like to use them against the enemy in trees because the nails will penetrate the trees all the way to the ground where our other rockets go off in the top of the tree.'

With the WDU-4/A available for antipersonnel use, another warhead containing heavier, 20-grain flechettes, the WDU-4A/A, was developed for use against lightly armored targets (US Navy, 1972b).

41. US Army, 1966b, pp. 23, 95. Despite the increase in velocity, the 5.56mm bullet, because of its much smaller size, has far less kinetic energy than the 7.62mm bullet and hence, in principle, less wounding capacity. The modern version of the 5.56mm bullet, the M193, weighing 55 grains (3.56 grams), has

1,640 joules of energy on leaving the barrel of the gun as against 3,272 joules for the 7.62mm NATO round, weighing 147 grains (9.5 grams; Sellier and Kneubuehl, 1994, pp. 365, 372).

42. According to Tompkins (1966, p. 123), the rifles were bought by the Advanced Research Projects Agency (ARPA), a Pentagon research organization whose creation was authorized in 1958 (Klare, 1972, p. 121). Michael T. Klare has reported that in 1962, at the request of the CIA, 30,000 AR-15s were sent to Vietnam for testing by Special Forces units in combat conditions under Project Agile, a top-secret Pentagon program for counterinsurgency research (*ibid.*, pp. 215, 219). In 1963 a further 104,000 rifles were ordered from the Colt company, which had acquired the production rights (SIPRI, 1978, p. 98).

43. V. Briggins, 'Lightweight Rifle Is Favored,' *Newport News Times Herald*, 2 February 1966.

44. Dimond and Rich, 1967, pp. 620–24. The information that wounds at close range (where the velocity of the bullet is highest) were less severe than those further from the muzzle of the gun contradicts the notion that velocity is mainly responsible for what Dimond and Rich called the 'devastating wounding power' of the M16 (AR-15) rifle, although with such a small sample the evidence could not be considered conclusive. It would, however, be consistent with the possibility that as the bullet travels through the air, its yaw increases, making it more likely to tumble when it hits the body.

45. The American change of heart is remembered with an I-told-you-so attitude by specialists in other countries who had favored a reduction in caliber from the start. When it was announced in 1951 that the British Army, following a recommendation of the 'Ideal Calibre Committee,' would adopt a new .28 caliber rifle designed at the Enfield factory, the full weight of the US military was brought to bear on the Churchill government and the British rifle was scrapped (*Jane's Infantry Weapons 1975*, pp. 295–9, 307). 'People in the United States have admitted privately that it was the biggest mistake they ever made,' a British Army weapons expert told me. 'All our work on a high velocity, small caliber rifle got dropped,' another British expert said. 'Then the US came up with 5.56 millimeters.'

46. SIPRI, 1978, pp. 99–104.

47. Ott, 1975, pp. 42, 55.

48. An ex-Marine with a penchant for colorful story-telling told me of his experience in Vietnam in 1968–9:

'I was stationed at Camp Carroll, on top of a mountain a few miles south of the DMZ [the Demilitarized Zone separating the two Vietnams]. There was a river and a road below the mountain and on the other side, to the north, two mountains. The gooks were in those mountains. They'd try to ambush our convoys on the road. The gooks had a cannon in a cave. Every afternoon they'd haul it out and fire three rounds. One of them was always a dud. Then they'd roll the cannon back in and we'd be firing at them with our artillery. We'd pour about 85 million rounds into the mountain and our planes would be flying over dropping napalm and butterfly [cluster] bombs. You'd see about 70,000 explosions from the butterfly bombs; it looked like a bunch of little explosions laid out all over the hill. It didn't seem to bother the gooks any.

They probably had caves 80,000 feet deep. The next day they'd roll out their cannon again and shoot their three rounds.'

49. Krepinevich, 1986, pp. 201–2, 222–4. Similarly, Eric M. Bergerud has written that according to records of the US 25th Infantry Division, stationed west of Saigon, 'the 25th artillery fired 122,000 rounds in direct support and another 85,000 rounds for harassment and interdiction in the first quarter of 1967 alone. For this expenditure, intelligence estimated that 231 enemy fighters were killed' (Bergerud, 1993, p. 77).

50. Truckenmiller, 1964.

51. US Army, Frankford Arsenal, historical summary for fiscal year 1967, p. 23; cf. Riffin, 1972, pp. 5–6.

52. The first munition using high fragmentation steel was the M409 152mm projectile. Although this is primarily an antitank round, using a conventional 'shaped charge' with the explosive surrounded by a conical copper lining (see Chapter 4), the use of high fragmentation steel in the outer wall gives the projectile an added antipersonnel capability. An Army manual states: 'For antipersonnel use, the round is fired so that the fuze will function on graze. Blast and fragmentation created by detonation of the explosive charge inflicts casualties' (US Army, 1967a with changes, p. 2-90.2.1).

53. Although the first high fragmentation steel, AISI 52100, had emerged from an earlier program, the effort to develop other varieties was clearly prompted by the needs of the Vietnam war. According to an Army report: 'About 1965, the Army initiated a dynamic program to develop wrought steels having high fragmentation...' The report cited the importance of fragments in producing casualties, and stated: 'Recent lethality assessments have shown that maximum effectiveness can be achieved in naturally fragmenting artillery shell when the average fragment weight is between 1 and 15 grains (depending upon the weapon size and military objective)' (Riffin, 1972, pp. 5–6).

54. Painter, 1974, p. 16; Benner, 1968, p. 8. According to an Army manual, the M548 105mm rocket-assisted projectile 'is a high-explosive, rocket-assisted round with extended range capability. Significantly more powerful and lethal than comparable HE Cartridge M1, it is employed against personnel and materiel targets.' The fragmentation of this round is enhanced by the fact that it is filled with Composition B rather than the TNT used in the original M1 round (US Army, 1967, with changes, p. 2-115).

55. Magis, 1967.

56. Riffin, 1972, p. 8.

57. US patent 3,880,081, 'High Boron Alloy Steel Fragmentation Munition' (29 April 1975, filed 19 December 1973).

58. Weymouth, 1952, p. 5.

59. There were approximately one hundred malleable iron foundries in the United States as of 1960, but only a few of them were capable of turning out shell casings, which had to be of higher quality and accuracy than ordinary commercial castings. The surfaces of the castings proved less smooth and accurate than had been expected, and expensive machining operations became necessary. Automobiles were selling well in those times of national prosperity,

and with the big demand for car parts, foundries preferred commercial orders to the less certain and more exacting ordnance production. Army procurement officials were in a difficult position: the commanders in Vietnam were asking for munitions at rates which at times surpassed those of World War II, but as it was not officially a war, there were no wartime controls that could be used to force manufacturers to produce what was needed. By 1968, 81mm mortar shells were being made of AISI 1340 high fragmentation steel; by 1973, 60mm mortar shells were also being made of this material (Benner, 1968, p. 8; US Army Munitions Command, 1973, pp. F-4, F-10).

60. US House of Representatives, Committee on Appropriations, *Department of Defense Appropriations for 1967*, hearings, vol. 4, pp. 92–3. The record is of a hearing held on 28 March 1966.

61. Green, Thomson, and Roots, 1955, pp. 370–71.

62. French and Callender, 1962, p. 112. According to the authors, the accident also demonstrated the fallacy of the pine-board test which had been used as a measure of missile effectiveness up to the late 1920s, when Army scientists in search of a new semiautomatic weapon bullet realized that there was no reliable criterion for wounding: 'For many years, ordnance engineers had been using the penetration of 1-inch pine boards separated by a small air space (1 inch) for judging the relative efficiency of bullets. Subsequent investigation revealed this test to be far from precise because of variations in pine boards, as well as many other factors beyond reasonable control.' In the accident, bystanders were hit by shrapnel balls which did not even penetrate their clothing. 'However, shrapnel balls had penetrated many pine boards in the usual tests.'

63. These rounds were for the 57mm recoilless rifle, the 76mm gun, and the 90mm tank gun. The heavy steel base and the longitudinal slits to facilitate rupture of these new canisters were improvements over World War II canister rounds, which often broke up while in the gun tube and damaged the bore (US Army Ordnance Corps, 1960, p. 11-20). The 90mm canisters were used in the Vietnam war.

64. Katterhenry, 1957.

65. *Ibid.* Whirlpool took up the work on flechette munitions when International Harvester gave up its Illinois ordnance laboratory in 1957. Soon there was a flurry of Army contracts for Whirlpool: 'Investigation and Design of Long Range Antipersonnel 155mm. Artillery Ammunition' (1957); 'Design, Development, Fabricate and Test 105mm. Beehive Ammunition' (1959); 'Design and Development of New and Improved Flechettes and Applicable Weapon Systems' (1961); and a contract with a classified title (1962) under which Whirlpool reported to the Army on 'Sting Ray' – apparently a projectile containing flechettes coated with a chemical agent. Perhaps this last munition was the source of the 'small, blue plastic flechettes' which a Pentagon official carelessly passed to a *Newsweek* reporter in 1963, provoking this comment from President Kennedy: '[Secretary of Defense] McNamara tells me those are as secret as anything going on in the Pentagon, and he's going to find out who the hell is passing them around' (Bradlee, 1975, 1976 edition, p. 152).

66. US Army Materiel Command, 1969.

67. Associated Press dispatch by Bob Horton, Palo Alto (California) *Times*, 14 December 1967.

68. *San Francisco Examiner*, 2 January 1968. The attack is mentioned in Eric M. Bergerud's history of the 25th Infantry Division, where the numbers are given as 355 NLF troops left behind dead and 21 Americans killed (Bergerud, 1991, p. 127).

69. Ott, 1975, p. 61.

70. Hammerman *et al.*, 1985, p. 218.

71. Ott, 1975, pp. 109–10.

72. *Ibid.*, p. 113; Rogers, 1974, p. 139. According to Ott, the artillerymen fired thirty Beehive rounds, 'the largest number of these rounds fired in a single engagement to date.'

73. A Beehive projectile is a flechette-filled round fitted with a mechanical time fuze that can be set to blow the shell open either at the muzzle or at any point up to the full range of the gun.

74. US Army, 1967a. A few figures are enough to show the tremendous increase in number and range of wounding missiles which these new munitions provided. The flechette-filled canister for the 90mm tank gun disperses a much greater number of wounding missiles, approximately 5,600 8-grain flechettes, as compared with the 1,280 slugs in the post-Korea canister from which it is derived; the number is even more impressive when compared with the maximum of 390 fragments in World War II canister rounds. It has a maximum effective range of 400 meters, twice the range of the post-Korea round, the difference being due to the better aerodynamic shape of the flechettes.

75. Hexner, 1970, p. 35.

76. US Army, 1972b. A 'mechanical time' fuze is a fuze which works by means of a clockwork device.

77. US Army Ordnance Corps, 1960, p. 12-2.

78. Green, Thomson, and Roots, 1955, pp. 363, 365.

79. US Army, 1966a, p. 4-84; US Army Ordnance Corps, 1960, p. 12-2.

80. Hexner, 1970, p. 36.

81. US House of Representatives, Committee on Appropriations, *Department of Defense Appropriations for 1968*, hearings, vol. 3, p. 208.

82. *Missiles and Rockets*, 28 March 1966, p. 141.

CHAPTER 4

CLUSTERS OF GUAVAS

Conventional ammunition – An aggressive ammunition program was started to improve conventional attack capability, and embraced the backfitting of existing ordnance and the development of new conventional weapons with increased effectiveness. Excellent progress has been made in Rockeye I, an antitank cluster weapon; Snakeye I, a retarded bomb; and Sadeye, a large area antipersonnel weapon...

Thus wrote the Secretary of the Navy in his annual report for the fiscal year 1961–2. Why an 'aggressive' program for the development of 'conventional' ammunition? What was a 'cluster' weapon? Why Sadeye, 'a large area antipersonnel weapon'?

When President John F. Kennedy took office in January 1961, he brought with him a sense of the threat posed, not by Soviet missiles, but by guerrilla campaigns and other forms of 'limited' warfare about which General Maxwell D. Taylor had warned in his book *The Uncertain Trumpet*, published in 1960. The Berlin Wall crisis of July 1961 gave President Kennedy a pretext for rebuilding the country's nonnuclear war capability, and his emergency budget, enacted in the wake of the crisis, included substantial funds for nonnuclear munitions.[1] The progress cited by the Secretary of the Navy in his report for fiscal 1962 was one of the first benefits of this new interest in 'conventional' weaponry.

Although most of the interest in the 1950s had been in preparing to destroy the Soviet Union with nuclear missiles and preventing the same thing from happening to the USA, the military laboratories which specialized in conventional weaponry had been quietly working away at modernizing the country's nonnuclear ammunition and absorbing the lessons of the Korean war. The Army had developed new fragmentation munitions (Chapter 2). The Navy had streamlined its high explosive bombs for external carriage on jet aircraft, and in 1959 it had begun work on the 'Eye' series.[2] The Air Force had commissioned a major project on the feasibility of laying land mines from the air. These strands of research were to come together in the cluster bombs that emerged in the 1960s.

A cluster bomb is a group of smaller bombs which are dropped together. The British had come up with the idea in World War I for incendiary bombing,[3] and at the time of World War II, clusters of fragmentation, chemical, and incendiary bombs were available. The fragmentation clusters made for a sort of two-dimensional form of strafing. '"Wicked little weapons," according to Brigadier General George C. Kenney, they proved their value in the battle for New Guinea and became increasingly popular,' in the words of a US Army history of the war. 'If accurately placed, they could harass front-line infantry and disrupt lines of communication far more completely than could machine gun fire.'[4] The chemical clusters were a means of spreading clouds of poisonous mustard gas over enemy troops. As for the incendiary clusters, they depended on the principle that a large fire is best obtained by lighting many small fires at once.

Intensively burning metallic incendiaries were used against London and Birmingham, and they worked well on the stone and brick cities of Germany.[5] Against the wood and paper construction materials of Japanese cities (where, in the words of an official US Army history, there were many 'household industries' supporting the war effort), it was thought by Allied military planners that the new preparation of jellied fuel, napalm, would be best for starting fires.

On the night of 9 March 1945, 2,000 tons of incendiaries, mostly clusters of 6-lb napalm bombs, were dropped on Tokyo. A strong wind caused the fires to spread rapidly and burn intensely, destroying 15.8 square miles in the center of the city. According to the Army history:

> Some people were able to escape through the wide fire lanes, but many others were encircled by the flames and died of suffocation and burns. Those who fled to the canals faced death in the scalding water or were crushed by the terrified mob which crowded in on top of them. This raid alone caused the death of an estimated 83,793 people and almost 41,000 more received injuries. Over one million people lost their homes.[6]

Compared to the bomb clusters of World War II, the cluster bombs of the 1960s embodied many advances. The little bombs, now called 'bomblets,' were smaller, more numerous, and covered a wider area. They came in many varieties, including some which employed the latest techniques of controlled fragmentation. They were scattered from 'dispensers' of various types, some of which were streamlined for external carriage on high-speed jet aircraft. Many were interchangeable: different types of bomblets could be used with different dispensers, and vice versa. They could be used to attack multiple targets, wide-area targets, and small or moving targets which the pilot of a jet aircraft could not easily hit with a single munition.[7]

All this, however, was not apparent at once. The news of the new weapons reached the public slowly, in snippets such as the reference in the Secretary of the Navy's annual report, and – later – in news reports from Vietnam.

Cluster Bombs against North Vietnam: Early Reports

In August 1965, five months after the United States began systematically bombing North Vietnam in Operation Rolling Thunder, *Newsweek* magazine reported:

> New orders have been crackling out of the Pentagon, with requests some-times going out by telephone and telegram – rather than mail – to speed up the process.... Some of the work is still classified, such as Honeywell's $3.3 million order for BLU-3 cluster bombs. These are the high explosive anti-personnel bomblets being dropped on North Vietnam.[8]

In 1966, at a closed Congressional hearing, a Navy admiral described the Sadeye as 'an air-launched cluster bomb designed to deliver a large number of bomblets over a target area, in level glide, dive, or toss delivery mode.' Another Navy witness noted that there had been 'a technical problem with the separation of the bands, the band from the dispenser, at the time of separation from the aircraft. That has been corrected,' he said.

In early 1967, at another of the annual closed hearings held to consider the Defense Department's budget requests, a member of Congress inquired about the BLU-26 bomblet.

> MR. RHODES [Republican, Arizona]   Mr. Chairman, may I ask what the BLU-26 is?
>
> MAJOR GENERAL GOLDSWORTHY [US Air Force]   It is about the size of a baseball with flutes on the outside. It is put into various dispensers which open at a given altitude and the flutes on the bomblet cause a pattern dispersion.
>
> MR. RHODES   Antipersonnel bomb?
>
> GENERAL GOLDSWORTHY   BLU-26 is antipersonnel. It has the steel ball bear-ings from which we get the lethal fragments.[9]

Later in the year, at another closed hearing, an Air Force witness described the 'operational test' of a cluster bomb against a target in North Vietnam. Anyone present who had followed these matters closely would have noted that the 'large area antipersonnel weapon' described by the Secretary of the Navy in his 1962 report was now an Air Force 'flak suppression' weapon with 'area target applications.' The testimony appeared in the obscure location of pages 513–14 of volume 3 of the printed record of the hearings of the Committee on Appropriations of the US House of Representatives on *Department of Defense Appropriations for 1968*. (The censor's deletions are marked by dashes.)

MAJOR GENERAL EVANS [Director of Development and Special Assistant for Counterinsurgency to the Deputy Chief of Staff for Research and Development, US Air Force] For flak suppression we developed a weapon which could be delivered in a dive mode and released above the zone of intense ground fire. To be most effective we wanted it to cover a wide area.

This was the CBU-24, which was operationally evaluated in SEA [Southeast Asia] in April of last year.

Last year we showed you a very brief film clip of it during its initial test.

It weighs about the same as a 750-pound bomb and contains about 700 bomblets.

The bomblet it disperses is called the BLU-26, shown here. Flutes on the outside cause the bomb to spin up when released, which, in turn, causes the fuze to arm and the bomb to disperse due to magnus lift.

The complete round resembles the M117 [750-lb high explosive] bomb in shape and size, and is no more difficult to load or handle on the aircraft.

Although this was developed as a flak suppression weapon, its area target applications will become obvious from the next film clip.

This is a film clip of the operational tests that were run in Southeast Asia in April of last year.

This is an F-105 carrying — these CBU-24 bombs.

You will see the bombs come off and then the two clamshells, the halves of the bomb case will open up and release the bomblets themselves.

There you see the opening of the clamshells. A couple of them collide in the air and that is why you see the explosions. Here is a target about 130 miles north of the DMZ [Demilitarized Zone], an actual North Vietnamese target, a communications center. This shows what — these CBU-24's are doing to that target area. The picture, of course, is taken by a follow-on F-105 aircraft to record the initial operational test and evaluation.

Here you can see the secondary fires and explosions that resulted from that one attack. Because of the extreme success of this weapon in Southeast Asia we have now received approval from the Defense Department to produce these at the rate of — per month.

Probably our most successful weapon development to date, and I might say the credit for it goes to the Armament Laboratory at Eglin Field, Florida.

Soon after the 'operational test,' news of the new weapon began to filter out of North Vietnam through reports from the occasional visitors to the country – members of the American peace movement, journalists, and other invited guests whom the North Vietnamese considered sympathetic to their cause. From these reports and such official US information as was later released, it became possible to piece together a picture of the weapon.

The CBU-24 (CBU = 'cluster bomb unit') consists of an SUU-30 dispenser (the 'clamshell' referred to by General Evans) containing some 640 to 670 1-lb, spherical BLU-26 bomblets.[10] Dropped from an airplane, the CBU-24 opens in the air, releasing the bomblets, which are aerodynamically designed to scatter in a pattern. When the bomblets hit the ground, they explode. Each bomblet has some three hundred $7/32$-inch steel balls embedded in its casing. The use of one CBU-24 results in some 200,000 steel balls shooting in all directions over a wide area.

The CBU-24 represents an extension over space of the principle of controlled fragmentation described in Chapter 2. Some elements of the weapon relied on existing technologies. The dispenser, virtually identical to the Navy's Sadeye, is similar to a leaflet bomb which opens in the air, scattering leaflets.[11] The bomblet – a round metal case with an explosive filler – is basically a hand grenade, and the use of pre-formed fragments in the form of steel balls is similar to the use of steel balls in the fragmenting face of the Claymore mine (Chapter 2).[12] One major innovation in the CBU-24 was the metal flanges on the outside of each bomblet, causing the bomblets to spin and disperse through an aerodynamic phenomenon known as magnus lift.[13] The fuze, contained within the bomblet and activated by impact when the bomblet hits the ground, was also an innovation. But the greatest innovation was the combination of all these technologies into a single 'large area antipersonnel weapon.'

After its successful 'operational evaluation,'[14] the CBU-24 went into production in the fiscal year 1966–7. The scale of manufacture soon became immense. In early 1968, for example, these contract announcements appeared in the *Commerce Business Daily*, a US Department of Commerce publication for firms seeking government business:

METAL PARTS KIT, BOMB, BLU-26/B FRAGMENTATION Contract F33657-68-C-0776 dtd 29 Jan 68 – 24000000 ea – $8,104,800 – Honeywell Inc., Ordnance Div., Hopkins, Minn.

BALL, CARBON STEEL, $7/32$" FRAGMENTATION Contract F33657-68-C-0668 dtd 9 Feb 68 – 4500000000 ea – $2,925,000 – Superior Steel Ball Co., New Britain, Conn.

The first listing showed that on 29 January 1968, the Ordnance Division of Honeywell Inc. had been awarded an $8,104,800 Air Force contract to produce 24 million sets of BLU-26 bomblet parts. The second showed that on 9 February the Superior Steel Ball Company, a New England ball bearing maker, was awarded a contract to produce 4.5 billion $7/32$-

inch steel balls – more than one hundred times the population of Vietnam, Laos and Cambodia combined.

The demand for CBU-24s was so immense that the producers were able to strike a hard bargain, as one Congressman found to his annoyance at a 1967 hearing. (The dash is the Air Force censor's.)

MR. MAHON [Democrat, Texas] You are requesting $24.4-million for industrial facilities. What are the Air Force requirements for — ?

MAJOR GENERAL GOLDSWORTHY There are new munitions that we are putting into production at an increased rate because of the requirement in Southeast Asia. They include the CBU-24/29, which is a bomb about the size of a baseball which is designed for wide dispersion. These facilities are all associated with increased production of munitions for Southeast Asia.

MR. MAHON Why is it necessary to provide private industry with facilities to manufacture $7/32$-inch steel balls? Cannot industry handle this without Government assistance?

GENERAL GOLDSWORTHY These are the little ball bearings that are pressed into the bomb, the little baseball-size bomblet. These $7/32$-inch steel balls have to be a polished and machined ball because of the manufacturing process. We could not get industry to respond to this requirement without additional facilities.

MR. MAHON Industry has been making ball bearings for generations. Do you have to do this to encourage them to accomplish the objective?

GENERAL GOLDSWORTHY Sir, there is an impact on their commercial consumption, roller skates and this sort of thing. They are quite familiar with the fact that our programs can vary. It can be a high priority one day and not the next.

MR. MAHON So, we are taking the gamble.

GENERAL GOLDSWORTHY We did our best to get them to produce these for us, but we reached the point where to bring in adequate production we had to provide this.

MR. MAHON As a result of the fact that industry does not take much of a risk here, did you get a better price or will you?

GENERAL GOLDSWORTHY We have quite a few manufacturers, and we have a different price from each one. In this particular case we did defray the cost of the equipment in the price.[15]

The Vietnam war was looking very different from different vantage points. Here was Congressman Mahon, intent on saving the taxpayers' money. There was General Evans, pleased to tell the committee about the 'extreme success' of the CBU-24 with its 'area target applications.' Here were the US officials insisting that only targets of 'steel and concrete' were being bombed. There were the terse daily announcements of bombing raids, giving not much more than the number of sorties flown, the aircraft used, and the general location and nature of the targets. And over there were the reports from inside North Vietnam, tainted and unreliable in the view of the Americans. As in the South, these war reports were inevitably affected by what the authorities, under wartime conditions, could or might choose to show to their visitors; for in North Vietnam, as in the United States, the authorities had their own ways of presenting the details of weaponry.

'Guava' Bombs as Seen from the Other Side: Allegations and Denials

Four months after the 'operational evaluation' of the CBU-24, Madeleine Riffaud, correspondent for Radio Luxembourg and the French communist newspaper *L'Humanité*, was probably the first Western visitor to learn about the new cluster bomb. Taken to the village of Phu Xa in the suburbs of Hanoi immediately after an American raid on 13 August 1966, she saw spherical bomblets which the North Vietnamese called 'guavas,' and the remains of the clamshell-type dispenser from which they came. A film with civilian victims of the raid was shown on French television.

Riffaud wrote that the Americans had 'made massive use against populated areas of ball-bearing bombs (called "pineapples," used since 1965) and also of "guavas," a new model, much more lethal, which projects in high density its fragments which are intended to penetrate the body in a spiral path, and its ball bearings which are so hard to extract.' The bombs were 'completely harmless against military or economic works. Dropped on a village, a market, a school, they can cause innumerable victims. Intended to kill.' A North Vietnamese officer told her in September that since the summer, ball-embedded cluster bomblets made up half the tonnage of bombs dropped on North Vietnam.[16]

In October, the North Vietnamese Commission for Investigation on the American Imperialists' War Crimes in Vietnam published a booklet, *American Crimes in Vietnam*. It described the 'pineapple' bomblet (the BLU-3), spewing forth steel balls on explosion, and referred to the 'guava' cluster bomb (the CBU-24) as a military improvement on the 'pineapple.' Echoing Riffaud's statement that 'guavas' were harmless against military works, it described them as being 'especially meant to kill civilians. Children most frequently fall victims to these fragmentation bombs.'[17]

In late October–November 1966, the American pacifist David Dellinger visited North Vietnam, defying the US-imposed ban on travel to the country. Taken under cover of darkness to visit towns and villages outside Hanoi, he was horrified by what he saw.

...the frequency of the [air] attacks soon forced us off the main routes, which are only two-lane highways at best. Each time I traveled we detoured through narrow dirt roads and traveled on dikes that might not have been intended as roads at all, except for carts pulled by oxen and on occasion by Vietnamese peasants. After a while I learned that no matter how many miles we left the highway we were never very far from bomb craters and bombed-out villages.

Traveling always by night (and making only occasional brief sorties by daytime) I was unable to get a clear picture of the statistics of the damage, but there was no doubt that it was extensive and ghastly. In Y Ngo, a village of 300 primitive houses, none of which would normally be considered suitable habitation for an American, 100 houses had been destroyed. In Yen Vuc, out of 262 houses, only 9 still remained.

When we came to a section that looked like a layman's visualization of the surface of the moon — barren and pockmarked with craters — I could imagine that we were approaching a bridge, but this did not always turn out to be the case. Sometimes it was clear that a whole hamlet had been wiped out in a determined effort to destroy a bridge that was at most twenty to thirty feet long. The stream had been quickly spanned again...[18]

About thirty-five miles south of Hanoi I visited the ruins of what once had been Phy Ly, a city with a population of over ten thousand. It was a gruesome Vietnamese Guernica. Not a building was still standing. Despite the fact that I think that the Air Force and the White House have grossly exaggerated American ability to carry out 'pin-point,' 'precision' bombing, I do not see how the total destruction of a city of this size can be passed off as an accident. As if a city of more than ten thousand people could be reduced to rubble and ashes by a few bombs that were aimed at a bridge or railroad terminal but missed their mark...

When I visited Nam Dinh [a textile city where earlier visitors had reported bomb damage to a school, a pagoda, and a textile mill], areas almost totally destroyed included the working class residential areas of Hang Thao Street, where according to official statistics 17,680 persons had lived and Hoang Van Thu Street, which had housed nearly 8,000.[19]

Adding to Dellinger's distress was the use of fragmentation cluster bombs:

Even apart from the widespread destruction of villages, cities and towns, I see no way to explain away the universal use of fragmentation bombs. Fragmentation bombs are useless against bridges and buildings of any kind but are deadly against people. In fact another name for them is antipersonnel bombs. I saw these bombs everywhere I went in North Vietnam.

There are different types of fragmentation bombs, but they all start with a 'mother' bomb. (The term itself tells us something about our culture. Do we know nothing more about motherhood than this? Or is it that we have accepted the fact that mothers produce offspring who are destined to become killers?) The mother bomb explodes in the air over the target area, releasing 300 smaller bombs, typically the size of either a grapefruit or a pineapple. Each of the smaller bombs then ejects a spray of 150 tiny pellets of steel, which are so small that they bounce uselessly off concrete or steel, though they are very effective when they hit a human eye or heart. Vietnamese doctors told me that they have difficulty operating on patients wounded by these bombs, because the steel is so small that it is hard to locate, except through X-rays. (There are more target areas in Vietnam than there are X-ray machines.)

Dellinger found that some bomblets were timed to go off later, prolonging the effect of the attack.

According to the Vietnamese, the general pattern of most attacks is to drop heavy explosive bombs and then to follow a few minutes later with fragmentation bombs and strafing, so as to interfere with relief operations and to kill those who are trying to flee the bombed-out area. From personal observation, I learned that the fragmentation bombs are equipped with timing devices so that they do not all eject their murderous barrage right away. When relief workers are trying to rescue the wounded, or later when the planes have departed and the all-clear has been sounded, hundreds of fragmentation bombs may explode, wounding or killing the innocent.

At first, Dellinger wrote, he had questioned claims of deliberate bombing of residential areas, schools and hospitals: 'Something, perhaps my own type of Americanism, rose up inside me and I tried to deny that Americans would knowingly bomb and strafe civilians, at least as part of deliberate governmental policy...' But later:

when I made two extensive trips outside Hanoi, I reluctantly agreed with the Vietnamese that the United States has consciously and deliberately attacked the civilian population in a brutal attempt to destroy civilian morale. The best defense my American pride could muster was to say that the American people would not knowingly tolerate such practices. I urged Vietnamese officials to invite other non-communist observers, including perhaps a few American newsmen or even someone like Senator Fulbright, to see the damage and report the facts to the American people. I argued that when the American people found out the nature and effects of the bombings, they would put an end to them.[20]

Shortly after Dellinger's visit, the *New York Times* reporter Harrison Salisbury flew to Hanoi. In the first of his dispatches, published on Christmas Day, he described the remains of a cluster bomb in Phu Xa, the village which Riffaud had visited, said to have been destroyed by bombing on 13 August, with twenty-four dead and twenty-three wounded.

The village has now been completely rebuilt, and has a small museum of mementos of the attack. In the museum is the casing of a United States fragmentation bomb, which bears the legend 'Loaded 7/66.' A month after that date it was said to have fallen on Phu Xa village, releasing 300 iron spheres, each about the size of a baseball and each loaded with 300 steel pellets about the size and shape of bicycle bearings. Those missiles are reported to have caused most of the Phu Xa casualties.

Two days after his first article appeared, the *New York Times* published Salisbury's account of a bombing raid on Hanoi carried out while he was there. The damage extended from a 'truck park,' listed in an American communiqué as a target but devoid of trucks, to the Vietnamese–Polish Friendship School three quarters of a mile away, which was destroyed. Salisbury wrote:

> It is the conviction of the North Vietnamese that the United States is deliberately directing bombs against the civilian population although ostensibly contending that 'military objectives' are the target.

America's leading newspaper had sent one of its most respected journalists behind enemy lines in a time of undeclared war, and had seen fit to print his reports containing allegations that the United States was committing war crimes and using an atrocious new antipersonnel weapon. The reactions were swift and sure. From the Pentagon came an assurance that it was US policy to attack only military targets and that 'all possible care is taken to avoid civilian casualties.' United Press International reported from Saigon that civilian casualties in the North had been caused by accidental explosions of North Vietnamese surface-to-air missiles. Former President Eisenhower said that he knew the bombing was 'aimed exclusively at military targets'; 'unfortunately,' he added, there were 'some civilians around these targets.' 'Is there any place in the world where there are not civilians?' he asked. The *New York Times*'s military correspondent wrote that the bombing of North Vietnam was the 'most restricted and restrained' campaign in the history of aerial warfare. The *Washington Post* revealed that the figures cited by Salisbury had come from North Vietnamese sources; their story was entitled 'Salisbury's "Casualties" Tally with Viet Reds'.' And the *New York Times* itself implicitly repudiated its own reporter in an editorial denying 'that there is even a shred of evidence to lend credence to the communist propaganda that the United States is deliberately bombing civilian targets and that the campaign in the north has been one of terror, aimed at urban and residential areas and nonmilitary targets.'

In London, where Harrison Salisbury's articles had been reprinted in *The Times*, the American Embassy issued a statement from the US Information Service in which the bombing of the North, with its un-intended but 'regrettable' civilian casualties, was contrasted with the communists' assassinations of village and province chiefs – which 'is nothing less than genocide.' Nothing in Salisbury's stories contradicted President Johnson's statement 'that he regrets every single civilian death' caused by the bombing, the statement said. The American effort in Vietnam involved 'an attempt to advance the rule of law among nations.' The statement acknowledged that the use of military power was 'rooted in the imperfection of man,' but considered that

> the mere fact that there are 'laws of war' indicates that an effort is still being made to impose upon the uses of power among nations some of the restraints that operate to good practical effect among individuals and groups within nations, and that are generally recognised as morally imperative. The basic American purpose in Vietnam – to prove that aggression does not pay – partakes of this practical idealism.[21]

When Harrison Salisbury's articles were republished in 1967 in the form of a book, there were some significant changes. In his first *New York Times* story he had written: 'Contrary to the impression given by United States communiqués, on-the-spot inspection indicates that American bombing has been inflicting considerable civilian casualties in Hanoi and its environs for some time past.' He had gone on to describe his visit to Phu Xa, and the cluster bomb said to have caused most of the casualties. But in Salisbury's book, Phu Xa first appeared on page 59, after an account of the author's pre-departure Christmas shopping in New York, the French pastry and the butter ('a little rancid') in his Hanoi hotel, and the 'dismal' destruction of houses in a 'dirty' little street in Hanoi (not, Salisbury thought, the result of 'a deliberate act' by an American pilot). The description of the baseball-sized bomblets with their '300 steel pellets' was omitted from the account; the cluster bomb dispenser casing which Salisbury had seen in the Phu Xa museum was now simply 'a fragment of a bomb'; and the casualties in Phu Xa ('not much of a village') had now been caused simply by a 'high explosive bomb.'

'What had happened here?' Salisbury wrote in his book. It seemed to him 'unlikely that an American pilot had deliberately aimed for the village.' 'This was war,' he mused. 'This was air war. It was being waged with new, extremely rapid, extremely sensitive aircraft. They were trying to attack very small, very precise targets. Were they being sent on missions that were beyond their capability?'

Abandoning his reporter's instinct, Salisbury was allowing America's good intentions to return to the fore and the CBU-24 to fade back into obscurity as far as the American public was concerned. And the perspective shifted from the damage to civilian life that Salisbury had seen, to the professional difficulties of the American pilots.

I suppose that the lazy dogs ['guavas'] and the pineapples were dropped by our planes on what they presumed were antiaircraft batteries, radar installations, or military outposts [Salisbury wrote later on in his book]. The trouble was that in heavily populated North Vietnam they inevitably took a toll among civilians.[22]

In March 1967 a *Chicago Tribune* correspondent provided another explanation for the civilian casualties: the North Vietnamese were capitalizing on America's humane approach to war by putting guns in residential areas.

CBU, cluster bomb unit used against AAA [anti-aircraft artillery] positions, is one weapon authorities in Washington prefer not to mention, not because they regard war as a jolly game of squat tag in which one should not be beastly to the enemy but because they are sensitive about world opinion, that most terrible of all bugaboos...

American planes also used general purpose bombs as a 'flak suppression' weapon. Both CBU and bombs cause civilian casualties when the AAA positions are in residential areas. Airmen believe the enemy puts them there deliberately to take advantage of our known reluctance to hit civilians.[23]

A month later it was reported from Saigon that a decision had been made to use antipersonnel bombs to protect American planes whether or not the flak guns were in villages:

...reliable US sources have said American jets regularly drop antipersonnel bombs on North Vietnamese antiaircraft batteries even when they are located in villages...

The sources said the North Vietnamese moved many of their batteries into the villages in hopes of escaping the American bombs. A decision was made to hit them despite the toll of civilians, the source said, because otherwise far more US jets would be shot down.[24]

In November 1967 a report by Joergen E. Petersen was published in the British newspaper *The Guardian*. Petersen had visited two hospitals in Hanoi, where he saw casualties from the US 'pellet bombs' (ball-studded bomblets).

I ... saw a 14-year-old boy who was not doing so well – he had been in a coma for four days. And I saw a woman of 29 who had been caught by a pellet bomb in one of the one-man concrete tube shelters with her two-year-old daughter on her lap. The bomb rolled down on them and the child caught the brunt of the pellets and was killed. The mother survived – with her legs, back, and shoulders one mass of little wounds.

I saw a row of women with less serious pellet wounds, and a group of boys. There was not a sound from any of them – not even the beginning of a smile. They just stared...

It seems inappropriate to comment on the bombing when you view it from one side, but the pellet bombs are slowly creating a serious change in the public mind here. During my last visit hardly anyone expressed pure hatred of the Americans. But now, apart from the cautious nature of official statements, which always distinguish between the American government and the American people, general hatred is mounting in the civilian population here because this weapon is seen as being directed only against the most unprotected part of the civilian population. The death rate from pellet bombs is highest among women and children.[25]

Was that perception correct? Were the clusters of 'guavas' and 'pine-apples' being used in a war against civilians?

A War against Civilians?

In April–May 1967, the first session of the International War Crimes Tribunal was held in Stockholm. The Tribunal had been set up on the initiative of the British philosopher Bertrand Russell to conduct 'a solemn and historic investigation' (in Russell's words)[26] into charges that the United States and its allies had committed war crimes and acts of aggression in Vietnam. Teams of investigators visited North Vietnam, bringing back reports of cluster bomb attacks and the results of examinations of cluster bomb victims in North Vietnamese hospitals. The US government was invited but declined to attend; Secretary of State Dean Rusk told reporters he had no intention of 'playing games with a 94-year-old Briton.' The Tribunal's two sessions went largely unnoticed by the world news media.

One of the documents introduced as evidence at the Tribunal was a US Air Force reserve officers' training manual, *Fundamentals of Aerospace Weapon Systems*. Within a nation, according to the manual, there were four types of targets: military, economic, political, and 'psychosocial.' This last included 'the moral strength of the people as manifested in their internal stability, unity, national will, and ability to influence other people' – in a word, morale. 'Some of the conventional targets for morale attacks have been water supplies, food supplies, housing areas, transportation centers, and industrial sites,' the manual stated. The four types of targets or 'components of a national structure' must be 'analyzed to determine which should be destroyed in order to cause the entire instrument or organization they make up to malfunction or break down completely. The destruction of certain of the components could render the whole useless to the enemy, and could, in fact, undermine one or more of the others, so closely are all the components of national strength related.'[27]

Dr Jean-Pierre Vigier, Director of Research at the French National Center for Scientific Research and former Officer-in-Charge of

Armaments Inspection of the French Army, presented his findings on the technical characteristics of cluster bombs used against North Vietnam, and commented on the general pattern of bombing, reflecting discussions with his colleagues in Paris:

> You see it's very hard to believe in so many so-called 'mistakes' [he said in response to a question]. When one states, as the US has in Vietnam, that the Air Force bombs 'only steel and concrete,' this doesn't sound very reasonable, because steel and concrete exist in a rather limited way in underdeveloped countries. What is really being done there, I think, is an attempt to break the morale of the population by hitting its psychosocial institutions; namely, churches, schools, medical facilities, and dikes...

Asked whether he thought that genocide was involved, Vigier replied:

> I'm not going to comment on the word genocide, I'll only comment on the technical aspect. Where underdeveloped countries are being warred upon by developed countries, the main military objective turns out to be the population itself. It is a battle of machines against people. As the US Air Force document states, the only way to break an underdeveloped country which maintains a will to resist is to completely destroy the people.... That's, I believe, why fragmentation [cluster] bombs have been used in such a high proportion; 50 per cent of all bombs falling on North Vietnam are fragmentation bombs. This is not an accident; this is the logical application of US theory of military weapons technique in warfare against an underdeveloped country.[28]

This was the clearest statement of the case that cluster bombs were being used in a deliberate and systematic attack against the people of North Vietnam, a case that fueled the protests against Honeywell and other antipersonnel bomb makers in the United States (Chapter 5).[29] But the case had been built by citing a US statement of bombing theory, examining the effects of the bombing, and inferring that these effects were the result of the application of the theory. What evidence could be found from US sources that the theory enunciated in the US Air Force manual was being deliberately applied in the bombing of North Vietnam?

On 13 June 1971, the first extract from the secret history of the US decision-making process on Vietnam policy commissioned by Secretary of Defense Robert S. McNamara appeared in the *New York Times*. Successive attempts by the US government to block publication through court injunctions were unsuccessful. Since then the 'Pentagon Papers' have provided a unique insight into US policy-making, and a source for countless books and articles on the war.

The chapters on the bombing of North Vietnam, making up two large sections of the published text, suggest that policy-makers approached the bombing in a much more conventional way than suggested by *Fundamentals of Aerospace Weapons Systems* and the discussions at the Russell Tribunal. Each new phase of Operation Rolling Thunder was marked by an expansion of targets, with emphases on bombing 'lines of communication' (from spring 1965), petroleum storage facilities (June–July 1966), and North Vietnam's only steel plant, electrical plants, and a cement plant (from spring 1967). In so far as the United States was trying to impede the efforts of the North Vietnamese to supply the guerrillas in the South, or to prevent them from sending troops there, each of these categories of attack could be envisaged as attacks on the North Vietnamese military effort.[30] There is nothing in the published volumes of the Pentagon Papers to suggest that an attack on the civilian population as such was ever contemplated.[31] And despite the wide use of cluster bombs, there is almost no mention of them in the top-level policy debates recorded in the Pentagon Papers, except in the discussions of plans for a barrier to seal North Vietnam from the South (see below).

The inference that there was no deliberate plan to attack North Vietnamese civilians is strengthened by another consideration. As a party to the Hague Convention No. IV of 1907 Respecting the Laws and Customs of War on Land and other treaties, the United States was formally committed to upholding the laws of war. US obligations in this regard had been set forth in the Army manual *The Law of Land Warfare* (1956). This manual stated, among other things, that the law of land warfare 'places limits on the exercise of a belligerent's power' in the interest of protecting combatants and noncombatants from unnecessary suffering, and 'requires that belligerents refrain from employing any kind or degree of violence which is not actually necessary for military purposes and that they conduct hostilities with regard for the principles of humanity and chivalry.' It cited the Hague Regulations of 1907 (annexed to the Hague Convention No. IV) prohibiting the bombardment of undefended towns, villages, dwellings, or buildings.

The manual stated further that the law of war is binding on members of the armed forces, that military commanders are responsible for war crimes committed in pursuance of an order of the commander concerned, that war crimes are within the jurisdiction of US military tribunals, and that 'The fact that the law of war has been violated pursuant to an order of a superior authority' does not constitute a defense, unless the defendant 'did not know and could not reasonably have been expected to know that the act ordered was unlawful.'[32] Had the US President decided that civilians should be attacked, the transmission of this order would have exposed each person in the chain of command down to the aircraft pilot to the threat of prosecution for war crimes.

Determined as US officials were to win the war, and for all that they did to mislead the public in pursuance of the war effort, it seems unlikely that they would have gone so far as to issue orders to commit acts that would unequivocally have been war crimes.

There are, however, other ways of explaining the widespread damage to civilians.

- Pilots often had considerable discretion about what to bomb. After the first Rolling Thunder attacks, whose targets were selected in Washington, the restrictions were relaxed, and from the latter half of March 1965 pilots were authorized to engage in 'armed reconnaissance' and attack 'targets of opportunity' in addition to preplanned targets.[33] A 'target of opportunity' was a military target which a pilot spotted and decided to strike, such as a truck; no attempt seems to have been made to determine whether or not the trucks attacked were carrying military supplies. The concept of a 'line of communication' was also broad, and could conceivably justify an attack on almost any road, bridge, or railway in North Vietnam.[34]

- The wide area coverage of a cluster bomb was intended either to allow for attacks on 'area targets' or to compensate for aiming errors, the idea being that a 'point target' anywhere within the area covered would stand a chance of being hit by one or more bomblets. Thus the area covered by a cluster bomb would often be many times greater than the area of the target ostensibly being attacked, such as an antiaircraft gun site.[35] Any civilians nearby who had not taken shelter stood a good chance of being hit. The risk was extended over time when bomblets with random delay fuzes were used.

- The bombing was often inaccurate. According to a recent study of the air war by Earl H. Tilford Jr, F-105 Thunderchiefs and F-4 Phantom jets bombing from an altitude of 6,000 feet 'could expect to put about 75 per cent of their load to within 400 feet of the aiming point. In bad weather, bombs often fell between 1,500 and 2,000 feet from the intended targets.'[36]

At a 1967 hearing, some two years after the start of Operation Rolling Thunder, a US Senate committee heard testimony from Admiral Ulysses G. Sharp, the man who, as Commander in Chief of US Forces in the Pacific, was the highest military commander in charge of the bombing of North Vietnam. (By then more than 400,000 tons of bombs had been dropped on North Vietnam, approximately one fifth of the total tonnage of air ordnance dropped by US forces in all theaters during World War II, according to the 1972 Cornell air war study.[37]) The dashes represent the Navy censor's deletions from the printed record.

SENATOR MILLER [Iowa]   Have we on any occasion in connection with any of the targets that have been struck in North Vietnam given any advance warning that civilians would be endangered and they should therefore evacuate if they want to protect themselves?

ADMIRAL SHARP   I do not believe so.

Does anybody know the answer to that question?

ADMIRAL JOHNSON [Commander in Chief, Pacific Fleet] — .

ADMIRAL SHARP   I do not believe we have.

SENATOR MILLER   — . Have you made any recommendations regarding the advance warning of the civilians?

ADMIRAL SHARP   I have not.

SENATOR MILLER   Have you been asked for a recommendation on this?

ADMIRAL SHARP   No, I have not. I think that is a good idea and we will work on that thought.[38]

Another contributing factor to the damage to civilians was that despite the huge numbers of cluster bombs dropped over Indochina, the secrecy and silence surrounding their use precluded any public debate which could have led to tighter restrictions. It is clear today that the silence was deliberate.

Michael Krepon, who interviewed officials involved in the decision to use the CBU-24, wrote that after a protracted internal debate over the use of napalm, which some civilian officials argued should be restricted for fear of provoking world opinion,[39] the Joint Chiefs of Staff 'were in no mood to engage in another debate over ordnance selection.' Vice Admiral Lloyd M. Mustin, Director of Operations for the Joint Chiefs of Staff, told Krepon that no formal request to use cluster bombs was ever made by the Joint Chiefs to any political authority:

'In our view, they were a purely conventional weapon, and we regarded them as available, and the less said, the better. Somebody somewhere would want to raise the argument, "Well, do we or don't we want to authorize the use of this weapon?" ... We in J-3 [Directorate for Operations] had ways of exchanging information with our subordinate echelons all the way out to pilots on the line, and we just said, "As far as we know, that's authorized to you, you've got 'em, use 'em when you want, and keep your mouth shut, or somebody will tell you that you can't."'[40]

Department of Defense procurement figures released after the war showed that in the six fiscal years from 1966 to 1971, the US military services ordered 423,778 CBU-24-series cluster bombs and 59,192 bomblet-filled units used in B-52 bombers,[41] making a total of approximately 285 million 'guava' bomblets – nearly seven bomblets for every man, woman and child in Vietnam, Laos, and Cambodia. As the CBU-24 was superseded by the CBU-58, which went into production in fiscal

1970,[42] it is reasonable to assume that most of the bombs produced were dropped on Indochina, inevitably causing civilian casualties and leaving many unexploded bomblets which would pose a long-term risk to civilian life.[43] It was, in effect, a war against civilians, even if the people in charge of the bombing could claim to be trying to minimize civilian casualties.[44]

The story of the CBU-24 is a depressing one for those who have tried over the years to impose limits under international law on the sufferings inflicted in war. A major military power, formally committed to upholding the laws of war, introduced a radically new weapon, carrying a high risk of indiscriminate effects on civilians, with no public discussion and little in the way of internal controls.[45] Protests from abroad could be shrugged off, and the US news media cooperated in maintaining a tranquil silence, discounting the charge that civilians were being attacked, and refraining from disseminating details of the new weapons. Ordnance, in any case, is not something that most people understand or are concerned about: napalm might seem horrifying because burning as a method of warfare was somehow outside the pale, but cluster bombs could be passed off as 'conventional ironmongery,' in Admiral Mustin's words.[46]

A major increase in antipersonnel battlefield lethality had been accomplished with no public debate and relatively little subsequent protest.[47] The 'success' of the CBU-24 would lead to a proliferation of cluster technologies to other countries, making it difficult today to impose any international controls on their use (Chapter 7). The military advantages of the new cluster bombs were quickly recognized. As in so many earlier chapters in the history of warfare, it would be the civilians, in Vietnam and other conflicts, who would pay the price for the technological innovations which their leaders had encouraged.

A Profusion of Clusters

The story of cluster bombs in Vietnam was not limited to the 'guava.' A few of the highlights can serve to illustrate the profusion of cluster weapons stimulated by the war effort, presaging the lines of development which future weapons would take in the United States and abroad.

The 'pineapple,' an antimateriel weapon turned antipersonnel

The BLU-3 is a cylindrical high explosive bomblet with 255 steel balls embedded in an aluminum case. Six metal tail fins are folded against the case. As each bomblet is released from the dispenser, the fins unfold, arming the fuze and stabilizing the bomblet so that it will land nose first. When it hits the ground, 'Impact detonates the high explosive filler which bursts the bomb case and drives the steel balls outward.'[48] The North Vietnamese nickname 'pineapple' comes from the resemblance of the yellow-painted bomblet with fins unfolded to the succulent tropical fruit. The dispensers for the BLU-3 consist of horizontal tubes slung under an airplane. The pilot flies along, and as he sees an appropriate target, he ejects the bomblets rearwards, one, two, or more tubes at a time, or in a ripple or a salvo.[49]

Larger and more powerful than the 'guava,' the BLU-3 bomblet is classified in Army manuals as an 'antimateriel' weapon.[50] A secret 1963 report on the 'operational test and evaluation' of the CBU-2/A cluster bomb (SUU-7A/A dispenser with BLU-3/B bomblets), conducted at Nellis Air Force Base, Nevada, concluded that the weapon was 'particularly well adapted to the destruction of ramped aircraft and the electronic equipment associated with mobile (or semi-mobile) radar-directed missile and cannon defenses' during the opening stages of a full-scale nonnuclear conflict, and 'highly effective' later on 'against vehicular convoys, materiel storage areas, and fuel depots.' It 'would also be effective against massed personnel in unprotected or lightly protected areas.... Conversely, used against widely scattered, poorly-equipped personnel such as guerrillas, it is out of its natural element and would not be as effective. If used in a guerrilla warfare environment, the weapon's security would be compromised without a likelihood of achieving justifiable results.'[51]

The needs of Vietnam changed the equation. Pursuant to a secret cable of 22 January 1965[52] from the Joint Chiefs of Staff to the Commander in Chief, Pacific (CINCPAC), in April the US Air Force Test Unit in Vietnam began tests involving 'the first use of CBU dispenser munitions against insurgent personnel targets throughout RVN [South Vietnam].' Even though it was impossible in all but one instance to visit the bombed areas afterwards for 'direct ground assessment of damage' and thus to determine whether the bomblets had had any effect at all, the evaluation concluded that 'the area coverage and delivery accuracy of the CBU munitions make them more effective against unprotected personnel targets than any other conventional ordnance of comparable weight available in RVN.'[53]

The secret cable of 22 January 1965 also informed CINCPAC that 'the CBU-2/A and the CBU-14, which used the same BLU-3 bomblet, are unclassified munitions and there are no special restrictions on their use. You are authorized and encouraged to employ these munitions in your area of responsibility, against suitable targets as indicated by operational considerations...' The message warned CINCPAC: 'It is important that no publicity be given to the use of these weapons...'[54] As the military advantage of secrecy would be lost once the bomb was used, the warning can only have been intended to forestall public criticism over the nature of the weapon.

By August 1965, *Newsweek* was able to report that orders for BLU-3s were 'crackling out of the Pentagon,' and that the bomblets were being dropped on North Vietnam (see above).[55] Orders for cluster bombs containing at least 37 million 'pineapples' were placed during the eight fiscal years from 1964 to 1971, indicating that after the 'guava,' the 'pineapple' was the bomblet most heavily used in the war.[56]

Among other uses, 'pineapples' were dropped on targets which could not be seen, and may not even have been there. This practice was described by Frank Harvey, an experienced reporter who was allowed to fly with US pilots in 1966:

> ...the deadliest weapon of all, at least against personnel, were CBUs – cluster bomb units.... If a pilot used CBUs properly he could lawnmower for considerable distances, killing or maiming anybody on a path several hundred feet wide and many yards long.
>
> The FACs [forward air controllers] favored CBUs for 'recon by fire' missions. They called in a fighter to cruise along a highway or canal, dropping CBUs. The bomblets made a distinctive noise, which from the distance sounded like rolling thunder and anybody hiding in the undergrowth waiting to ambush a convoy could hear the CBUs coming. If a FAC saw people break out and run in front of the plane, he'd officially flushed some VC [Vietcong] and could call in a Huey [helicopter gunship] or two and wipe them out.[57]

One of the places bombed with 'pineapples' was the Plain of Jars in northeastern Laos, a rural area controlled by the communist Pathet Lao and used by the North Vietnamese as a diversionary theater of combat. At first, US aircraft had to be diverted from other areas of operations to attack northern Laos, but after the bombing of North Vietnam stopped with the end of Operation Rolling Thunder in November 1968, 'there were plenty of planes and bombs for Laos.'[58] A UN adviser, Georges Chapelier, wrote: 'By 1968 the intensity of the bombings was such that no organized life was possible in the villages,' and: 'the bombing climax reached its peak in 1969 when jet planes came daily and destroyed all stationary structures. Nothing was left standing. The villagers lived in trenches and holes or in caves. They only farmed at night.'[59]

Fredric R. Branfman described the destruction of the Plain of Jars as marking 'a new era' in which war 'is not fought by men but machines, war which can erase distant and unseen societies clandestinely, unknown to and even unsuspected by the world outside.' Survivors interviewed by Branfman described the destruction of their families, homes, and livestock, and drew pictures of attacks using 'pineapples' and other bombs. Not until October 1969, as the survivors were evacuated to refugee camps, did the United States publicly acknowledged that it had been bombing northern Laos since 1964.[60]

Rockeye, an antitank bomb with an antipersonnel 'fringe benefit'

Unlike the weapons described earlier in this chapter, the Rockeye dispenses bomblets which are designed principally for use against tanks. In common with other antitank munitions, the bomblet contains a 'shaped charge': the explosive charge facing the nose of the bomblet is hollowed in the shape of an inverted cone. On explosion, a layer of metal lining on the inside of the cone is converted into a long, thin jet of molten particles which will bore through armor, injuring the tank crew and setting fire to fuel and explosives inside the tank.[61] At the same time, the metal case surrounding the bomblet breaks into fast-moving fragments which will inflict casualties on people nearby.

The double punch of the Rockeye was described at a closed Congressional hearing in 1966.

> MR. SIKES [Democrat, Florida]   In the justification I note this: 'The Rockeye II is a cluster bomb which contains antitank and antipersonnel bomblets.' Does that mean one or the other and not both in the same cluster?
>
> ADMIRAL SHINN [Chief, Bureau of Naval Weapons]   They are the same, sir. They spread and if you have a concentration of personnel, would be damaging to the personnel.
>
> MR. SIKES   Are the bomblets all the same?
>
> COMMANDER HALEY [Director, Plans and Programs for Munitions, Bureau of Naval Weapons]   Same bomblet.
>
> MR. SIKES   Surely a bomblet effective against people is not necessarily effective against tanks.
>
> COMMANDER HALEY   Basically this is a shaped charge head. It is the same as we use on rockets and many other items. The fringe benefit that you derive from this is the antipersonnel effect.[62]

The origins of the Rockeye go back to the late 1950s, when the US Navy began considering how to redesign its arsenal of nonnuclear munitions to meet the demands of 'limited' war.[63] Pilot production of the Rockeye II began in 1967, and the weapon was authorized for use with A-4 fighter aircraft in August 1968, but it was not until 1972, in the renewed bombing of North Vietnam which began in April, that reports of Rockeye use reached the West. North Vietnamese press releases stated that 'perforating' bombs were being used on dikes and in populated areas of the port city of Haiphong. Some bomblets penetrated the concrete lids of the one-person underground shelters which had been built across the country to protect people from the American air raids.

These reports led once again to charges that the United States had introduced a munition designed for enhanced effect against the civilian population. The use of plastic tail fins, shattering when the bomblet explodes, gave rise to charges that the Americans were employing an antipersonnel weapon designed to produce plastic fragments undetectable by X-rays.[64]

After the use of Rockeyes in Indochina subsided, the US armed forces placed further large orders to build up their war reserve stocks. These cluster bombs were to see service nearly twenty years later in the 1991 Gulf war.

Combined-effects bomblets

A cluster bomb, engineers found, could be made even more useful if extra damage-producing elements were built in. An incendiary element, for example, could be added to a fragmentation bomblet, as an Air Force witness told a Congressional subcommittee in 1972:

> ...the BLU-61 [2.2-lb fragmentation] bomblet, which the gentleman is holding up here, we put lots of these in dispensers, drop them on light materiel targets. They do fine from the standpoint of explosives and shrapnel. But in order again to set on fire the fuel, we added a liner in the thing to help make it burn. This liner is zirconium. It was a fairly high cost item. Our engineers felt that perhaps by using particles in the explosive itself it would work just as well and it would be cheaper. This did work just as well. The liner has been replaced by zirconium particles in the explosive, and this year it is going to save us about $2 per little bomblet, which means for the inventory for 1972, the buy, about $8-million cost savings.[65]

The Rockeye bomblet would be 'damaging to personnel' nearby, but only as a 'fringe benefit.' In a revised version, known as the CBU-59/B antipersonnel/antimateriel (APAM) bomb, the metal casing has a controlled fragmentation element for enhanced antipersonnel effectiveness. A new dual-purpose fuze has been added so that if it strikes a soft target such as the earth, the fuze will ignite an impulse charge, producing gases which propel the bomblet back up into the air, where it explodes, yielding a more lethal spray of fragments than if it exploded on the ground.[66]

Fuzes for enhanced effectiveness

The operation of a cluster bomb involves a complicated sequence of events where timing is of the essence. This is why fuzing is so important. Thus, the opening of the Rockeye II dispenser in the air is initiated by a mechanical time (clockwork) fuze mounted in the dispenser; the length of time during which the dispenser falls before opening (and, hence, the altitude of opening and the pattern of bomblets on the ground) can be preset before the airplane takes off. The Rockeye bomblet fuze has a variable mechanism which explodes the bomblet at the proper standoff distance for maximum effect when striking armor, while allowing the bomblet to penetrate a soft target such as earth or a sandbag before exploding. As mentioned above, the antipersonnel/antimateriel version of the Rockeye has a dual-action fuze which causes the bomblet to pop up in the air if it hits a soft target such as the ground.

One of the most ingenious features of the 'guava' bomblet is the impact fuze, the M219. Set inside the bomblet, the fuze comprises three hammerweights which are held together in the center by springs. The fuze is armed (made ready to fire) by centrifugal force when the bomblet is released from the dispenser and starts to spin. In the words of an Army manual:

Arming occurs when the centrifugal force on the hammerweights (induced by spinning of the bomb) is sufficient to overcome the force of the spring bearing against the weights. The hammerweights move back, releasing the firing pin from the rotor.... The fuze is sensitive to impact from any direction. Initiation of the fuze is accomplished by movement of one or more of the firing pin hammerweights.[67]

The M218 random delay fuze for the 'guava' bomblet, whose 'murderous' action David Dellinger observed in North Vietnam, is armed in the same way as the impact fuze, but the firing mechanism is different. (The description is from a 1968 proposal to the Army by Honeywell Inc., developer and manufacturer of the fuze, citing the M219 and its predecessors as 'an excellent demonstration of designing fuzes for automated high volume production.')

Upon seeing an arming speed of 2400 rpm, the rotor arms in the manner of the M219. This permits a spring driven, four-bladed wiper to rotate over a disc and mylar sac assembly containing silicone gel. This wiper continues through 270 degrees, providing a delay action which occurs in a deliberately random manner, after which time the fuze fires.

Another Honeywell project was the development of a proximity fuze that would make 'guava' bomblets explode in the air, enhancing the effect against personnel. The same proposal stated:

Under contract to the Air Force Armament Laboratory, Honeywell has developed a new proximity fuze design (including the safing and arming mechanism, a reserve battery, a new miniature electric detonator, and a monolithic integrated circuit) for the BLU-26/B bomblet. This program has particular interest in that a very low cost design has been created; it is anticipated that the total munition cost will be less than $8.00 in high production.

Another fuze provided a solution to a perennial problem in Vietnam: how to strike at guerrillas sheltering in the jungle. The 1965 Air Force evaluation of the BLU-3 'pineapple' in South Vietnam, mentioned above, found that the bomblet was 'not ideally suited for use against personnel and light materiel targets concealed under a tree canopy' because many of the bomblets exploded in the canopy. It recommended that 'A new bomb and fuze should be developed for this type of target that assures canopy penetration and approach to ground level before detonation.'[68] The response was the BLU-24/B (dubbed 'orange' by the Vietnamese), an antipersonnel fragmentation bomblet, made of cast nodular graphitic iron, with an adaptation of the M219 fuze design which employed a spin decay mechanism so that the bomblet would not explode until it penetrated the canopy and the rate of spin decreased. According to the abstract of a 1967 Air Force Armament Laboratory report:

> The BLU-24/B was designed to penetrate jungle canopy. The curved vanes in the bomb cause the bomb to rotate rapidly, arming the fuze.... The bomb fuze fires only when the bomb's rotational rate decreases below 2,000 rpm (caused by friction between bomb and target).[69]

Different combinations of bomblets and dispensers

'We make every effort to utilize a dispenser for more than one bomb,' an Air Force witness told a Congressional subcommittee in 1967. 'For example when the SUU-14 — carries the BLU-3 — bomb, it is called the CBU-14, when it carries the BLU-24 — bomb, it is called the CBU-25 and when the BLU-17 — bomb is loaded it is designated the CBU-22.... Whenever possible, new bombs are developed to be compatible with an existing dispenser. This has resulted in appreciable savings in development and production costs.'[70]

Three basic types of cluster bomb dispensers emerged from the profusion of US developments in the 1960s and 1970s. They were free-fall dispensers, opening in the air, exemplified by the SUU-30 'guava' dispenser and the Rockeye II dispenser; rearward-ejection dispensers, the SUU-7 and SUU-14, used to dispense 'pineapples' and other bomblets; and downward-ejection dispensers dropping clusters of bomblets from large round or square tubes. When other countries took up the challenge of developing their own cluster bombs, a fourth type, sideward-ejection, was added to the list (see Chapter 7).

The most gigantic cluster bomb which the world has seen to date is the Hayes dispenser, named after its developer, Hayes International Corporation. It is a huge boxlike aluminum contraption comprising twenty-four rectangular cells, each of which is loaded with three square boxes or 'adapters' containing bomblets. Two dispensers can be fitted in the bomb bay of a B-52 bomber; smaller versions are available for the B-57 and the C-123 cargo plane. A B-52 with two Hayes dispensers can drop astronomical numbers of small munitions: 10,656 'pineapple' bomblets, 25,488 'guava' bomblets, or 77,040 0.3-lb spherical M40 fragmentation grenades in a single bombing run.[71]

Cluster bomb adapters containing 'pineapple,' 'guava,' and 'orange' bomblets were procured by the US armed forces between the fiscal years 1965 and 1970. It is likely that most or all of them were used in Indochina, where B-52s dropped over two and a half million tons of bombs in the course of the war.[72]

The most comprehensive published list of US cluster bombs of the Vietnam war era is in the Stockholm International Peace Research Institute study *Anti-personnel Weapons*. Six pages of small print contain details of over ninety post-World War II bomb and mine clusters ranging from the Mk 12 Padeye dispenser munition to the GBU-2 guided cluster bomb, and from the CBU-1 to the CBU-72; while another three and a half pages list bombs and bomblets in the BLU series.[73] Included are cluster bombs dispensing antipersonnel, antimateriel, antitank, incendiary, chemical, smoke, anti-intrusion, fuel-air explosive, and training bomblets, as well as aerial mines. Most of the weapons listed are developmental models which never entered service inventories, but at least twenty went into production. Were the lists to be reissued today, further models would have to be added.

'Improved Conventional Munitions' for Artillery

Another idea for attacking the enemy with bomblets, cheaper than dropping them from airplanes, was to deliver them by artillery shells. During the Vietnam war, the US Army introduced cluster shells for its 105mm, 155mm and 8-inch howitzers. Fired from a gun, the shells open in the air and release their payloads of small, spherical fragmentation bomblets which hit the ground, pop back up, and explode.[74] A later model, introduced in the 1970s, contains 'high explosive, dual purpose' bomblets with a shaped charge and a controlled fragmentation casing; these can penetrate armor and are also effective against personnel – the same combination as in the antipersonnel/antimateriel version of the Rockeye bomb.

Unlike other weapons projects with suggestive titles, such as some of the Eye-series bombs (Fireye or Deneye, for example), bomblet-filled shells were given the innocuous name 'Improved Conventional Munitions,' or ICMs for short. The Army program under which they were developed had an even blander title, 'Selected Ammunition,' giving no hint of the innovations being prepared.

A 1978 Army manual states that ICM rounds differ from ordinary high explosive artillery shells 'in that the submunitions (grenades) are distributed almost uniformly throughout the pattern area. Thus, the density of fragmentation from ICM is more uniform than the high explosive ammunition. For this reason, ICM will prove to be more effective when employed against area personnel targets.' Six howitzers, each firing an antipersonnel ICM round, can be expected to inflict casualties over a radius of 135 meters, as against 105 meters for an ordinary high explosive round, according to the manual.[75] The fragmentation bomblets in the antipersonnel ICM shells 'are designed to provide maximum effectiveness against troops in the open over rolling terrain.' This round, the manual states, 'is optimized for antipersonnel effect. Effect against materiel targets is limited to comparatively minor damage. Although grenade fragments will puncture vehicle tires, windows, radiators, and gasoline tanks; will render ammunition and electronic equipment unserviceable; and may cause secondary fires, the frequency of this type of effectiveness is not sufficient in itself to justify expenditure of these projectiles as antimateriel weapons.' The dual-purpose munition, however, 'has an increased lethality against personnel and an added capability against light armored vehicles such as ... armored personnel carriers or trucks.' In comparison to other types of shells, dual purpose ICMs are listed as the preferred munition for attacks on trucks, anti-aircraft weapons, self-propelled field artillery, surface-to-surface missiles, radar, and command posts containing 'personnel and light materiel targets.'[76]

Bomblet-filled shells were first used in combat on 12 February 1968 by a US 105mm howitzer battery operating in I Corps (northern South Vietnam), according to an unofficial Army history:

> ...in I Corps area on 12 February 1968, Battery C, 1st Battalion, 40th Artillery (105mm.), while in support of a South Vietnamese unit, became the first US Army artillery unit to fire improved conventional munitions in combat. The target was 40–50 North Vietnamese troops in the open. The battery fired 54 rounds of the new ammunition, resulting in 14 enemy killed.... FIRECRACKER became the code word used when a forward observer wanted improved conventional munitions.[77]

The US Army ordered at least 118,000 bomblet-filled artillery shells between the fiscal years 1969 and 1973, according to Defense Department procurement records obtained by the Stockholm International

Peace Research Institute.[78] The office of the Army Project Manager for Selected Ammunition wrote in a report to the Army Materiel Command in 1972 that the cluster shells 'provided our field forces with far-reaching improvements in firepower and tactical capabilities, the first real breakthrough in this area since World War II.'[79]

Aerial Mines

The technologies of the new cluster bombs made for yet another innovation of the Vietnam war: they opened up the possibility of seeding land mines from the air, either in support of tactical operations or behind enemy lines. Once available, air-delivered antipersonnel mines were dropped in huge numbers, largely against unseen targets. As with cluster bombs, few – if any – restrictions appear to have been placed on their use. These new 'aerial mines' were to have a major impact in increasing the suffering inflicted on civilians through the waging of war.

The origins of aerial mines can be traced back to a US Air Force program called Project Doan Brook. Research under the project was carried out by the Case Institute of Technology in Cleveland, Ohio, from May 1951, eleven months after the outbreak of the Korean war, to October 1959. According to the unclassified abstract of the contractor's secret summary report, submitted to the Air Force in 1960: 'The original task of the Project was to establish the technical and tactical feasibility of an air-laid land mine. Subsequently, the main effort was concentrated on (1) the design and development of aerial mines to be employed against various targets and (2) the study of the tactical applications of these weapons.' Under the project the Case Institute also compiled a secret handbook of 'operational and service instructions on the air-laid land mine hardware, as well as the aerial mining doctrine, which have been developed by Project Doan Brook.'

Three new air-delivered antipersonnel mines were first used in the Vietnam war:

- The gravel mine, unofficially nicknamed the 'teabag' mine because of its appearance or the 'leaf' mine because of its fluttering motion as it falls to the earth. An Army witness described it at a 1967 Congressional hearing as 'a small canvas-covered charge of lead azide which is laid from helicopters, airplanes, or can be spread from the ground by individuals or from a truck.'[80] It is rectangular, $2^3/4$ inches by 3 inches, approximately three-quarters of an inch thick, and weighs slightly over two ounces. The canvas pouch is water repellent and is colored olive drab, straw, or brown, providing good camouflage when the mine is lying on the ground.[81]

- The Dragontooth, a tiny plastic mine weighing only seven-tenths of an ounce.
- The Wide Area Antipersonnel Mine (WAAPM, pronounced 'wop 'em'), an adaptation of the 'guava' bomblet; it is a spherical metallic object with external flanges and a fuze similar to that of the 'guava.' When the mine hits the ground, eight tripwires are deployed by means of springs, and when one of them is disturbed, the mine explodes, shooting fragments in all directions. The appearance of the mine with its tripwires earned it the Vietnamese nickname 'spider mine.'

As with cluster bombs, there are various aerial dispensers. Gravel mines, for instance, can be carried in tubular canisters slung under a helicopter or a low-speed airplane, and ejected rearwards by means of pistons as the aircraft flies along; or they can be dropped in much larger numbers from the cells of a SUU-41 downward-ejection Tactical Fighter Dispenser by high-speed jet aircraft. Some 4,800 Dragontooth mines are dropped from the cylindrical canisters of a SUU-13 downward-ejection dispenser slung under a jet fighter, while the WAAPM is dispensed from the SUU-38 Tactical Fighter Dispenser.[82]

Another development was cluster shells for sowing mines by artillery, known as the Area Denial Artillery Munition (ADAM).[83] Still other equipment was designed to scatter mines from ground vehicles.[84]

At hearings on the US 'electronic battlefield' program held before a special US Senate subcommittee in 1970, an Air Force witness stressed the antipersonnel character of the Dragontooth mine:

SENATOR GOLDWATER [Republican, Arizona]   How much damage can it do?
MAJOR ANDERSON [Directorate of Operations, Department of the Air Force]   How much damage, sir?
SENATOR GOLDWATER   Yes.
MAJOR ANDERSON   It is purely antipersonnel. If a person steps on it, it could blow his foot off. If a truck rolls over it, it won't blow the tire.[85]

Aerial mines were one of several new pieces of equipment which came together in one of the most extraordinary chapters of the Vietnam war, the 'electronic battlefield,' a supreme example of the attempt to solve a military problem by technological means. As recorded in the Pentagon Papers and retold by freelance writer Paul Dickson, the impulse for the project came from a January 1966 memo from Professor Roger Fisher of the Harvard Law School to his friend John T. McNaughton, Assistant Secretary of Defense, proposing that North Vietnam be sealed off from the South by the creation of an air-seeded barrier of barbed wire, mines, and chemicals. McNaughton passed the idea to Secretary of Defense Robert S. McNamara,[86] and in April 1966 McNamara requested a group of about forty-five of the country's top university scientists, known as the JASON Division of the Institute for Defense Analyses, to consider the idea, including the possibility of using various warning systems and reconnaissance methods.

The top-secret JASON report, submitted to McNamara in August 1966 and later quoted in the Pentagon Papers, suggested the creation of an antipersonnel barrier and an antivehicle barrier along the Demilitarized Zone separating the two Vietnams and into the Laotian panhandle to cut the Ho Chi Minh trail over which the North Vietnamese were supplying the guerrillas in the South. Both barriers would use 'currently available or nearly available components' including land mines, cluster bombs, night vision devices, and electronic sensors. Both would be serviced by aircraft that would patrol to collect the impulses given off by the sensors, reseed the mines, and strike at targets. A signal from the sensors indicating enemy movement would be flashed back to an American base, and from there, strike aircraft would be sent to knock out the infiltrators with 'guava' bomblets. Among other items needed, JASON envisioned a monthly consumption of approximately 20 million gravel mines and 20,000 CBU-24 cluster bombs,[87] making up 'by far the major fraction' of the $800,000,000-per-year estimated cost of the barrier.[88]

The JASON report led to the setting up of a huge secret research project, stimulating the development of further munitions and other equipment[89] and ushering in new means of waging war by remote control, known popularly as the 'electronic battlefield' and referred to by Senator Goldwater at the 1970 hearings as possibly 'one of the greatest steps forward in warfare since gunpowder.'[90] The 'McNamara wall' along the Demilitarized Zone envisioned by the JASON group was never built, but an air-supported anti-infiltration system employing aerial mines and sensors began operating in Laos in December 1967 under the code name Igloo White.[91]

Two and a half years later, Senator William Proxmire, well known as a critic of government inefficiency and overspending, caused a storm by raising questions about the electronic battlefield publicly on the floor of the Senate. He was concerned, he said, not only about the cost, the possible unreliability of the equipment, and the lack of Congressional control, but also about the risk of indiscriminate effects against civilians:

One of the biggest problems is that it may be an indiscriminate weapon. The sensors cannot tell the difference between soldiers and women and children. It has been pointed out that in such underdeveloped parts of the world as Vietnam, whole villages may be wiped out by seeding wide areas with air dropped explosive devices designed to kill anyone who ventures into their neighborhood. Once seeded, we would lose control over these devices and they could represent a permanent menace to the civilian population, much like old land mines.[92]

The ensuing controversy prompted the Senate Committee on Armed Services to organize three days of closed hearings by a special sub-committee comprising three Committee members friendly to the armed services. Military officers gave details of the electronic battlefield, and the Senators asked mild questions about costs, Congressional oversight, and the possible duplication of effects of different munitions. There is no indication in the printed record of the hearings that anyone raised Senator Proxmire's question about the effects of the electronic battle-field on civilians.

In December 1972, five years after the inception of Igloo White, the *Philadelphia Inquirer* reported that the electronic battlefield program in Laos was being curtailed, 'both because of the prospects of an Indochina ceasefire and the enormous cost of the program.'[93] The *Washington Post* reported that the sensor system 'produced more information than could be absorbed and used properly, was foiled on numerous occasions by North Vietnamese tricks and bypass roads, and required continual reseeding with new sensors.' General John W. Vogt, commander of the 7th Air Force, told the *Washington Post* 'he would not quarrel with the assessment that it "was not cost-effective. It was very expensive to operate, complex, and took a lot of resources."'[94]

Even as antipersonnel mines were being strewn across Laos in a futile attempt to block the Ho Chi Minh trail, US commanders in South Vietnam were finding new tactical uses for the new air-delivered mines. In an article entitled 'Economy of Force in the Central Highlands,' Major General Donn R. Pepke, commander of the US Army 4th Infantry Division, wrote that his forces had used Wide Area Antipersonnel Mines 'to canalize the enemy into areas where we could mass the combat power available to destroy him.' In late 1969, he wrote,

> it was decided to encircle known enemy base and supply areas with CBU-42/ A [WAAPM] munitions in conjunction with B-52 strikes. The purpose of this method of employment was to compress enemy movement and deny him freedom of exfiltration while artillery and tactical air were programmed into the clearly defined target areas.[95]

An Army manual, issued in May 1969, outlined the novel tactical and strategic actions made possible by the new technology of scatterable mines:

> A scatterable landmine system adds a new dimension to the field of mine warfare. Properly employed, scatterable landmines provide the commander

with a rapid, flexible, and effective means for delaying, harassing, containing, or canalizing the movement of enemy ground forces while simultaneously reducing the significant manpower and materiel requirements previously associated with the employment of landmines.

In particular: 'Whereas ground emplacement of mines permits some control over the enemy's forward movement, techniques of scatter mining allow lateral and rearward control as well.'

In addition to traditional types of minefields for which scatterable mines could now be used, scatter mining made possible the emplacement of new types of minefields for which new terms had been created, the manual stated. These included the 'obstacle,' 'retrograde,' 'anvil,' and 'interdiction' minefield – this last being defined as 'one which employs scatterable mines deep into enemy areas.'[96]

An Air Force manual, issued in a preliminary form in 1972, outlined another use for aerial mines, or 'Air Delivered Target Activated Munitions': area denial. It noted that 'Bomber aircraft, because of their large load carrying capacities and saturation capabilities, are well suited for mass delivery of ADTAMs in area denial operations.'[97]

Enormous numbers of aerial antipersonnel mines were produced for use in the Indochina war. Defense Department procurement figures indicate that 37,400,000 XM41E1 gravel mines were ordered in the fiscal years 1967 and 1968, and 31,473,400 Dragontooth mines in the fiscal years 1966 to 1968. It is likely that other procurements of aerial mines were hidden in the secret funding of the electronic battlefield program.[98]

The Munitions of Vietnam: Implications for Future Wars

It is a modern military conceit that tactics determine weapons – that tactical needs stimulate new inventions in weaponry. Except for occasional products of government arsenals the reverse is almost always true. New weapons have a way of appearing without being demanded...

Every really new weapon in history has produced changes in tactics, affecting not only the new weapon itself but nearly everything else in the arsenal at the time.

John S. Tompkins, *The Weapons of World War III*[99]

The Korean experience and the challenges of the Vietnam war stimulated the development of many munitions which saw their first use in Vietnam. By 1967 a US Army general was able to tell a Congressional subcommittee that 'virtually all of the arms now available to the troops in Vietnam have been developed and deployed since the Korean war.'[100] What were the implications of the cluster bombs and other new weapons for the battlefields of the future? How would they affect soldiers and civilians in future wars?

As in Korea and earlier wars, the US effort in Indochina was characterized by the use of massive firepower. As in Korea, massive firepower resulted in immense destruction without, in crucial ways, altering the course of the war. It was after Korea had been bombed to the point where 'there were no more targets' that the Chinese invaded, forcing the UN army to abandon half of the country which it had 'liberated' from the communists. In Vietnam, even as the bombing of the North was escalated, top US officials were receiving assessments that the bombing was not hindering the North Vietnamese war effort.[101]

These facts make it hard to assess the actual impact of the new munitions in strictly military terms. There were reports of Beehives, cluster bombs, and bomblet-filled shells killing groups of enemy troops and fending off attacks, and there was plenty of enthusiasm on the ground for weapons such as the 40mm grenade launcher and the 2.75-inch rocket. But great quantities of munitions were used against vague targets, in area bombardment, 'harassment and interdiction' fire and similar practices whose results could not be accurately assessed. The failure of huge operations such as Rolling Thunder and Igloo White cast doubt on the effectiveness of the munitions used, or at least on the ways in which they were used. The 15 million tons of munitions expended in the war[102] did not prevent the North Vietnamese victory in 1975.

As in Korea, there seems to have been little concern for the effects which the new techniques of machine warfare would have on civilians. In South Vietnam, US forces were instructed to observe 'rules of engagement' intended to protect civilians,[103] but there seem to have been few restrictions on area bombardment and other inherently indiscriminate practices. The risk of indiscriminate effects of cluster bombs and other wide-area weapons on civilians seems scarcely to have been considered.

The new cluster weapons made for a substantial increase in antipersonnel battlefield lethality. It was to be expected that when the new munitions are used against troops, there will be substantially more casualties than what the old munitions would have caused. Also, the advent of the new cluster weapons meant that there would be far more individual high explosive munitions per tonnage of munitions expended. With cluster bomblets exploding near each other, there will be an enhanced risk of soldiers being hit by fragments from several bomblets and suffering multiple injuries.

The new munitions tended to be described in curious and often misleading terms. Thus, war correspondents loved to write about the 'punch' provided by a new weapon and the 'punishment' being inflicted on the enemy, while the notion of 'pinpoint bombing' was flattering to American technology and fostered the idea that civilian casualties were being minimized. Yet US officials were silent about many of the new weapons, fearing that their seeming cruelty would cast doubt on the morality of the US war effort and spark protests, as was already happening over napalm.

The North Vietnamese and the National Liberation Front of South Vietnam, for their part, decried the cruelty of napalm and flechettes, and portrayed the new cluster bombs as weapons used in a murderous attack on a simple people – something that was not hard to do, as the evidence of destruction was there for any visitor to see. 'Ask your President Johnson if our straw huts were made of steel and concrete,' a twenty-year-old North Vietnamese woman wounded in an air attack told David Dellinger.[104] This portrayal of the Vietnamese as victims served to rally international support and to deflect attention from the ruthlessness of the North Vietnamese war aims, and of the methods used by the guerrillas in the South.

A different attitude toward munitions is shown in a little book called *The Inventor of Twig-Triggered Mines*, translated into English and printed in one of the 'liberated zones' of South Vietnam. It wove together the stories of Ut Duc, a young Hero of the South Vietnam People's Liberation Armed Forces, who used remnants of a US antipersonnel bomblet to devise a mine triggered by the disturbance of a twig, and a majestic flamboyant tree, damaged in the merciless US bombardment but now sending up a fresh shoot which symbolized the resistance of Vietnam to the American onslaught.

> 'Didn't I say it would never die!', smiled Ut Duc.
> 'And what else is my Dad doing out there?', Tac kept asking.
> 'Somebody's mine went off close to the tree and splashed American blood all over,' answered Sau Lap.
> 'And American flesh too!', cut in Binh.
> 'That's right, there's GI flesh too. The old man said he couldn't bear seeing American blood all over the tree. Furthermore the bits of flesh will stink most awfully and he feared that the tender shoot would not grow so he is staying behind to clean the place up and fetch some water to wash the shoot and the tree at the same time.'[105]

The dialogue may have been fanciful, but the production of homemade munitions from unexploded US ordnance was real enough, contradicting the notion that the fighting in the South could be stopped by bombing the North or blocking the Ho Chi Minh trail. A 1969 US Marine Corps study found that

US dud explosive ordnance, especially bombs, provide the VC [Vietcong] with a ready source of raw materials from which they fabricate their homemade ordnance. Without exception, the most common VC explosive is tritonal or H-6, removed from dud US bombs. The VC have recovery teams stationed throughout areas under their control. These teams are charged with the mission of locating and recovering dud ordnance. The smaller items such as grenades, BLU-3/B, mortar, artillery, rockets, etc. are recovered and salvaged to be converted into booby traps or land mines. In some instances the item is simply renovated and fired back at Free World Forces...[106]

Much unexploded ordnance was recovered and reused, but the introduction of the new cluster weapons dispersing massive numbers of high explosive submunitions would pose a long-term threat to civilian life in the areas attacked. Long after the fighting ended, civilians would be risking life and limb from unexploded bomblets and mines as they farmed, grazed livestock, or moved around in an area. Manufacturing defects, damage in delivery, or the failure of a fuze to function on impact with certain surfaces can be expected to result in a certain percentage of unexploded munitions, or 'duds.' Assuming a dud rate of 5 per cent, the deployment of (say) 285 million 'guava' bomblets would leave 14 million unexploded bomblets on the ground. Similarly massive numbers of gravel mines, Dragontooth mines, and other antipersonnel munitions were strewn across areas of Indochina.[107] The remnants of these attacks would constitute an immense, long-term problem for the people of those countries.

At one of the annual closed hearings in 1967 on the Pentagon's budget request for the coming year, a series of presentations on new Air Force weaponry ('Our development strides in conventional munitions are, perhaps, our greatest contribution to Southeast Asia operations,' an Air Force witness had stated) provoked this interchange:

> MR. SIKES   Are you making the battlefield too dangerous for our own people to fight in? Or are you making the waters so dangerous that friendly forces cannot use them when the fighting is over?
> MR. LIPSCOMB [Republican, California]   That is not the Air Force problem.
> General Evans   Yes, sir, — .
> MR. SIKES   How will mine danger be overcome?
> General Evans   — .[108]

The dashes representing the Air Force censor's deletions left Representative Sikes's questions unanswered in the public record of the hearing. Mr Sikes's questions are still unanswered today.

Notes

1. Klare, 1972, pp. 35–42.

2. According to a fact sheet on the 'Eye'-series bombs prepared by the US Naval Weapons Center in 1982, the program was initiated at the Naval Ordnance Test Station (NOTS) in China Lake, California, in 1959 at the request of the Navy's Bureau of Ordnance 'to develop new free-fall bombs and bombing systems that would improve the Navy's air-attack capability against a wide variety of tactical targets. Existing stockpiled munitions and submunitions were to be modernized and new air-launched, free-fall conventional ordnance to be developed for limited-war applications.' In 1959 the laboratory started work on Bigeye (a binary nerve gas dispenser), Gladeye (a downward-ejection 'modular dispenser for delivery of small tactical devices and bomblets from high-performance, tactical aircraft'), and the Snakeye retarding tail assembly allowing for low level skip-bombing with the new streamlined general-purpose bombs. Other weapons subsequently added to the program were Sadeye; the Rockeye antitank cluster bomb, described later in this chapter; the Deneye aerial mine dispenser; the Weteye chemical bomb, dispensing the nerve gas Sarin (GB); Misteye, a Sadeye dispenser delivering chemical and biological bomblets produced by the Army; Fireye, an improved firebomb; and Briteye, a flare system. Some of these weapons went into production, while other projects were cancelled at various stages of development.

The initiation of the 'Eye'-series program evidently arose from a concern that the Navy's conventional ordnance was inadequate to meet the demands of limited war. In 1958 the US Navy Commander in Chief, Pacific had expressed concern 'over the continued whittling away of US military strength actually in place in the Pacific which is gradually reducing the capability of [Pacific Command] forces to meet the many emergency situations which may arise in limited war as well as the ever present threat of general war,' and in 1959 his successor 'noted the fact that his command possessed thousands of tons of World War II bombs that could not be effectively used with modern aircraft,' according to an official history (Marolda and Fitzgerald, 1986, p. 14). In January 1959 the Navy's Bureau of Ordnance 'issued an operational requirement for improving World War II conventional free-fall weapons that were being used on modern, high-speed aircraft,' according to a 1964 description of the NOTS program. The NOTS free-fall weapons program began in July 1959.

3. SIPRI, 1973, p. 80; 1978, p. 18.

4. Green, Thomson, and Roots, 1955, p. 461. For details of World War II fragmentation bombs and information on the development of postwar US 'general purpose' (high explosive) bombs, see DeMarco, 1990.

5. Clusters of 4-lb magnesium bombs were used against German cities. The 4-lb magnesium bomb 'had a high degree of penetrability and an intensive burning action. These qualities made it particularly suitable for use against construction in Germany, 95 percent of which consisted of brick and stone,' according to a US Army history of the war (Kleber and Birdsell, 1966, p. 622). Thus, for example, 1.3 million 4-lb magnesium bombs were dropped on Hamburg by the Royal Air Force in a series of seven raids in 1943: 'German officials stated that 45,000

people lost their lives, although this number was admittedly inaccurate: "Exact figures could not be obtained out of a layer of human ashes'" (*ibid.*, p. 619; cf. SIPRI, 1975, p. 34). Magnesium bombs were also used by German forces against Great Britain.

6. Kleber and Birdsell, 1966, pp. 628–30. The firebombing of Tokyo caused more deaths than the atomic bombs dropped on Hiroshima or Nagasaki (SIPRI, 1975, p. 37).

Altogether, sixty-nine Japanese cities were ignited by incendiary attacks, contributing to Japan's surrender. In the judgment of another Army history: 'the tremendous destruction wrought in the Orient' by 6-lb napalm bombs 'showed how accurate had been the foresight of those who planned this bomb four years earlier' (Brophy, Miles, and Cochrane, 1959, p. 186).

7. The idea behind this last type of use is to compensate for aiming imprecisions in free-fall bombing from modern high-speed aircraft by using an area weapon against a point target. With reference to the Rockeye II antitank cluster bomb (see below), this rationale was described in a confidential 1964 Navy report stating that the bomb 'was designed to approach the effectiveness of a homing or guided bomb through the less expensive method of clustering many bomblets within a large container. Thus, one or more bomblets will hit the target if the cluster is dispersed with sufficient accuracy to superimpose the dispersal pattern over the target.'

The origins of modern cluster weapons are still surrounded in secrecy. A request in 1994 for the release under the Freedom of Information Act of sixteen technical reports on the development of cluster weapons in the 1950s and 1960s was refused by the US Air Force on the grounds that they contained information which is currently and properly classified in the interest of national defense, as well as information with military or space application for which an approval, authorization, or license would be required for its lawful export. A request for the release of the 1960 summary report on Project Doan Brook, the 1950s Air Force program for the development of aerial mines, described below, was refused on the same grounds.

8. *Newsweek*, 2 August 1965. The BLU-3 was the 'pineapple' bomblet, described below.

9. US House of Representatives, Committee on Appropriations, *Supplemental Defense Appropriations for 1967*, hearings, p. 350.

10. CBU-, SUU- and BLU- are US Air Force designations. 'SUU' stands for for 'suspension unit, utility' and 'BLU' for 'bomb, live, unit.'.

A US Army manual gives the weight of the BLU-26/B bomblet as 0.935 pounds and the diameter as 2.78 inches, including the external flanges (US Army, 1970, p. 1-11). The bomblets are filled with Composition B, like the M26 hand grenade (Chapter 2), or 70/30 cyclotol, a mixture of seven parts RDX with three parts TNT. These explosives have greater brisance than TNT, producing a faster explosion which gives the steel balls greater velocity and, hence, greater range and greater wounding effect. A $^7/_{32}$-inch steel ball would weigh approximately 10.5 grains, or about five times the ideal antipersonnel fragment size cited by the Army's Project Manager for Selected Ammunition (Chapter 2). The larger size would give the balls greater range, and allow them to damage light materiel as well as human targets.

11. The SUU-30 is a steel case divided longitudinally into two halves which are held together at the nose and the tail. A mechanical time fuze is set before takeoff of the aircraft, to go off a given number of seconds after the bomb is dropped. When the fuze goes off, the dispenser opens, and incoming air forces the two halves apart, releasing the contents.

12. The idea of such a grenade had existed since the early 1950s. Steel balls had been considered as a source of fragments in the US Army Ballistic Research Laboratories hand grenade study of 1951–2, and the BRL study also considered spherical hand grenades (Dunn and Sterne, 1952).

13. The idea of the flanges apparently goes back to a secret Army project in the early 1950s to disseminate radioactive particles as a means of warfare: 'The most significant development in aerial dissemination came in the investigation of spherical munitions as a means of solving the biggest problem in aerial RW [radiological warfare], that of dispersion. Since spheres lack good ballistic characteristics they provided far greater dispersion. BW [biological warfare] likewise benefited from this work since it, too, requires adequate dispersion for maximum effectiveness. *The use of ribbed spheres to impart a spin to the bomb* further increased the pattern size' ('Radiological Research and Development,' in 'Summary History of Chemical Corps Activities 9 September 1951 to 31 December 1952,' prepared by the Historical Office, Office of the Chief Chemical Officer, US Army, February 1953; emphasis added).

14. According to the US Department of Defense definition, 'operational evaluation' is 'The test and analysis of a specific end item or system, so far as practicable under service operating conditions, in order to determine if quantity production is warranted considering *a.* the increase in military effectiveness to be gained, and *b.* its effectiveness as compared with currently available items or systems...'

15. *Supplemental Defense Appropriations for 1967*, p. 346.

16. Riffaud, 1967, pp. 49, 103–13, 207.

17. DRV Commission, 1966, p. 26.

18. Dellinger, 1967, p. 14.

19. *Ibid.*, pp. 10–11.

20. *Ibid.*, pp. 6–9.

21. 'Two Kinds of Civilian Casualties in Vietnam,' London, US Information Service, 4 January 1967.

22. Salisbury, 1967.

23. Chester Manly, 'Air Raid Photos Show Accuracy of US Bombers,' *Chicago Tribune*, 7 March 1967.

24. 'Antipersonnel Bomb Use in North Verified,' Associated Press, *Washington Star*, 10 April 1967.

25. Joergen E. Petersen, 'Pellet Bombs Cause Mounting Hatred for US in Hanoi,' *Guardian*, 2 November 1967.

26. Limqueco and Weiss, eds, 1971, p. 57.

27. Duffet, ed., 1968, pp. 246–7. *Fundamentals of Aerospace Weapon Systems* was a publicly available document, issued by the Air Force Reserve Officers' Training Corps at the Air Force's Air University in 1961.

28. *Ibid.*, pp. 256–8.

29. The Tribunal found that the US government and US forces were 'guilty of the deliberate, systematic and large-scale bombardment of civilian targets, including civilian populations...' (Limqueco and Weiss, eds, 1971, p. 185).

30. As Earl H. Tilford Jr has written in his recent detailed study: 'Rolling Thunder began as a campaign of *strategic* persuasion. It switched very quickly to interdiction, a *tactical* mission. Throughout the three years and nine months of concerted bombing, the focus was primarily on interdicting the flow of supplies toward the battlefields of the South' (Tilford, 1993, p. 71; original emphasis).

31. As Tilford has written, civilian advisers on the bombing policy 'were sure that there was a threshold of pain beyond which North Vietnam would not go,' while the generals and admirals 'reasoned that since North Vietnam had a smaller industrial base, their leaders would hold it all the dearer and, thereby, be intimidated' (*ibid.*, p. 69). In this reasoning by US policy-makers, the notion of pain seems to have referred to a sensation expected to be experienced by North Vietnamese leaders, causing them to make a rational calculation to desist from the war effort, rather than to the pain experienced by North Vietnamese civilians affected by the bombing.

32. US Army, 1956, paragraphs 2–3, 39, 501, 505, 509.

33. According to the NATO definition, 'armed reconnaissance' is 'An air mission flown with the primary purpose of locating and attacking targets of opportunity, i.e., enemy materiel, personnel, and facilities, in assigned general areas or along assigned ground communications routes, and not for the purpose of attacking specific briefed targets.' A 'target of opportunity' is defined by NATO as 'A target which appears during combat and which can be reached by ground fire, naval fire, or aircraft fire, and against which fire has not been scheduled...'

34. In the Department of Defense definition: 'lines of communications (logistics)' are 'All the routes, land, water, and air, which connect an operating military force with a base of operations and along which supplies and military forces move.'

35. According to Michael Krepon: 'Soviet antiaircraft units used by the North Vietnamese were only about ten to 12 feet across, an extremely difficult target to knock out even though only a small amount of damage could render them inoperative. CBUs, *by literally pockmarking an entire area*, could either knock out the antiaircraft weapon or prevent it from firing...' (Krepon, 1974, p. 598; emphasis added).

36. Tilford, 1993, p. 75. According to W. Hays Parks, Chief of the International Law Team of the International Affairs Division of the Office of the US Army Judge Advocate General: 'Collateral [civilian] casualties occurring because of weather phenomena or conditions are equally beyond the responsibility of attacker or defender' (Parks, 1990, p. 190).

37. Littauer and Uphoff, eds, 1972, p. 281.

38. Admiral Sharp's testimony may be contrasted with this passage from the public statement of 4 January 1967 issued by the US Information Service (cited above): 'The policy of taking all feasible measures to minimize civilian casualties, both in North and South Vietnam, has been followed as rigorously as possible and remains in force.'

39. As Krepon noted (1974, p. 600), the restriction on the use of napalm in

any combat situation was lifted only on 9 March 1965, when President Johnson approved its use against North Vietnamese targets (US Department of Defense, 1971, vol. 3, pp. 278, 334; cited below as *Pentagon Papers*).

40. Krepon, 1974, p. 600.

41. SIPRI, 1978, Table 2.3, p. 30.

42. *Ibid*.

43. In Xieng Khouang province, one of the most heavily bombed areas of northern Laos, the province containing the Plain of Jars (see below), antipersonnel bomblets were reported to be the most commonly encountered type of unexploded munition after the US–Indochina war. In 1979 the USSR initiated an aid program to clear unexploded munitions from farm land in Xieng Khouang province. Over the course of eighteen months some 5,000,000 hectares were cleared of 12,700 explosive remnants of many types, with CBU-24 bomblets predominating (E.S. Martin and M. Hiebert, 'Explosive Remnants of the Second Indochina War in Viet Nam and Laos,' in SIPRI, 1985, pp. 44–7).

44. According to W. Hays Parks (1982, p. 13), proposed lists of targets in the bombing of North Vietnam were reviewed each week by President Johnson and a few top advisers according to four criteria, one of which was the estimated civilian casualties. President Johnson then personally selected the targets for attack. In Parks's view, 'Rolling Thunder was one of the most constrained military campaigns in history' (*ibid*., p. 21).

45. According to Krepon (1974, p. 602), 'no formal rules of engagement were placed on where, when and how CBU's were to be used.' Krepon has suggested that 'Lack of supply proved to be the most effective political check on indiscriminate use, because once they were operational, civilian officials had little to say about CBU's.'

46. *Ibid*., p. 600.

47. Julian Perry-Robinson of the Science Policy Research Unit at the University of Sussex, England, has calculated that an F-4 Phantom jet delivering nineteen 750-lb CBU-58 cluster bombs (an improved version of the CBU-24) has an antipersonnel lethality index of 150,000,000, as against an index of 9,600,000 for a Phantom delivering an equivalent load of nineteen 750-lb general-purpose (high explosive) bombs. By way of comprison, a Lance missile with a developmental 0.05 kiloton airburst nuclear warhead has an index of 60,000,000 on the same scale. An M16 rifle has an index of 4,200 (Perry-Robinson, 1983, pp. 160–61).

48. US Army, 1967c, p. 2-13.

49. *Ibid*.

50. The BLU-3 weighs 1.73 pounds and contains nearly twice as much explosive as the BLU-26. The $^1/_4$-inch steel balls weigh 16 grains, as against the $^7/_{32}$-inch, 10.5-grain balls in the 'guava' bomblet. The BLU-3 is filled with 70/30 cyclotol, a high-brisance explosive.

51. US Air Force Tactical Air Command, 1963, pp. 4–5.

52. Earlier, in August 1964, the Joint Chiefs of Staff (JCS) had authorized the 'use of CBU-2/A munitions against suitable targets on Yankee Team escort and SARCAP in Laos' and the 'use of Lazy Dog on suitable targets within RVN [South Vietnam]' by Farm Gate aircraft (the quotations are from the authorization as cited by the Commander in Chief, Pacific (CINCPAC)). Yankee Team was a

program involving US jet aircraft flying reconnaissance missions over Laos; Farm Gate was a US Air Force program in South Vietnam involving unconventional warfare operations using small aircraft (Cable, 1991, p. 83; Tilford, 1993, p. 45). Lazy Dogs were small, solid pieces of iron shaped like miniature bombs; they were dropped from airplanes using a dispenser known as the Mk 44 missile cluster adapter and were considered as possible payloads for Sadeye and Gladeye dispensers (cf. Tompkins, 1966, pp. 112, 115; US Army, 1966a, p. 2-65). In a secret cable of 26 September 1964 relaying the JCS authorization, CINCPAC noted: 'Introduction of these weapons into combat environment for first time provides unique opportunity to monitor and record weapon effectiveness, develop optimum delivery techniques and tactics and to gather associated data which would prove invaluable in later use or to discover possible weakness or improvements in weapons' (cable from CINCPAC to CONUSMACV, cited in Kahin, 1986 (1987 edition), p. 531, note 5).

53. US Air Force Test Unit, Vietnam, 1965, covering message and page v.

54. Quoted in Kahin, 1986 (1987 edition), p. 531, note 5.

55. When the North Vietnamese began telling visitors about the American cluster bombs in 1966, they said that the 'pineapple' was first used on 8 February 1965 against Le Thuy, a village near the coast some 40 kilometers north of the Demilitarized Zone separating the two Vietnams (Vigier, in Limqueco and Weiss, eds, 1971, p. 118). 8 February was the second day of raids in Operation Flaming Dart I, a bombing attack on North Vietnam which preceded Operation Rolling Thunder. In a press conference describing the raids of the previous day, US Secretary of Defense Robert S. McNamara said: 'The planes carry bombs, high explosive bombs and rockets.' He did not speak of cluster bombs (*New York Times*, 8 February 1965, p. 15).

56. This estimate is based on figures for procurement of the CBU-2 and CBU-14 cluster bombs, the canister with BLU-3 bomblets, and the ADU-253 cluster adapter given in SIPRI, 1978, Table 2.3, p. 30.

57. F. Harvey, 1967, p. 57. 'Reconnaissance by fire' is defined by NATO as 'A method of reconnaissance in which fire is placed on a suspected enemy position to cause the enemy to disclose his presence by movement or return of fire.'

58. Tilford, 1993, p. 120.

59. Quoted in Branfman, ed., 1972, p. 19.

60. *Ibid.*, pp. 4–5, 128–31. As in North Vietnam, US officials claimed that the air war was not directed against civilians. Former Ambassador William H. Sullivan testified at a closed session of a US Senate subcommittee in 1969: 'The United States Air Force contribution [in Laos] was limited to striking at the logistic routes ... choke points ... or at points of concentration which fed into the area where the actual ground battling was taking place ... it was the policy not to attack populated areas' (quoted in *ibid.*, p. 5).

61. 'Damage is actually produced by the tiny, hot, high velocity fragments of liner metal making up the jet. Depending upon the quality of the armor plate and upon the amount of explosive in the charge, varying amounts of metal may be spalled off the rear face of the armor at sufficiently high velocities to injure crew members. Fire very often results because the cramped space and very large amounts of explosives and inflammable fuels make it highly improbable for a jet

to perforate a tank without striking such inflammable material' (US Army Materiel Command, 1963, p. 10-31).

62. US House of Representatives, Committee on Appropriations, *Department of Defense Appropriations for 1967*, hearings, vol. 4, pp. 238–9.

63. A Navy civilian weapons development official involved in the program told me that the idea for the Rockeye came when an official at the Navy's Bureau of Ordnance in Washington suggested that if tail fins were fitted to the many obsolete antitank warheads left over from the Navy's 2.75-inch rocket program, and enough of the warheads were dropped from a dispenser, they would be likely to hit some targets. The name 'Rockeye' came from the surplus rocket warheads used as bomblets in this 'Rockeye I,' and also from the use of a Zuni 5-inch rocket motor to retrofire the bomblets from the aircraft, causing them to disperse radially to form a pattern of six overlapping circles. Engineers at the Naval Ordnance Test Station (NOTS) in China Lake, California, developed the Rockeye I in accordance with these ideas, but the bomblet size proved not to be ideal, so the engineers designed a smaller bomblet and redesigned the cluster bomb. The result was 'Rockeye II.' Honeywell Inc. assisted the Navy in developing the dispenser, bomblet, and bomblet fuze, and went on to become the main producer of Rockeye II, receiving over $100 million in production contracts.

An early, confidential NOTS report, dated October 1959, calculated the likely effectiveness of 2.75-inch antitank warheads against tanks when delivered either from a cluster weapon or in salvos of rockets. The report noted: 'tanks are perplexing targets for aircraft, since they are small and hard targets, making both acquisition and kill very difficult.... One way to solve the problem of a small target and large delivery error is to use a weapon consisting of a cluster of warheads. By this means the target can be attacked with greater hope of success (provided each warhead is potent enough that there is reasonable expectation that a hit on the target will result in a kill)...'

The work on this report was done under Project Freefall, described as 'a program to develop new air-delivered weapons for use in nonnuclear war and to utilize currently-stockpiled ordnance to provide interim conventional-war capability' – evidently a precursor of the Eye-series program (Dunn, 1959, pp. iii, 1).

64. See, for example, Fredric R. Branfman, 'The Rockeye Missile: The Culmination of US Antipersonnel Technology,' published in *American Report*, 4 December 1972. The US Army Materiel Command manual cited above (1963, p. B-6) indicates that a shaped charge can be used to perforate concrete.

65. US House of Representatives, Committee on Armed Services, *Department of Defense Authorizations for 1973*, hearings, vol. 3. Zirconium is a metal which, when abraded, produces sparks hot enough to ignite hydrocarbon vapors (SIPRI, 1975, p. 100).

66. US Navy, 1972a, pp. 2-1 to 2-8. In the Mk 20 Rockeye II, which weighs 490 pounds, 247 bomblets are dropped from a free-fall dispenser which opens in the air, releasing the bomblets. The CBU-59 uses the same dispenser as the Rockeye, but the bomblet is smaller: a CBU-59 contains 717 bomblets and weighs 750 pounds. The CBU-59/B went into pilot production in the fiscal year 1971. Since then, most antitank cluster bombs developed in other countries have followed the example of the CBU-59 in combining an antitank shaped charge

with an antipersonnel controlled fragmentation casing.

67. US Army, 1970, p. 1-8.

68. Earlier, a limited 'effectiveness test' of the BLU-3 in 'simulated jungle terrain,' conducted at Eglin Air Force Base, Florida, had 'revealed that three out of four bombs were either duds or ineffective tree bursts.' A secret report on the test was issued in November 1964 (US Air Force Special Air Warfare Center, 1965, p. 24).

69. US Air Force Armament Laboratory, Eglin Air Force Base, Florida, 1967, 'Ballistic Results of the Engineering Evaluation of the CBU-25/A,' final report, 4 January–20 April 1966, abstract.

The BLU-24/B is a 1.6-lb, cyclotol-filled spherical fragmentation bomblet with plastic fins which was known in Vietnam as the 'orange' bomblet. It is used with the SUU-14 dispenser in the CBU-25 cluster bomb. The scale of its use in Indochina is indicated by the fact that the US armed forces ordered 186,783 CBU-25s between the fiscal years 1966 and 1973 (SIPRI, 1978, Table 2.3, p. 30).

70. US House of Representatives, Committee on Appropriations, *Department of Defense Appropriations for 1968*, hearings, vol. 4, pp. 99–100. The dashes are the Air Force censor's.

71. US Army, 1970. Hayes International Corporation, an Alabama company, began working on cluster munitions in 1957, when 'a group was established [at the company] to meet the growing requirements for systems and techniques involved with the delivery of various submunitions,' according to a company brochure. 'In 1958 Hayes designed and fabricated a prototype system for dispensing biological bomblets. It was recognized that the system as evolved had other potential applications for delivering a variety of munitions that required pre-packaging before they could be successfully contained within an aircraft bomb bay. This led to further developmental work and became a stepping stone to gradual broadening of the [Hayes] Airborne Weapons Group capability base into a variety of programs relating to limited wars...' The brochure stated that the Hayes dispenser 'resembles a fine Swiss watch in intricacy and complexity of parts, all designed with micrometric attention to exacting interface requirements aimed at providing our Air Force bomber/attack aircraft with the ultimate refinements of state of the munitions-dispensing art technology.'

72. SIPRI, 1978, Table 2.2, p. 27. Some 30 per cent of the tonnage was dropped on Laos and 56 per cent on South Vietnam; the remainder was dropped on North Vietnam and Cambodia. Air Force field survey information cited in the SIPRI study indicated that the B-52s, dropping about 23 tons of bombs on a typical raid, killed from 0.7 to 3.5 enemy soldiers per bomb load (*ibid.*, p. 27).

73. *Ibid.*, Tables 5.11 and 5.12, pp. 147–58.

74. There are 18 bomblets (called M39 'grenades') in the M44 105mm shell, 60 M43 'grenades' in the M449 155mm shell, and 104 M43 grenades in the M404 8-inch shell. A similar shell for the 4.2-inch heavy mortar, the M453 shell, has 32 M36 grenades. These shells are referred to as 'antipersonnel' ICMs, as against the 'dual purpose' ICMs introduced later.

75. US Army, 1978, Table 4-1, p. 4-2. Other comparisons of the effects of ICM and high explosive rounds are classified. Perry-Robinson has estimated that a 155mm ICM has approximately four times the antipersonnel lethality of a

155mm high-explosive round (1983, Table 10.2, p. 160).

76. US Army, 1978, pp. 2-4, 4-1, 4-5, 4-12 to 4-15.

77. Ott, 1975, pp. 147–8.

78. This figure comprises 86,000 155mm shells procured in fiscal 1969 and 1973 and 32,000 8-inch shells in fiscal 1969 and 1970. It is likely that earlier production figures were classified.

79. US Army Project Manager for Selected Ammunition, 1972, 'Program Achievements 1962–1972,' submission to US Army Materiel Command for the AMC tenth anniversary.

80. US House of Representatives, Committee on Appropriations, *Department of Defense Appropriations for 1968*, hearings, vol. 4, p. 391.

81. These details refer to the XM41E1 and XM65 gravel mines as described in US Army, 1968, p. 1-9. The mine contains a mixture of 3.2 grams of lead azide with 7.1 grams of RDX. Lead azide is a high explosive which is sensitive to impact and is used to set off less sensitive explosives such as RDX.

82. The process of dropping Dragontooth mines from the SUU-13 dispenser was described by an Air Force witness at the US Senate Electronic Battlefield hearings as follows: 'The first step is canister ejection, followed by release of the individual mines from the canister. The mines disperse as they flutter to the ground. Application of sufficient external force, such as a foot step, activates the mine' (US Senate, Committee on Armed Services, *Investigation into Electronic Battlefield Program*, hearings, Washington, 1971 [cited below as *Electronic Battlefield hearings*], p. 138).

83. The M692/M731 155mm shell contains 36 antipersonnel grenades fitted with tripwires and bounding mechanisms (SIPRI, 1978, Table 7.2, p. 189). Honeywell Inc. was the developer of the ADAM; its first development contract on the project was awarded in 1969 (Prokosch, 1972, p. 72).

84. The generic term which the US Army introduced to refer to the new mass-sown mines is 'scatterable mines.' It is related to the term 'scattered laying (landmine warfare),' defined by NATO in the 1970s as 'the laying of mines without regard to pattern.' In the modern NATO definition, a scatterable mine is 'A mine laid without regard to classical pattern that is designed to be delivered by aircraft, artillery, missile, ground dispenser or by hand.'

85. *Electronic Battlefield* hearings, p. 138. Major Anderson used similar language in describing the effect of the gravel mine: 'The only kill mechanism is blast, gravel will blow a man's foot off but it will not blow a hole in a truck tire' (*ibid.*, p. 140).

86. McNaughton specified that to the extent necessary the barrier would run from the South China Sea across Vietnam and Laos all the way to the border with Thailand, a straight-line distance of about 160 miles (*Pentagon Papers*, vol. 4, p. 114).

87. The extent of mining envisioned with gravel mines is indicated by the JASON proposal that 'The actual mined area would encompass the equivalent of a strip about 100 by 5 kilometers.' The gravel mines would be 'both self-sterilizing for harassment [so that friendly forces could enter the area from time to time to watch roads and plant more mines] and non-sterilizing for area denial.' The 'guava' clusters would be used against both troops and trucks in 'attacks on area-

type targets of uncertain locations' (*Pentagon Papers*, vol. 4, pp. 121–2).

88. *Ibid.* The JASON report emphasized the novelty of what was being proposed. In comparison to earlier proposals for a barrier, the scientists wrote, 'the new aspects are: the very large scale of area denial, especially mine fields kilometers deep rather than the conventional 100–200 meters; the very large numbers and persistent employment of weapons, sensors, and aircraft sorties in the barrier area; and the emphasis on rapid and carefully planned incorporation of more effective weapons and sensors into the system.' The need for large quantities of munitions in such electronic barriers was recognized in the Air Force doctrine developed for operations of this kind. Under the heading 'Air-Supported Barrier,' a secret 1970 Air Force manual (declassified the next year) stated:

> An objective of the Air Force is the integration of surveillance elements with *large quantities of target-activated area denial munitions* backed up by *large numbers of strike sorties* to form an effective air barrier system. The need to restrict or block enemy movement exists at most levels of military conflict. In areas remote from the ground battle, situations can arise in which certain enemy politico-economic areas should be isolated and/or in which a series of air-supported barriers along enemy LOCs [lines of communication] should be established. In proximity to the ground battle, air-supported barriers can be established to detect/monitor/impede/destroy/channel enemy attacks and withdrawals. (US Air Force, 1970, p. 2-3; emphasis added)

89. The JASON report envisaged a continuing program of research and development to improve the barrier: 'Weapons and sensors which can make a much more effective barrier, only some of which are now under development, are not likely to be available in less than 18 months to 2 years. Even these, it must be expected, will eventually be overcome by the North Vietnamese, so that further improvements in weaponry will be necessary.' Among the efforts needed was 'rapid development of new mines (such as tripwire, smaller and more effectively camouflaged Gravel, and various other kinds of mines).'

The JASON report led to the setting up of a research and development program with the innocuous title 'Defense Communications Planning Group.' Its task was to implement the anti-infiltration systems conceived by the JASON group. The DCPG was to work on a 'high-priority, top secret and low profile' basis, reporting directly to the Secretary of Defense, and with virtually unlimited funding. Participants in the program later likened it to the Manhattan Project, which produced the atomic bomb; or the Polaris program, which yielded the first nuclear submarine (Dickson, 1976, pp. 32–5).

The Wide Area Antipersonnel Mine was one munition whose development was stimulated by the JASON study, to judge from the timing. 'Development of this mine began in 1966,' Honeywell wrote in a 1968 proposal to the Army. 'Production tooling was also initiated in 1966. Initial mine deliveries occurred in January 1968. We are now building toward a sustained production rate of 225,000 per month, and the automatic assembly and inspection equipment has a growth potential to a rate in excess of 300,000 per month.'

90. *Electronic Battlefield* hearings, p. 3.

91. Klare, 1972, p. 186. At the Electronic Battlefield hearings (pp. 146–7),

Major Anderson described the use of Wide Area Antipersonnel Mines in a 'munitions package concept' designed 'to cut the enemy's lines of communications and keep them cut for extended periods of time':

> First, the road is cut at a point difficult to bypass, using highly accurate guided weapons.... Next, antimateriel land mines are emplaced. These mines will destroy a truck if one enters the mined areas. Third, antipersonnel land mines are emplaced over the antimateriel mines to deter the enemy's mine-clearing operations. WAAPM has been used in this role. Fourth, sensors on both sides of the munitions package determine if truck traffic is getting through the package. Sensors in other locations are used to determine other routes taken by the enemy if he cannot get through the munitions package. By creating a difficult-to-bypass chokepoint, munitions packages can also result in a concentration of enemy vehicles. These can then be attacked using CBU-24 and general purpose bombs.

92. Quoted in Dickson, 1976, p. 103.

93. *Philadelphia Inquirer*, 14 December 1972.

94. Michael Getler, 'Computers Call the Shots for Bombers,' *Washington Post*, 12 December 1972.

95. Pepke, 1970, pp. 34–5.

96. US Army, 1969, pp. 4, 7–9.

97. US Air Force, 1972, p. 7.

98. SIPRI, 1978, Table 2.7, p. 36. On the secret funding of purchases of Wide Area Antipersonnel Mines by the Defense Communications Planning Group, see *Electronic Battlefield* hearings, pp. 131–3.

99. Tompkins, 1966, p. ix.

100. US House of Representatives, *Department of Defense Appropriations for 1968*, hearings, vol. 3, p. 223.

101. For example: 'As of July 1966 [sixteen months after the inception of Rolling Thunder] the US bombing of North Vietnam had had no measurable direct effect on Hanoi's ability to mount and support military operations in the South at the current level' (JASON report, August 1966; *Pentagon Papers*, vol. 4, p. 116). Similar assessments were made by various agencies in November 1966, January 1967, December 1967, and January 1968.

102. The figure is from SIPRI, 1976, Table 2.1, p. 13 (the figure of 14,265,000 given in the SIPRI table is in metric tonnes).

103. A brief survey and analysis of the US rules of engagement is provided in SIPRI, 1978, Appendix 9D, pp. 257–67.

104. Dellinger, 1967, p. 3.

105. Vien Phuong, 1970, p. 110.

106. Swearington, 1969.

107. For example, Martin and Hiebert (in SIPRI, 1985, pp. 39–43) have called attention to the large number of 40mm grenade rounds – estimated at over 140 million – fired in South Vietnam, and the high number of postwar civilian casualties caused by them.

108. US House of Representatives, Committee on Appropriations, *Department of Defense Appropriations for 1968*, hearings, vol. 3, pp. 489, 514.

CHAPTER 5

TACKLING THE
MERCHANTS OF DEATH

For many people who took part in the amorphous, chaotic movement to stop the Vietnam war, the horror of antipersonnel weapons was the ultimate proof of the malevolence of the war effort. When horror turned to outrage, it became a motivating force. Actions sprang up, locally and nationally. In the course of the war thousands of citizens took part in protests aimed at stopping the production of weapons destined for Indochina. If the lawmakers in Washington would not listen, here was one small way in which people throughout the country could make their own small attempt to halt the war effort.

Notes from a Napalm Scrapbook

Some years ago I began keeping a scrapbook on napalm. The first item was an article from the journal *Industrial and Engineering Chemistry*. Several Harvard University chemists wrote that in 1942 they had combined gasoline with a naphthenate-'palmitate' thickener, yielding a jellied fuel.[1] Their 'napalm' was one of the important military inventions of World War II. Carried in big canisters or 'firebombs,' it was used against enemy troops and villages, and in incendiary bomb clusters it accounted for the destruction of dozens of Japanese cities (Chapter 4).

Other items in my scrapbook took up the story after World War II:

we ... fired whole villages with the occupants – women and children and ten times as many Communist soldiers – under showers of napalm, and the pilots came back to their ships stinking of the vomit twisted from their vitals by the shock of what they had to do. (From a US Air Force history of the Korean war)[2]

Enemy personnel in the open are excellent targets.... Lightly built dwellings and factories such as are found in the Orient make excellent firebomb targets.... The basic objective of firebomb missions is to kill, injure, neutralize, and demoralize. (From a US Army manual, 1960)[3]

Skin is easily damaged by heat, the degree of damage depending upon the amount of heat. (*Napalm and Other Incendiary Weapons and All Aspects of Their Possible Use*, Report of the UN Secretary-General, 1973)[4]

At Stanford University in California in the winter of 1965–6, students involved in the antiwar protests learned that portable field units for mixing napalm were being developed by United Technology Center, a division of the United Aircraft Corporation. The plant was in a place called Coyote, some twenty miles south of Stanford. The students had gone there to hand out leaflets, but security guards were on hand to photograph any workers who accepted them, and as the plant was in the country, there were no bystanders who would see the message. Soon, however, the company's work expanded.

The *Wall Street Journal* reported on 14 March 1966: 'United Aircraft Corp. received an $11,015,049 Air Force contract to produce ordnance items in Redwood City, California.' A local newspaper was more precise: the 'ordnance items' to be produced were napalm bombs. The producer was United Technology Center, and the locale was a city of 56,000 on the San Francisco Bay between Stanford and San Francisco. The port of Redwood City agreed to allow a sublease of public land to the company as the site for its firebomb plant. Here was a target close to home.

The Stanford protestors joined forces with local residents, and the Redwood City Committee Against Napalm was born. Poring through the city charter, they discovered a proviso that decisions of the port commission could be overturned by popular vote. A petition campaign was organized to force the city to hold a referendum.

The students composed a leaflet on the improved form of napalm, Napalm B, to be produced in Redwood City. It was thickened with polystyrene, making it adhere to the target more firmly than the World War II variety. They cited a report in the magazine *Chemical and Engineering News* that the consumption of polystyrene in Napalm B was expected to be so great – 25 million pounds a month – that normal industrial supplies would be strained.

The leaflet quoted news reports from Vietnam. One reporter had tried to help carry a GI accidentally struck by napalm: 'I held a leg of the most seriously burned man. I wasn't tender enough. A big patch of burned skin came off in my hand' (San Francisco *Chronicle*, 17 November 1965). Another report referred to thousands of refugees, many of them wounded, who flocked from a cluster of destroyed hamlets in Binh Dinh province:

Most of the wounds are the simple type inflicted by shell and bomb fragments, but others are the gruesome variety caused by napalm. One distraught woman appeared at a field medical station holding a child in her arms whose legs had literally been cooked by napalm. The child is not expected to live. (San Francisco *Chronicle*, 15 February 1966)

This was another report:

> As the communists withdrew from Quang Ngai last Monday, US jet bombers pounded the hills into which they were headed. Many Vietnamese – one estimate was as high as 500 – were killed by the strikes. The American contention is that they were Viet Cong soldiers. But three out of four patients seeking treatments in a Vietnamese hospital afterwards for burns from napalm were village women. (*New York Times*, 6 June 1965)

The committee mailed the leaflet to all registered voters, and its members began going from door to door collecting signatures on their petition. A business enterprise which would otherwise have gone unnoticed had become a matter of public controversy.

Some sense of local opinion could be gained from that excellent institution, the Letters to the Editor page in the *Redwood City Tribune*. 'The good name of Redwood City with its old slogan "Climate Best by Government Test" appeals far more to me than "Napalm City by the Dead Bay"!' wrote one resident. Others disagreed. 'I see the "Do Gooders" are still panicked by the napalm issue in Redwood City,' one reader wrote. Another likened the committee to Judas, betraying 'our young men ... over in Vietnam, being shot at, many being killed.' This reader deplored their appearance at a church on Palm Sunday with posters displaying a photograph 'of unknown origin, of a Vietnam child, presumably, suffering from burns purportedly the result of an American napalm bomb.'

Another reader questioned the 'sincerity of the local napalm-banners' in view of 'the "conspiracy of silence" exhibited by this and other similar groups when it comes to identifying and exposing the actual enemy.' In his view, 'In so far as napalm is concerned it is a legitimate and destructive weapon of war, horribly effective and quite suitable for fighting communism and its dedicated agents.'

The response to the petition drive exceeded the committee's expectations. Two thousand, four hundred signatures were required; 3,761 were gathered and submitted by the deadline. The committee, too, had grown in the process. By the end of the drive, more than one hundred people had volunteered to collect signatures. But the city officials refused to certify the petition, and a local court upheld them on a technicality, ruling that the petition was incorrectly worded. The committee appealed to a higher court in San Francisco, but the court refused to hear the appeal. By now the plant had been erected and the bombs were in production.

The committee's effort had come to an end, but there were many people who wanted to continue the protest. They called for a big rally, organized a vigil at the plant, and began experimenting with other nonviolent tactics. What was happening in Redwood City had begun to attract national and international attention.

One month after the petition was handed in, another Redwood City group, calling itself 'Neighbors For Vietnam Victory Now!', placed an advertisement in the *Redwood City Tribune*. 'Were You Fooled by the NAPALM Petition?' it read. '*Many of us were – after all everyone is for* MORALITY. But now that we see big organization at work, national press and TV coverage, simultaneous demonstrations elsewhere, the same pattern as in other demonstrations, and the same viet-niks and America-haters getting into the act, we detect the SMELL OF A BIG FAKE.' The petition was 'an attempt to deprive our boys overseas of an important weapon,' they said, and it was rejected because 'we can't vote on an issue directed against our country.' They urged citizens to display their American flags, avoid the coming anti-napalm rally, and 'if the demonstrators pass you, treat them to a stony silence.'

If there was a sinister fakery in the Redwood City campaign, I could not detect it – in the magazine editor and the Unitarian minister who were the leading figures of the committee; in the school pupils and grownups who kept a 24-hour vigil at the plant for two months; in the local artist who created a lurid oil painting with the words 'STOP NAPALM' against a background of smoke and charred buildings; or in the young Stanford professor who made his own brief contribution to stopping the war effort when he spotted a truck loaded with empty bomb cases speeding down the freeway toward the plant, and managed to make it stop by pulling alongside in his car, gesticulating wildly, and shouting, 'Hey, one of your bombs is falling off!'

The vigil was a form of protest that was catching on across the country. Of all the vigils during the Vietnam war, this one must have enjoyed one of the most poignant sites. It was held just outside the plant, in the port, between the plant entrance and the road. The plant was no more than a small loading facility, and as the whole operation took place outdoors, in the mild California climate, the protestors could watch it from the other side of the wire-mesh fence which separated it from the road. The empty aluminum bomb shells were brought in by truck, in wooden crates (thoughtfully marked 'Do Not Drop'); the polystyrene powder, used to thicken the napalm, came in by train and was mixed with the incendiary fuel in vats. The mixture was then piped into the bomb cases through a tube, and the filled bombs were loaded on barges, to be towed across the San Francisco Bay to a naval storage site from which they would be shipped to Vietnam. Some of the polystyrene had spilled by the railway tracks; when the protestors took the white powder in their hands, they found it was sticky to the touch.

The vigil brought together many of the same sorts of Americans who would take part in peace actions elsewhere throughout the war. There were the teenagers, whose direct, moral approach cut through the hesitancies of their elders. There were the timid, whose distress at the war overcame their fears and impelled them to take a stand. There were the special people, often ill at ease in their own society, for whom the war in Vietnam revealed some searing truth about the evils of American life. These special people often acted on their own, in unusual ways; they could not be stopped.

One of them, whose exploits I chronicled for the *Stanford Daily*, was a bearded 51-year-old psychiatrist named Oliver Henderson. One day Dr Henderson and a young electrical engineer stood in the road in front of a truck which was being used to deliver bomb casings to the plant, and refused to move. The two men were arrested. Two others were arrested the next day when they did the same.

Later, Dr Henderson began going down to the plant with a United Nations flag and a megaphone and speaking to the workers, using what he called 'hypnotic techniques.' 'Your fingers will become heavy like lead because you don't want to work,' he would say. 'Your skin will tingle and itch as long as you work on the dirty bomb. When you have meat for dinner tonight you won't be able to eat it because it will be charred by napalm.' He approached the whole enterprise with good humor; he didn't mind appearing ridiculous – it was a way of getting through. After a few visits the workers became friendly and greeted him when he arrived; and when he heard that one worker had quit (possibly from pangs of conscience?), he was elated. The management responded by playing loud records – 'especially Tchaikovsky's *Pathétique* symphony, which is perfect for me,' he said.

After the vigil finished, there were sporadic protests throughout the year, and at Christmas a religious service was held outside the plant. Early in 1967, the American flag in front of the plant was quietly taken down and the machinery was dismantled. The Air Force contract with UTC had not been renewed. Whether this was because of the protests or whether it was simply on grounds of efficiency, no one could tell. The company kept silent.

In the meantime, I had received a helpful explanation on the exclusively military character of napalm. I wrote a letter of protest to the President of the United States, and received a reply from an official in the office of the Secretary of the Air Force. He told me:

Napalm was used extensively during World War II and has been in our inventory ever since. It is mixed in California for employment in Vietnam against selected targets such as caves, reinforced supply areas, and the like, which do not involve civilians.

The Corporate Image

As things quietened down in Redwood City, the protests were spreading elsewhere. 'Committees against Napalm' were formed in several cities. Attention shifted to the Dow Chemical Company, maker of the polystyrene thickener in the UTC bombs, whose own contracts for napalm soon dwarfed those of UTC.

Unlike UTC and its parent company, Dow offered scope for nationwide protests. Its best-known product was Saran Wrap, a clear plastic tissue which clung to the food it enclosed, as Dow's jellied fuel clung to the skin. Saran Wrap was to be found in households across the country; any local antiwar group could go to the nearest supermarket and call for a boycott. Further opportunities for protest were afforded by the frequent visits of Dow recruiters to university campuses.

In New York, seventy-five people designated 19 March 1967 'Napalm Sunday' and marched from the Metropolitan Museum of Art to St Patrick's Cathedral 'to demonstrate against the war and the use of napalm in Vietnam,' as one of them wrote in *Win*, a magazine connected with the recently formed New York Workshop in Nonviolence.

> We marched in threes, and each trio had signs that, when combined, read 'Napalm Burns People,' supplied to us by the Village Peace Center. We were led by two girls who carried a sign reading 'Which way will your loved ones come back?' Behind them limped a boy covered with bandages. Four boys carried a coffin decorated with an American flag.[5]

In California, also in March, twenty-five members of Students for a Democratic Society (SDS) held a sit-in at Pomona College and succeeded (in their words) in preventing an 'obviously upset' Dow representative from holding recruiting interviews for prospective employees. When the Dean of Students remonstrated with them, they replied that 'Pomona College was not founded for the purpose of training people to burn children.' Their report was published in the national newspaper of SDS, an organization which combined activism with sociopolitical analysis. The report concluded: 'In addition to the bad publicity we gave Dow in Los Angeles papers, we were happy to have awakened a consciousness in the minds of everyone in the community on the effects of napalm and Dow's part in making it.'[6]

Drawing on the practice of Chinese restaurants which give their customers fortune cookies at the end of a meal, members of the New York Workshop in Nonviolence showed up at the giant antiwar march on 15 April 1967 and handed out cookies containing this message:

> 'Help! I'm a prisoner in a US peasant-cooking factory!'
> *Anonymous Dow employee*[7]

The protests were not stopping Dow from making napalm, but they were having an effect on one of the company's most valuable assets: its corporate image. Weapons work was something most companies would rather not have the public know about.

A man came to see me, during my Stanford days, to ask if I could write an article on flechettes. He had learned about them when a neighbor, working at an FMC Corporation plant, brought some home from work and passed them around as a curiosity. I took one in the palm of my hand. It was like a small finishing nail, about an inch long, with four small fins at the blunt end.

My visitor was a man who had spent his life working in a razor-blade plant. Like many other Americans, he had invested in the stock market, and among his holdings were shares in FMC.[8] He had come to me because of my connection with one of the new 'underground' newspapers which had been raising questions about the responsibility of US corporations for war crimes in Indochina. He had come across newspaper accounts of the use of flechettes in combat, and had kept copies.[9] In 1968, as a shareholder, he went to the company's annual meeting in San Jose, California. Armed with his press clippings and enlarged photos of flechettes, he rose to his feet and asked for comment on the FMC flechette munitions.

'The weapon was developed by the government and is manufactured by FMC as a patriotic contribution to defense,' the Chairman of the Board said.

The stockholder quoted from an Associated Press story which said that the Pentagon had decided not to announce the development of the flechette shell, possibly because of 'the ugly nature of the weapon.' He was told: 'We make a lot of mean weapons, classified and unclassified, and we don't want to talk about them.'

The manufacture of antipersonnel weapons was not the sort of thing that would help FMC's public image. A better image was given by a company magazine, *FMC Progress*. FMC's honorary chairman, John D. Crummey, had been honored at a 'community recognition dinner' sponsored by the First Methodist Church of San Jose, the magazine reported, and the California state legislature had passed a resolution applauding Mr Crummey's 'worldwide philanthropic efforts,' and commending Mr and Mrs Crummey for 'substantial interest in character building agencies such as the YMCA, YWCA, Boy Scouts and the Salvation Army.'

FMC was contributing to America's well-being, according to an ad in another magazine. While FMC flechettes were 'shredding' Vietcong and nailing them to trees, the company ran an ad showing a man in pyjamas relaxing in front of a TV with a bag of corn chips in his lap. 'We're helping satisfy millions of munchers,' FMC proclaimed. 'There are roughly 194 million munchers in the United States. Last count. Every day they consume hundreds of thousands of dollars' worth of fresh, flavorful products. Potato chips, corn chips, pretzels, nuts. You name it and munchers devour it.' FMC was helping by providing packaging machinery.

The notion put forth by the FMC chairman that a company would make weapons simply as 'a patriotic contribution to defense' was belied by the vigor with which weapons makers competed for government contracts and put their engineers' brains to work designing new weapons with a good sales potential. FMC had lucrative contracts to make poisonous nerve gas, armored personnel carriers, and naval gun mounts, and the company had helped develop a supersonic firebomb and a chemical dispenser to poison crops in military operations. These facts could be found in government documents and military magazines, but the company saw no need to keep the public informed.

A large company is a complex and multifaceted object; no one person looking from outside can see all the facets. Some people can usefully be told of a company's antipersonnel work, but they are a specialized lot. The ads in defense industry publications such as *Ordnance* showed a world strange and wondrous to ordinary mortals.

Antipersonnel, antiarmor, antimateriel: Looking for a munition to defeat a target?[10]

Firebombs must be ignited. The igniter prototype for one Navy bomb was a difficult-to-weld assembly. Versions made of steel and then aluminum did not meet reliability requirements. Edsel's suggestion: Replace them with an aluminum impact extrusion that is more reliable. Costs less, too. (Advertisement by the Aluminum Company of America citing the achievement of one of its engineers, Edsel Johnson)[11]

BANG! BANG! You're *alive*! – Little boys will always play guns. Rules will change only when the world grows up … in a peace for all time, all people. To bring that peace closer, General Time's Ordnance Group works to keep today's peacemakers stronger. And tomorrow, our complete capability will work to make the good life even better. A better time with *The Big Time*. (Ad for General Time Corporation, maker of fuzes for flechette-filled Beehive shells)[12]

Ordnance Engineers. FMC, one of the top 100, is building for the future near San Francisco. – Ordnance is a big thing with us. It has been in the past and will continue to be in the decades to come. Contact us in confidence if you want the chance to prove yourself in an environment dedicated to product superiority.[13]

Had the antiwar movement accepted that these companies' robust statements were simply expressions of a 'patriotic contribution to defense,' it should have left the companies in peace and concentrated its efforts on the policy-makers in Washington. But a few hours' research in the business section of any sizeable public library was enough to show that the corporate conglomerates also had good connections in places of influence. Here was another facet.

The huge General Tire and Rubber Company, best known for its automobile tires, was one such conglomerate. Its subsidiary, Aerojet-General, had helped develop antipersonnel mines and cluster bomb dispensers, and an Aerojet-General subsidiary made components for 'guava' bomblets and 2.75-inch rocket warheads. General Tire's RKO chain of TV and radio stations could be depended on to present the Vietnam war to the public in a suitably patriotic manner. One of the three brothers at the head of General Tire was the editor of *The Pope Speaks*, a quarterly journal of papal documents which reprinted the Holy Father's declarations on subjects such as 'The Ideal of Christian Businessman' and 'Aid For Underdeveloped Countries' while omitting most of his statements on the Vietnam war.

Avco Corporation, I knew from my research, had worked for the military on 'Services and Materials for an Investigation of Improved Antipersonnel Kill Mechanisms,' and had done a 'Feasibility Study of a Repeating Antipersonnel Mine.' In response to a request to supply information for my book, Avco kindly put together a list of its US Air Force contracts for 'Fire Bomblet,' 'Jungle Canopy Bomb Fuze,' 'Napalm Bomb Igniter,' 'Grape Munition,' and 'Fragmentation Wrap.' The company had done a study of 'an artillery delivered, random detonating antipersonnel mine' and a project on 'Antipersonnel Warheads' whose objectives were 'to develop better and less costly methods of fabricating small antipersonnel warheads, to improve warhead fragmenting characteristics, to evaluate new materials, and to minimize the number of components in a warhead.' It had done 'lethality studies and tests' in which 'Special emphasis has been given to combined effects munitions (fragmentation and incendiary) to optimize the lethality of the munition. This work has been applied to the design of warheads for mines, projectiles and bomblets.' All of this would have been news to a person who listened to one of Avco's radio stations or went into an Avco finance office to ask for a home loan.

Scovill Manufacturing Company was a long-established New England firm making such items as paper clips and zippers. The *Wall Street Journal* reported on 25 October 1966 that Scovill had received an Army contract for $4,171,813 for 'metal parts for cluster bombs'; this was one of a series of 'guava' bomblet contracts awarded to Scovill. The company's dynamic new president, Yale graduate Malcolm Baldridge (later US Secretary of Commerce), was praised in *Forbes* magazine in 1965 for his 'ruthlessness' in firing three hundred staff and shifting operations to the southern United States, where labor was cheaper. While 'guavas' rained on North Vietnam, Scovill placed an ad in the *New York Times* Sunday magazine (11 June 1967) showing three cool young ladies in bathing suits:

> *Get with the joiners.* Joiners that show up in swingiest swimsuits. Flip little zippers known as Nylaire. Willowy zippers that drape and shape to a fabric. Their teeth won't bite because they come covered up – inside and out. And special locking action means stay-up without slip-up. A Nylaire zipper has top-to-bottom stamina. Yet you barely know it's there. In a swimsuit it's the joiner with the gentle touch. And for a zipper, what could be hipper?

Different antipersonnel weapons makers varied in the style of their public image and in their techniques for reacting to antiwar protests. One of the kindliest was Honeywell Inc. of Minneapolis, Minnesota.

A Company with Human Feelings

Minnesota, a dynamic and progressive state, the 'Land of a Thousand Lakes.' The capital, St Paul, an old town of railroads and breweries on the banks of the great Mississippi; its twin city, Minneapolis, cultural center and home of the university. A great place to live; and Honeywell of Minneapolis contributed to the quality of life with its thermostats for the control of central heating, so welcome in cold Minnesota winters.

'The Washington scene is fascinating,' said US Senator Walter Mondale. 'But, believe me, the best place to be a politician is Minnesota. This is a vast and exciting physical and political environment. And the things that count here are lakes and rivers and people.'

'There's a really great thing about Minnesotans,' said Hubert H. Humphrey, Minnesota's other Senator, a man who, as Lyndon B. Johnson's Vice-President, had been one of the main apologists for the Vietnam war. 'If you try to maintain the kind of honesty and morality they stand for – and it's pretty rigid – they'll forgive any crazy ideas you have. No matter how liberal. Lots of the great liberal ideas of this nation came from Minnesotans.'[14] And Honeywell, with its employment program for disadvantaged Indians and black people, had earned a reputation as a liberal and respected citizen of the community.

Geography and water imposed on the state 'an image that has as much truth as poetry,' the *National Geographic* reported. Minnesota's way of life seemed 'permanently positioned in the middle of the American dream ... the vision that brought immigrants to our shores, that bent men to the plow, that promised in return for honest labor a life of some plenty, some peace, and some dignity. A life in which people respect their community, and each man repays something of what he thinks he owes to it. A life formed by a closeness to nature.'[15]

Honest labor and a vision of a just reward had made Honeywell a leading company of Minnesota. Now it was threatened by a handful of activists who felt they owed to all humanity a respect for life and the preservation of nature. Moved by the 'horrifying realization' (as one of them later wrote) that antipersonnel cluster bombs were being produced in Minneapolis, they tried, in the vibrant political environment of Minnesota, 'to build a political power base which could force Honeywell directors to cease all war production and convert to production of creative products.'[16] And Honeywell, hurt by the accusations of its critics, claimed a common humanity with them:

> Honeywell management shares the feelings of those who would like to see the Vietnam war ended [the company stated in a press release in April 1969]. We vigorously support the efforts the government is making to find a solution to the complex problems that surround this conflict. Until such solutions are found we believe the government has an obligation to provide our armed forces engaged in the conflict with the equipment they need to maintain a strong military posture. As a technologically-based company we have the capability to provide a variety of equipment as a supplier to the defense department. We believe it is entirely appropriate and correct to do so as a matter of good citizenship. For those who do not share our views about what a company should do in the support of its democratically chosen government we endorse their right to legal and peaceful protest.[17]

As a supplier to the Defense Department, Honeywell had worked hard to identify and develop materiel that would enable the nation's armed forces to engage enemy personnel. A Honeywell study for the Tactical Air Command (cited in a 1963 Honeywell proposal to the Army) had shown that fragmentation cluster bombs, directed against targets on the ground, 'would provide an effective system for defeating area targets.' Another study (cited in the same proposal) had identified the 'employment parameters' that would yield 'maximum effectiveness' in an attack using a leaflet bomb filled with grenades – something like a Sadeye filled with 'guavas.' In an internal report in 1963, a Honeywell mathematician had calculated the effectiveness of a weapon system delivering an elliptical pattern of rockets against 'personnel targets.' Another, in 1964, wrote a report explaining 'methods used in calculating the effectiveness of some antipersonnel weapon systems.' This report introduced the notion of 'expected fraction of casualties,' defined as 'the average fraction of troops within a given target area that are expected to be incapacitated in a single event,' as a measure of the effectiveness of antipersonnel bomblets against 'troops randomly distributed within the targets.'

One of Honeywell's outstanding product lines was military fuzes. Honeywell 'entered the fuzing business in the early 1950s,' the company reminded the Army in a 1968 proposal, 'with contracts to develop bomblet impact fuzes and to produce the M517 81mm. mortar proximity fuze.' Thanks to Honeywell's expertise in automation, the BLU-26 ('guava' bomblet) impact fuze was being produced with only eight-tenths of a minute's total direct labor, and the delay fuze, which caused the bomblets to explode at random moments after arming, had been cut in price from $3.13 to $1.24. 'Dozens of fuzes of virtually all types' had been developed at Honeywell, the company told the Army, and Honeywell had produced 'over 200,000,000 fuzes. We are presently producing fuzes at the rate of about 7,000,000 per month.' Indeed:

> Honeywell's Ordnance Division has been involved in munition R&D [research and development] and production for many years, and has an excellent record of carrying these munitions and munition components through development into production. In fact, we feel that during the past several years *we have emerged as the country's leading developer and supplier of munitions.* (emphasis added)

This was the corporation that a few activists in Minnesota had decided to take on. They organized meetings, built up a membership, and tried to learn more about the company. One member of the project, posing as a student, went to the Honeywell office and was given an armful of press releases. Another looked into the company's connections with the University of Minnesota, which owned Honeywell shares. Another got a job in a Honeywell weapons plant.

From various sources, the Honeywell Project composed its basic leaflet, wherein they declared that the company was:

> involved in genocide. Honeywell Inc., one of the top 20 US prime defense contractors, with defense sales of 478 million dollars annually, is producer of the deadly antipersonnel fragmentation bombs which have been responsible for much of the civilian casualties in the Vietnam War.

Reports from both North and South Vietnam indicate that villagers, mostly women and children, are being exterminated by the use of this immoral weapon.... Genocide is the same wherever it occurs. Honeywell is directly involved in the genocide in Vietnam because it produces these inhuman weapons.

'Genocide is the same wherever it occurs': this was not the language of the Honeywell management, who shared the feelings of those who wished the war ended. The bombing of Vietnam had, however, been good for Honeywell's weapons business. 'Continued depletion of weapon stockpiles in Southeast Asia,' the company told stockholders in its annual report distributed in 1968, 'hastened production of current munitions and conversion of several of our engineering development programs into full-scale production.' A cessation of hostilities in Southeast Asia would mean a drop in requirements for some munitions, but other, 'new systems' would be needed for Air Force and Navy stockpiles.

Honeywell spoke to its stockholders in phrases of prosperity and careful planning, and its posture, when it was confronted by the protestors, was one of dignity and fair-mindedness. Good citizens serving a democratically chosen government, Honeywell could afford to be calm. Through a connection with an arm of that government, the Federal Bureau of Investigation, which had infiltrated the Project with informers, Honeywell managers must have known their adversaries' every move in advance. This side of the story, however, emerged only later.[18]

In April 1969, a week before the annual stockholders' meeting, at which a demonstration was planned, three Project members managed to secure an interview with Honeywell chairman James H. Binger and his vice-president for personnel and labor relations. Marv Davidov, Honeywell Project coordinator, outlined the nature of the project (as he later wrote in a report to Project members and friends), and spoke of their concern.

I said, 'These bombs have been used against people in North Vietnam since 1965.'
    Binger said, 'And the South, too.' (No arrogance in his statement.)
    I asked if he would like to see photos of bomb damage to children. He said, 'No, I've already seen many of them.' ...
    The two moments when both men exhibited a gut reaction occurred when I said that we plan at some future time civil disobedience at the homes, country clubs, businesses and churches of decision-makers.
    Binger asked what that meant. I merely defined civil disobedience.
    I said that we will connect with the Japanese, French, German, English, Italian and Australian peace movements to focus on Honeywell's overseas operations. Binger said, 'Oh!' – and moved in his chair. *Obviously*, we must do something *here*.

At the stockholders' meeting, a representative of the Honeywell Project presented 'the case of the People vs. the Honeywell Corporation of America.' Citing Nuremberg principles on the responsibility of accomplices to crimes against civilians, he said: 'The case for the prosecution is straightforward. Our argument is that it is illegal, immoral and inhuman for Honeywell to manufacture armaments for the mass destruction of civilian poor. In addition, we argue that Honeywell's mass production of weaponry constitutes a direct attack on poor and working people in this country and throughout the world.'

James H. Binger replied: 'You have been very eloquent. I know you've covered a number of matters of grave concern to our management and our stockholders. This does not mean that we arrive at the same conclusions. I think this is not a place where rebuttal is required or desirable. I think each of us has his thoughts about the important, serious problems that you have enumerated. I thank you again.'[19]

Honeywell's annual report distributed in 1969 said that aerospace and defense sales had risen 45 per cent over the previous year. The Ordnance Division had 'increased production of equipment needed in Southeast Asia,' and was pursuing 'a number of important research and development programs' with the 'common objective of providing greater tactical air strike effectiveness and flexibility in support of our ground combat forces.' And a Honeywell engineer suggested in an interoffice memo of 1969 that 'spin angular deceleration' should be explored as an 'impact signature' which could be used in fuze designs. 'It may be in Honeywell's interest to consider a major expansion into this area,' he wrote. 'If not, we should try to encourage some agency of the government to fill this gap.'

Four months after the stockholders' meeting, parishioners arriving for the Sunday service at James Binger's church were greeted by Honeywell Project members holding photos of 'guava' bomb victims, and given a leaflet whose imagery had something in common with the 'hypnotic techniques' of Redwood City protestor Dr Oliver Henderson:

Here at St. Martin's-by-the-Lake you are participating this morning in the familiar ritual during which, each Sunday, many of us take time to put our daily lives in perspective. The rich and orderly service helps us to celebrate life and its blessings and to remind ourselves once again of our obligations as Christians.

In Vietnam many churches as well as schools and hospitals stand in ruins. The shadow of these ruins falls far. Some of you may have noticed it dulling the Sunday morning atmosphere here at St. Martin's, casting its pall over the bright flowers and altar hangings, lending an ominous note to the sacred music.

James Binger, Chairman of the Board at Honeywell, belongs to St. Martin's and helps support it. Since 1965, Honeywell has contracted to manufacture an illegal and barbaric weapon used extensively against the civilian populations both in North and South Vietnam. [The leaflet continued with a description of cluster bombs and the assertion that their use was illegal under international law.]

The minister, who had been told of the demonstration beforehand, said in a sermon that he had once been a pacifist but could no longer accept absolute truths. James H. Binger told a Project representative: 'You have every right to express your point of view and you are certainly doing that.'

The 1970 annual meeting marked the climax of Honeywell Project activities. The Project had grown, and its message had spread afar. There were demonstrations at Honeywell sales offices across the country, and actions in France, Sweden, Denmark, and Great Britain.

In Minneapolis, hundreds of people arrived at the meeting bringing shares of stock or proxies entitling them to admission. Several hundred got inside, but hundreds more were refused entry. Those inside protested, but Binger said that adequate opportunity had been given to all stockholders and proxy holders to participate in the meeting. Several people by a window of the meeting room cried that police with gas masks were using tear gas and advancing on the thousand and more demonstrators outside. This provoked many demands that the police be called off on the part of the protestors inside (described in the *New York Times* as 'young persons in hippie clothes and war paint').

The meeting was in a turmoil. James H. Binger told the protestors: 'By your disorderly conduct you have forfeited your right to an opportunity during the meeting when you can present your points of view and make your arguments in an orderly way.' He declared the management's slate of directors elected by management-held proxies representing 87.7 per cent of the stock, and declared the meeting adjourned after only fourteen minutes. Stewart Meacham, an official of the American Friends Service Committee, the service arm of the Religious Society of Friends (Quakers), who attended the meeting, wrote at the end of a long report:

I was saddened somewhat by the feeling that I had that the passion and the deep desire of these young people to see a more hopeful future and a more decent society is not finding expression through ways that can really lead to the world they yearn for and are ready to run great risks for. At the same time there is no question but that many of them are completely committed to achieving a society that will not be run by large bureaucratic structures which assign people dehumanizing roles and order them about. The ease with which the company turned aside this challenge on April 28 and the coldness with which it was willing to do it heightens one's sense of admiration for the young people on the one hand and deepens one's despair on the other ... I ... came away feeling less hopeful than I at times have felt about whether the beautiful life-affirming spirit of the youth culture can survive and triumph or whether it will become embittered, frustrated and unable to find deep enough soil in our society for the roots it needs to be sinking in these troubled days.[20]

Two days after the annual meeting, the neutral land of Cambodia was invaded by American forces armed with Honeywell munitions. This happened even though Honeywell 'share[d] the feelings of those who would like to see the Vietnam war ended' and 'vigorously' supported the government's efforts to resolve the conflict – but then, it was in order to end that conflict, and to get at the enemy facilities which Junction City and similar operations had failed to destroy, that America crossed the Cambodian border and plunged a peaceful country into the carnage and devastation that Vietnam and Laos had already seen.

Within the United States, the invasion touched off the most acute political crisis of the war. Hundreds of universities closed for the rest of the spring because of the unrest. But in Minneapolis, the Honeywell Project was in trouble. After the excitement and frustration of the annual meeting, it was hard to say what to do next.

In 1971 the group that confronted Honeywell at its annual meeting was the Council for Corporate Review, an offshoot of the Honeywell Project. As its name suggested, the politics of the Council were milder than those of the Project. Where the Project had talked of building worker and community control, the Council wanted to change the company from within. 'I'm finding out how possible it is to change a corporation from the inside,' Charles A. Pillsbury, a director of the Council and young member of one of Minneapolis's leading industrial families, had told a reporter in 1970. 'I might learn, at the end of this, that I'm wasting my time.'

For the Honeywell Project, as Marv Davidov later told me, the annual meeting was 'a theater at which we could present our program.' For the Council, it was an opportunity to enter into the corporation's decision-making process. The Council drew up proposals for corporate reform and submitted them as stockholders' resolutions; resolutions on war production and on Honeywell's South African business were rejected as illegal by the company management.

At the annual meeting, after nearly three hours of debate, Charles Pillsbury, upset, called James Binger (with whom his mother played tennis) 'the Krupp of Minneapolis,' and asked him: 'How does it feel to be a war criminal?' Binger replied that he found those remarks

'personally disagreeable,' and said: 'Mr. Pillsbury, I ask you to stop this.'
The best received of the Council's three proposed resolutions got seven-
tenths of one per cent of the stockholders' votes.[21]

On American Independence Day, 1971, anonymous individuals
strewed the Woodhill Country Club golf course with mutilated dolls
stained with Chinese red paint, and planted white wooden crosses on
the fairways. An airplane flew over the next day and bombarded the
course with weighted balloons carrying the message: 'This is a Honeywell
antipersonnel fragmentation bomb, you're dead.'

> *Achtung!* [said the leaflet which was left with the dolls, and it gave the names
> of James Binger and other Honeywell 'war criminals' who belonged to the
> club.]
>
> These executives and others like them enjoy an opulent life style. We have
> left some reminders of the price some people pay for this luxury...
>
> It hasn't been divinely ordained that some people should play golf and sip
> cocktails while other people are murdered to support them. We could have
> defoliated your greens, napalmed your fairways, and fragged your veranda.
> Enjoy yourselves while you can.
>
> Fuck You, The Viet Cong

In 1972 the Honeywell Project held a 'Corporate War Crimes Investigation.' Denis Brasket, dissident Honeywell engineer, gave an account
of his futile attempts to discuss the morality of weapons work with his
colleagues.[22] Danny T. Notley, a Vietnam veteran who said he had been
ordered to fire a 40mm shot-filled cartridge into a group of people in
a Vietnamese village temporarily occupied by his Army squad,[23] testified
at the investigation. So did Fredric R. Branfman, who had interviewed
peasant survivors of the bombing of Laos (Chapter 4). Honeywell
management were invited, but did not attend.[24]

The next challenge came from an offshoot of the antiwar movement
that was in some ways a more formidable opponent than Honeywell's
previous challengers – Clergy and Laity Concerned, a national peace
group with strong Christian ties. When CALC published details of
Honeywell's antipersonnel weapons, Honeywell – who had sought every
opportunity to enhance the antipersonnel lethality of America's munitions – issued a new statement refuting the charges of immorality and
illegal corporate behavior:

> It is essential for the survival of our democracy that corporations carry out
> public policies declared by elected representatives of the people. It would be
> intolerable if every corporation in the land had its own domestic and foreign
> policies and attempted to use its power to implement them.
>
> An aspect of the current protest that is difficult to understand is the idea
> of laying at the doorstep of any corporation the responsibility for an un-

popular and tragic war. Honeywell has been on record for a number of years as wanting the war ended as quickly as possible. Honeywell people share the same human feelings and respect for life that our critics claim as their justification ...

It is apparent that the current wave of protest has as its principal emotional appeal the idea that certain weapons are more horrible than others and that those who make them are war criminals.

There are no nice weapons. It is one of the tragedies of humanity that weapons exist at all, but the stern lesson of history is that those who cherish freedom must be prepared to fight for freedom.

Antipersonnel weapons of the type most frequently criticized have the same purpose as hand grenades, conventional bombs or bullets. They were not developed for use against civilian population, as has been charged. They were developed for use against military targets and are effective because they cover a wider area than conventional explosives. To the best of our knowledge that is how they are used.

We flatly reject the charge that manufacturing these weapons makes Honeywell people war criminals. This is a slanderous charge that is utterly devoid of merit. It appears to us that few international lawyers agree with such charges and no court of the United States has entertained this argument.[25]

CALC's chapters across the country called for boycotts of Honeywell cameras and other products. Their appeals brought results. A New York hospital stopped buying Honeywell medical equipment in protest over antipersonnel weapons; a California architectural association asked its members not to specify Honeywell thermostats in their plans; and the city council of Ann Arbor, Michigan, drawing on principles established in World War II war crimes trials, voted not to buy Honeywell products for the city.

CALC was joined in the campaign by the American Friends Service Committee, another peace organization with a nationwide structure. On the day of the annual meeting in 1973, some two hundred campaigners from across the country showed up in Minneapolis. Their resolutions got less than 3 per cent of the vote.[26]

On the weekend after the annual meeting, there was an unexpected encounter between Chairman Binger and Honeywell Project organizer Marv Davidov at a showing of French films at the University of Minnesota. By Davidov's account, the two men had not changed their views:

Surprises come hard but a tall distinguished gray haired man in double breasted blue blazer and turtle neck with appropriate matching pants entered. Binger.

Naturally, I began a conversation. Putting my hand on his shoulder I said quietly, 'Say Jim, what are you doing here?' He looked up also surprised and said he was there to study French. 'As you know we have business activitiy in France. I'd like to learn to speak directly to our people over there.'

Davidov asked what he thought of the stockholders' meeting and Binger said that the CALC people had talked too much. The first film began and the two went to their seats in separate parts of the room.

> After the film in which one child had said to another, I don't like you because your father is a capitalist, Binger walked up. We went to the Newman Center across the street. He bought coffee from the machine for both of us and I was thinking of asking him to buy Newman for us. We sat at a table in the empty lunchroom. I began by trying to tell him it's our good fortune to meet in an informal situation like this. I had not met with him since before our action at the 1970 shareholders' meeting. I said that as a human, Jim Binger, he seemed not a bad sort although I'm not sure I would want him as a friend, but as Board Chairman of Honeywell he created in me among other emotions intense anger. We never got far in that direction because a friend of mine joined us…
>
> Binger mentioned he was getting many letters and referred directly to the exchange last year between he and Dr. Yarborough from Albert Einstein medical school in New York.… [Dr Yarborough had threatened to boycott Honeywell products.] Honeywell's answer in part is, thousands of man hours and millions of dollars in cancer research and you have not eradicated cancer and what right do you have as one Federal contractor to question the activity of another, Honeywell. Yarborough's answer was eloquent.
>
> Anyway, we said if decision making power were organized differently people would probably choose to eradicate cancer rather than Indochinese. At this point Binger got a little nervous and wanted to return to the French lesson.
>
> Ironically, the next French film was a film on cancer. It was a radical critique of the French medical establishment. The creation of a powerful medical technology benefits industry at the expense of the citizen and sends many to their premature death. The message comes to you profoundly in the cinematic description of a relationship between a mother dying of cancer and her son. Against the wishes of medical consultants the son tells his mother the nature of her illness and together they begin to resist it. She fights consciously and their honesty joins them as never before.
>
> At intermission Binger came up and we asked him what he thought of the film. His answer was, 'I will have to go up closer to the sound during the next film.' The French lesson prevails.
>
> I am more convinced than ever before that Binger sees reality from his class and power position just as we all see reality from the vision of our politics.

After the 1973 shareholders' meeting, the AFSC and CALC went on to other projects involving militarism, corporate power, and the changing face of the Indochina war. In Vietnam, following the Paris Peace Agreement of 1973, US ground forces were being withdrawn, and the US role was concentrated on bombardment and support for the anticommunist forces.

In 1975 the North Vietnamese army swept through South Vietnam. The US Embassy and the remaining US forces were hastily evacuated. In Cambodia, Pnomh Penh was overrun by the Khmer Rouge, ushering in a four-year regime of one of the most murderous sets of rulers in modern history. Laos, too, was now under communist rule. Indochina was left destroyed, impoverished, and littered with unexploded bomblets.

In August 1975, Honeywell was awarded a $1,100,312 US Army contract for bomblet delay fuzes. In November, the company received a $29,059,872 contract to replenish stocks of Rockeyes which had been used against North Vietnam. In April 1976 Honeywell won a $69,428 contract to 'conceptually define an antiarmor cluster munition' and a $315,000 contract for bomblet-filled warheads for the Lance surface-to-surface missile.

'Sales of both ordnance and aircraft-related products' maintained 'the high levels' achieved in the previous year, Honeywell told the stockholders in its annual report distributed in 1976. The war was over, but the new antipersonnel weapons were now well established, and there was plenty of business to be done.

Notes

1. Fieser *et al.*, 1946.
2. W. Karig, M.W. Cagle, and F.A. Manson, *Battle Report: The War in Korea* (New York, Rinehart, 1952); cited in SIPRI, 1972, p. 82.
3. US Army field manual FM 20-33, *Ground Flame Warfare*; cited in SIPRI, 1972, pp. 79–80.
4. UN Secretary-General, 1973, paragraph 105.
5. Jack McGuire, 'Napalm Sunday,' *Win* magazine, 7 April 1967, p. 2.
6. Mike Truman, 'Dow Run Out of Town,' *New Left Notes*, 1 May 1967. SDS involvement in the anti-Dow protests is described in Sale, 1973.
7. 'Fortunes Cookieless,' *Win*, 12 May 1967, p. 13.
8. FMC stood for Food Machinery and Chemicals.
9. Two of them were the Associated Press and United Press International stories on the use of flechette-filled artillery rounds in Vietnam, cited above in Chapter 3.
10. Ad in *Ordnance*, May–June 1966.
11. *Ordnance*, November–December 1966.
12. *Ordnance*, May–June 1970.
13. Ad in *Ordnance*, March–April 1972.
14. David S. Boyer, 'Minnesota, Where Water Is the Magic Word,' *National Geographic*, vol. 149, no. 2 (February 1976), p. 204.
15. *Ibid.*, p. 202.
16. Honeywell Project coordinator Marv Davidov, quoted in 'An Example of Action Research on the Military Industrial Complex: The Honeywell Project,' in Kanegis *et al.*, 1970, pp. 73, 79.

17. Press release issued on 28 April 1969, one day before the annual stock-holders' meeting, as quoted in Kanegis *et al.*, 1970, p. 85.

18. The infiltration of the Honeywell Project was disclosed by a US Senate select committee in 1976. Citing memoranda of April 1970 between the FBI field office in Minneapolis and FBI headquarters in Washington, the committee described the infiltration of the Honeywell Project:.

> An illustrative example of attacks on speaking concerns the plans of a dissi-dent stockholders' group to protest a large corporation's war production at the annual stockholders meeting. The [FBI] field office was authorized to furnish information about the group's plans (obtained from paid informants in the group) to a confidential source in the company's management. The Bureau's purpose was not only to 'circumvent efforts to disrupt the corporate meeting,' but also to prevent any attempt to 'obtain publicity or embarrass' corporate officials.

Commenting on this and other activities of the FBI's COINTELPRO project, the Senate committee concluded that the FBI was 'squarely attacking' the exer-cise of the constitutionally protected rights of freedom of speech and association (US Senate Select Committee to Study Government Operations with respect to Intelligence Activities; final report; *Supplementary Detailed Staff Reports on Intelligence Activities and the Rights of Americans*; book 3; US Senate report No. 94-755; Wash-ington, 1976, p. 28).

19. Kanegis *et al.*, 1970, pp. 83–7; Hallock Seymour, 'Honeywell Is Urged to End Arms Output,' Minneapolis *Star*, 30 April 1969.

20. Stewart Meacham, 'A Report on the Honeywell Stockholders Meeting April 28, 1970'; reprinted by the Council for Corporate Review.

21. Thomas R. Linden, 'War Foe Plans Proxy Fight to End Honeywell's Arms Output,' *Los Angeles Times*, 4 February 1970; Richard Gibson, 'Peaceful Dissent-ers Try, Fail to Change Honeywell Policies,' Minneapolis *Star*, 11 May 1971.

22. 'I said to some of the engineers, I said, "Look. Let us say that the Defense Department comes down next week with a request for a proposal to design a rack. And let's say they specify a 100-pound rack, a rack designed to take hundred-pound bodies or smaller." (This would clearly be a rack to be used for interrogation purposes of children by the intelligence agencies.)

'I said, "Let us suppose for instance that this comes down – you'll all sit down and start designing a rack. One of you will order chimpanzees to use for a test program, because you can get them for about 20 dollars each, to test this rack. Others of you will do the stress analysis on the rack and none of you will think about – 'What is it that I'm doing? I'm designing a rack to dismember children.'"

'And as I told this story, they all waited for the punchline. Of course, I didn't have a punchline. But they all waited, and they said, "Well, what's your point, now, get to it," you know.

'So that was a rather fruitless endeavor. There wasn't much that could be said to people whose minds are closed' (Denis Brasket, testimony at the Corporate War Crimes Investigation, 1972).

23. In 1971 Notley had described the incident at the International Commission of Enquiry into United States Crimes in Indochina in Oslo (Browning and Forman, eds., 1972, pp. 169–75).

24. 'Corporate War Crimes Investigation,' Honeywell Project leaflet, 1972.

25. 'Honeywell Responds to War Production Critics,' Honeywell press release, 18 April 1972.

26. Molly Babize, 'The Honeywell Campaign,' *Spark*, vol. 4, no. 1, Spring 1974 (published by the Committee for Social Responsibility in Engineering, New York); 'The Honeywell Campaign,' in *Corporate Action Guide*, published by the Corporate Action Project, Washington, 1974.

CHAPTER 6

BANNING ANTIPERSONNEL WEAPONS THROUGH INTERNATIONAL LAW

Scarcely a decade after a host of new antipersonnel weapons began being tried out on the testing fields of Vietnam, a conference of diplomats, military officers, and doctors met in Switzerland to consider banning or restricting their use. The Conference of Government Experts on Weapons that May Cause Unnecessary Suffering or Have Indiscriminate Effects opened in Lucerne in September 1974 under the auspices of the International Committee of the Red Cross (ICRC), the Swiss-based organization which works for the application and development of the international laws that regulate the conduct of armed conflict, known as 'international humanitarian law.'[1]

The impulse for the conference came from Sweden. Inspired by public outrage in its own country over the Vietnam war, and in keeping with Sweden's long interest in disarmament, the government first raised the issue in 1971 at a conference of government experts organized by the ICRC on developing the laws of war. To obtain the necessary technical background, the government convened a group of Swedish military and medical experts to study the effects of recently developed weapons from the point of view of international law. Its report, issued in 1973, offered language for a series of possible antipersonnel weapons bans.[2]

Prompted by a proposal from Sweden and eighteen other governments, the ICRC in 1973 convened a 'working group' of official experts from different countries to explore possible bans or restrictions on antipersonnel weapons, but the importance of this group's findings was diminished by the refusal of the United States to participate. The working group's report none the less served to keep the issue alive. When the Conference of Government Experts (a title denoting something more exalted than a mere 'working group' of 'experts') opened in Lucerne in 1974, the Americans were there in force.[3]

Lucerne, 1974: Taming the Rash Swedes

For Lucerne, it was a big event. This serene old town on the side of a breathtakingly beautiful mountain-rimmed lake attracted its share of tourists, but it was the first time in memory that an international governmental conference had been held there instead of in the usual Geneva site. There were banners welcoming the conference, and the city buses had signs announcing that it was taking place. But at the conference itself, held in a hall slightly outside the town, the sense of isolation was complete, and the outside world could hardly know what was happening there.

The United States was represented by a weapons systems analyst from Aberdeen Proving Ground, two military surgeons, field officers, and international affairs specialists from the Defense and State Departments. They sat on the left of the room, near their colleagues from the UK and other NATO countries. On the right were North and South Vietnam, not speaking to each other, and several Soviet experts 'sitting with their big ears flapping,' as one Western delegate remarked in private. At the back of the room were observers from the Stockholm International Peace Research Institute (SIPRI) and the group I represented, the Friends World Committee for Consultation, an international organization of the Religious Society of Friends (Quakers), long known for their opposition to war. Altogether forty-nine countries were represented, as well as six national liberation movements, several of which have since come to power. Laos and Cambodia, two countries which had suffered immensely from antipersonnel weapons, were not there, and the South Vietnamese opposition force, by then known as the Provisional Revolutionary Government of South Vietnam, which also had much experience of the weapons, was excluded from the conference as a result of US pressure.

The conference had before it a proposal from Sweden and six other countries (Egypt, Mexico, Norway, Sudan, Switzerland, and Yugoslavia) which, if adopted, would have banned many of the most important antipersonnel weapons used in Vietnam. The language was forthright, and the categories of weapons covered were comprehensive:

- 'Cluster warheads with bomblets which act through the ejection of a great number of small calibered fragments or pellets are prohibited for use.'

- 'Weapons which act through the release of a number of projectiles in the form of flechettes, needles and similar, are prohibited for use.'

- 'Projectiles of small caliber weapons may not be so designed or have such velocity that they are apt to deform or tumble on or following entry into a human body or to create shock waves which damage tissue outside their trajectories or to produce secondary projectiles.'

- 'Antipersonnel land mines must not be laid by aircraft.'
- 'Incendiary weapons shall be prohibited for use...'[4]

The grounds for banning these weapons under the existing doctrine of the laws of war were that each of them was either *cruel* (causing 'unnecesary suffering' or 'superfluous injury,' in the accepted phrases) or *indiscriminate* (such that civilians were likely to be hit if a military target was attacked). One of the means used at the conference to discredit the proposals was therefore to show that antipersonnel weapons are neither indiscriminate nor cruel.

Comparing an 'average,' 65-grain fragment from an old shell with an 'average,' 1.5-grain fragment from an 'improved' munition, a US munitions expert told the conference that the old fragment would cause a worse wound because of its greater mass. The newer munition would have a greater tendency to inflict multiple wounds – the average person hit would be struck by 2.58 fragments as against 1.22 fragments from the old shell – but the person hit by the old shell would still be hurt more badly because the old shell fragments were so much larger.

> The question might well arise as to why these munitions are considered 'improvements' over the conventional variety, if lower levels of incapacitation are caused by them [he said]. The answer is that we consider them more effective because very basically, under the assumption of the uniform distribution of targets about the burst, the measure of effectiveness of a fragmenting munition is found by summing the 'probability of incapacitation' which was determined for each target. Thus, the fact that the improved munitions are judged to be more effective than the conventional weapons; and that for the targets hit, a lower average level of incapacitation is caused by the improved munitions; lead one to the conclusion that the improved weapons wound more targets.[5]

On flechettes, a US expert acknowledged that 'All flechettes tumble at some striking velocity'; and with one flechette, he said, it had been found that 'relatively quick tumbling occurs ... for striking velocities greater than 3,000 feet per second.' But 'Due to their great stability within the target, the wounding capability of flechettes at velocities where no tumbling occurs is significantly lower than that of either fragments or flechettes at striking velocities which result in tumbling'; and 'there is little difference between the wounding power of fragments and flechettes which tumble due to their high striking velocity.'

Which flechette was being compared to which fragment and how bad the wounds from that fragment were, the expert did not say; nor did he refer to the risk of multiple wounding from the thousands of flechettes in a Beehive or canister shell. He did not mention the fact that flechettes from the 2.75-inch rocket warhead introduced in Vietnam would indeed hit the body at more than the tumbling threshold of 3,000 feet per second (Chapter 3). Nor did he mention a US Air Force project in the late 1960s to speed up flechettes or fragments by expelling them with a propellant charge from the nose of an air-to-ground warhead, resulting in 'fragments highly lethal to personnel targets', according to the contractor's report.[6]

On napalm, an American expert presented information on some five incidents in which firebombs had been 'dropped inadvertently on friendly combat units in the field' (in the words of the conference report). Out of 53 personnel affected,

> Only four of them died. Out of the 45 burned in the two major incidents, only five men received greater than 10 per cent third-degree burns, even though they were right in the fireball. Of the 45 men, 44 had still been capable of performing their required military duties until evacuated. These findings refuted the argument, in the view of the expert relating them, that napalm was an all-or-nothing weapon.[7]

Antipersonnel cluster bombs also were not very harmful, to judge by the experts' statements. 'In the CBU flak suppression role, they drive crews from their weapons into shelters,' a member of the US delegation told the conference. 'The pellets don't have a strong penetration capability, so the crews are protected. So are civilians if they take cover, as they almost always do. The other choice would be general-purpose bombs which would result in increased casualties.'

'Do I understand the American expert to say that CBUs just drive people into shelters for a few moments?' asked a startled non-governmental expert.

'Yes, in many circumstances,' the American responded.

Along with showing that antipersonnel weapons were neither cruel nor indiscriminate, another tactic of the Americans and their NATO allies was to debunk the Swedes' figures. The Swedish study group report had estimated the area coverage of the CBU-24 cluster bomb as 300 by 900 meters, and this figure (without the bomb being mentioned by name) had been reproduced in the 1973 ICRC experts' report. Nonsense! cried the government experts at Lucerne. 'The size of the area is classified but it is only a fraction of that stated in the ICRC report,' a Dutch major said. It was not for him to reveal secrets about the new American weapon, but he could assure the conference that the Swedish figure was all wrong.

In a statement to the conference, I mentioned the hugest cluster bomb of all time: the Hayes dispenser, two of which are used to drop 25,488 'guava' bomblets or 77,040 M40 grenades from the belly of a B-52 bomber. A weapon of that scale can hardly help but be indiscriminate; but there was no discussion of this point by the government experts. (When I mentioned the Hayes dispenser again at the second ICRC government experts' conference in Lugano, a member of the US delegation told me he doubted such a weapon existed at all!)

The Swedish proposal to ban bullets which 'have such velocity' as to deform or tumble in the body had been based on an idea of Callender and French, dating from US wound ballistics research before World War II (Chapter 1). The Swedes had suggested that the devastating effects of cavitation or 'explosive' wounding began to appear as bullets stuck the body at velocities of 800 meters per second or more. This figure had found its way into the 1973 ICRC experts' report. The practical implications were enormous: a cutoff figure of 800 meters per second at a range of 100 meters would have meant banning the US M16 rifle while allowing the Soviet AK47, whose bullet was larger but traveled less fast.

At Lucerne various experts denounced the 800 meters per second figure; among them one of the Americans, who presented evidence that 'projectiles with velocities less than 800 meters per second produce significant cavitation effects' and that 'there is no discontinuous or quantum jump in the cavitation effects of projectiles as their striking velocity nears or exceeds the 800 meters per second limit.' The Americans had found that flechettes could tumble when striking the body above a certain velocity, as mentioned above, but they did not believe that there was a corresponding threshold for bullets, or at least that the threshold was at 800 meters per second.

Impressed by these denials, the Swedes softened their position. Pressing the point home, a British expert remarked that he was glad the 'mystical' figure of 800 meters per second had been dropped. He added: 'While welcoming this new approach, it does tend to leave the Swedish proposals rather in the position of a policeman who, having accused a motorist of exceeding the speed limit, is now unable to state what the speed limit, if any, might be.'

Pursuing the idea that the terrific wounding effect of the M16 might none the less be due to the high bullet velocity, a Swedish delegate quoted from three articles published between 1967 and 1969 by a US Army surgeon who had observed M16 wounds in Vietnam:

'The M16 rifle is a devastatingly effective combat weapon with tremendous wounding and killing power related to its high velocity and air transit characteristics.' (1967)

'In general the M16 with its high velocity of 3,250 feet per second has massive tissue destruction emphasizing the importance of velocity in the wounding power of a missile.' (1968)

'The importance of the wounding power of missiles has recently been emphasized with reference to the numerous agents utilized in the fighting in Vietnam. High velocity missiles are usually associated with extensive tissue injury. The M16 missile with its high velocity has created massive wounds previously not encountered from such a small bullet...' (1969)

The author of these articles was none other than a member of the US delegation, a military surgeon who had been at the conference earlier but had since flown home. To answer the Swedish use of his findings, the Americans flew him all the way back to Lucerne, where he gave a rambling statement, referring to his youth at the time and to the limitations of wartime statistics, without, however, explicitly retracting what he had written.

The Swedish proposals were being demolished without anything better being offered in their place. But what was saddest about the Lucerne conference was its failure to come to grips with one of the direst developments of the Vietnam war: the emergence of wide-area antipersonnel weapons.

'I have no doubt that if each person in this room were asked what constituted an area target and what the word "large" meant, we would get many different answers,' a British colonel told the conference. 'We in the artillery are more precise. A point target is a single target such as a tank, a vehicle or perhaps a bridge. An area target is a group of point targets which occupy an area on the ground, but not necessarily a very large area...

'In my experience application of artillery fire is a fine art. The modern tendency is to make it more scientific, more accurate and more discriminate ... artillerymen are usually reluctant to blaze off rounds unless targets are well defined.... Hence, surface-to-surface artillery used in the normal way is a discriminate system; it could be used in an indiscriminate way, but by its technical nature it is discriminate.'

Speaking in his 'personal capacity' as a government expert,[8] the British colonel of artillery was participating in a general assault on the concept of indiscriminate weapons. In pretending that artillery was normally used discriminately, he ignored the US practice of massive artillery fire in World War II, Korea, and Vietnam. By saying that artillery was discriminate by nature, he ignored the new forms of ammunition designed to give artillery shells a wider area coverage. The bomblet-filled Improved Conventional Munitions with their 'far-reaching improvements in firepower and tactical capabilities, the first real breakthrough in this area since World War II' were not mentioned by the British expert; nor was the US Area Denial Artillery Munition, nor anything similar that had been developed in Europe.

The British had a special interest in the conference because they, too, had a new cluster bomb, the BL 755. It dispensed what a Royal Air Force captain blandly referred to as 'a number of dual purpose sub-munitions' – in fact, quite a large number of bomblets consisting of a shaped charge surrounded by a coil of notched wire designed to break into approximately 2,000 fragments on explosion. The BL 755, the captain told the conference, was 'designed to replace high explosive (HE) bombs in attacks on armored and soft-skinned vehicles, parked aircraft, antiaircraft batteries, radar installations, small ships and head-quarters or maintenance areas.' (In the original version of his statement, the list of targets included 'troop concentrations,' but this phrase had been crossed out by hand.)

'The method of ejection of these bomblets is designed to create an even distribution over a small area on the ground,' the captain continued. 'This area, less than one hectare, will take into account the movement of the target (e.g. a tank) during the bomb's time of fall and the errors in delivery resulting from ballistic disturbance at weapon release. With modern weapons aiming systems, the delivery errors to be expected are of the order of 30–60 meters and it is significant to remember that a 500-kilogram [high explosive] bomb must fall within 10–15 meters of a tank even to stop it, let alone to destroy it.

'The implication for this conference is that a far greater weight of HE must be delivered into an area to achieve the same probability of destroying tanks when using blast bombs rather than BL 755.'

There was more to it than that, however. The real significance of what the captain was saying was that in order to destroy a *point* target (a tank), an *area* weapon was being used. And from the fact that the weapon disseminated antipersonnel bomblets throughout that area, it followed that personnel within the area had become part of the target, and would inevitably be part of it whether they were soldiers or civilians. The target itself had become enlarged as a consequence of the design of the weapon.

The alternative to a cluster bomb, the captain said, was to use several high explosive bombs; but from a humanitarian point of view, a better alternative to using an area weapon against a point target would be to improve the accuracy of delivery of a point weapon, a weapon which could destroy a tank without the wider side-effects of the BL 755.

The Lucerne conference might have felt itself under more pressure to move toward banning the new weapons if representatives of the countries where they had been used had said more about their terrible effects. But the delegations of those countries seemed reluctant to go into details – understandably, one does not tell one's adversary which blows are landing hardest.

From the socialist side, a North Vietnamese delegate cited cases, already known through North Vietnamese publicity, of a fisherman and a farmer who had been injured by flechettes. From the Western side, a South Vietnamese governmental expert denounced the enemy's home-made bamboo mine, which produced 'flechettes' of bamboo on explosion and said the enemy had also used a directional mine that projected 850 thin nails in a 45-degree angle.

An Egyptian expert said that 105mm Beehives and the 2.75-inch flechette-filled rocket had been used against his country in a recent war. (By whom and in what war he did not say, as one of the conference rules was that 'the Conference shall ... abstain from any discussion of a controversial or political nature.')

Despite the devastation which their citizens had suffered from cluster bombs and other antipersonnel weapons, the North Vietnamese were not very interested in working to have them banned under international law. 'A weapon used by the imperialist is an imperialist weapon,' their delegation head told me. 'In the hands of a liberation fighter, it is a sacred tool.'[9]

Some experts (according to the conference report) thought that 'because the effects of potential future weapons could have important humanitarian implications, it was necessary to keep a close watch in order to develop any prohibitions or limitations that might seem necessary before the weapon in question had become widely accepted.' Another expert, though, seemed unwilling to accept any limit on future weapons developments. In his view, 'if a nation was forced into war, its right to throw its ingenuity and technology into the balance could not seriously be questioned.'[10]

There was no meeting of the minds at Lucerne. Summing up the results, the president of the conference was able to say only that it had 'contributed to an increase in knowledge and understanding of the subject' and that a second conference could usefully be convened.[11]

Lugano, 1976: An Emerging Consensus

When the second Conference of Government Experts opened in Lugano in January 1976, there had been some significant changes. The Vietnam war was over. The North Vietnamese had won; they did not attend the conference. The United Kingdom was working for an agreement on the marking of minefields. The Swedes now had more co-sponsors for their proposals; these were still formally before the conference, but – curiously

– the Swedes themselves seemed to have lost interest in them, preferring to focus their attention on rifle bullets and the scientific questions raised in Lucerne about cavitation and the causes of bullet wounding.[12]

The Americans had some more data on napalm to present. Out of forty-eight soldiers accidentally burned by napalm in Vietnam in 1968–9, three-quarters 'had 20 per cent or less of the total body area burned,' they disclosed. Apart from those who died, a follow-up study had shown only one of the victims to have 'medical/mental problems' that were considered by the US Veterans Administration 'to be related to the firebomb accident.' (Twenty-one of the victims, though, complained of 'the sensitivity of the burned areas' to 'heat and cold.')

The Canadians also had some interesting data to offer. They had covered several dozen live goats with army blankets and dropped a napalm bomb on them. Two of the goats had slightly reddened skin as a result, and six had singed hairs: the blankets evidently gave considerable protection. The Canadians also tried some experiments using live human subjects. A burning blob of napalm on the bare skin became unbearable after one second, they found. But a single layer of cotton protected the skin against burning for six to seven seconds, and of the napalm blobs striking a person in a simulated direct hit, 69 per cent could be extinguished with the bare hands.

When the conference reached the topic of flechettes, the discussion was desultory. Fearing to see the Swedish initiative dropped, I tried to evoke the horror which such weapons can arouse among ordinary people.

> Mr. Chairman [I said], I think we must take into account what, for lack of a better term, I will call the 'public conscience.' Of course, no one can say exactly what it is; and, yet, it is a force to be reckoned with.
>
> In 1974, I left at the end of the Lucerne conference and on the train, I met a young Swiss couple, very much in love, who asked me what I was doing. By way of illustration, I pulled a flechette out of my pocket. The young man looked at it gravely; the young woman shrank back in her seat in horror. She didn't want to look at it; she understood what it was for.
>
> Some years ago, in one of my classes, some of my students asked me to describe my research on munitions development. I gave a long account of the various cluster bomb systems used to deliver incapacitating fragments on to personnel targets scattered over large areas. One of my students came up to me afterwards, rather depressed. 'I had no idea there were such things,' he said. 'I thought a bomb was a bomb.' He meant, something that goes off with a big bang and perhaps kills a few people. The concept of maximizing anti-personnel effect over a considerable area was a new one to him.
>
> Mr. Chairman, as we all live together in one world, perhaps it is a good thing if there are some common understandings regarding our conduct toward

our fellow human beings. Within a country, we have laws prohibiting murder and theft; and yet, a student of jurisprudence might agree that it is not so much the law, or the fear of punishment, as it is well-inculcated moral precepts that deter most people from committing those crimes. And the law itself is largely the embodiment of public morality, and grows out of it. Perhaps, then, it is a good thing that people shrink from flechettes and are horrified by cluster bombs, and that thousands and thousands of people protested the use of napalm in a recent armed conflict; perhaps these reactions can serve as a guide to the examination of munitions from a humanitarian point of view.

'As one who shares humanitarian concerns, I would welcome more information on the wounding effects of flechettes,' a British expert responded. 'Will a leather vest, for example, protect against flechettes?' He was following the Lucerne approach of debunking claims for weapons bans by suggesting that flechettes were really not so harmful after all.

As in Lucerne, the Western experts were ready with technical details to confound the uninitiated.

I ran into a member of the US delegation at a cocktail party. 'Why do you keep talking about SPIW?' he said, challenging me for having referred in a speech to that most benign of weapons, the needle gun. 'Have you seen flechette wounds?'

'No, have you?' I said.

He admitted that he hadn't. 'Have you asked Bo Rybeck about flechettes?' he wanted to know. (The Americans had been relaying to everyone the incautious disclosure by Dr Rybeck, one of the Swedish experts, that the flechette 'wounds' produced in Swedish ballistic tests had not been severe.)

I pointed out to him that the Swedish experiments went up to velocities of only about 600 meters per second – well below the velocities where tumbling might be expected to occur – and that they did not involve flechettes with points designed to curl or deform, like those which Irwin R. Barr had patented. That shut him up; but how many other delegates circulating in the corridors and cocktail parties of Lugano would have had the technical knowledge to spot the flaw in the American's aspersions?

In Lucerne, I had had the honor of being invited to lunch by a member of the military side of the US delegation; and he took malicious glee in the thought that the State Department would pay for the meal. He was furious, I could see. What was all this nonsense about flechettes? He had used them in Vietnam, and they were effective, no question about it. He had wanted to tell that to the conference, but his delegation head wouldn't let him. 'I'm my own man,' he told me. 'I can say what I want'; but his delegation had told him to keep quiet.

He bore no rancor toward the enemy: he was out to kill them, they were out to kill him – it was as simple as that. ('I wanted to get their ass' was the way he put it.) He would have enjoyed a friendly chat with the boys from the Provisional Revolutionary Government ('How many of you did I get?'), and he was sorry they had not been allowed to attend the conference. He had approached the North Vietnamese delegation, and he could not understand why they turned their back on this man, who had crossed the ocean to destroy their country.

As for the Swedes, they were the prize hypocrites, as far as he was concerned. For all their humanitarian talk, didn't they have a large military budget and plenty of men under arms? A ban on certain anti-personnel weapons would have suited them quite well. Their Foreign Ministry, in trying to secure prohibitions of cruel and indiscriminate weapons, was in his view only the 'tool' of some unnamed Swedish military interest.

I asked one Swedish diplomat to define Sweden's humanitarian foreign policy for me. 'Sweden's humanitarian outlook stems from a long tradition,' he said. 'It has a domestic side as well as a foreign one. Our prisons are more humane than in other countries. They are models of comfort. The prisoners have private rooms with TV. Their sweethearts can visit them, have intercourse. It is not necessary to starve a man to death sexually in order to rehabilitate him.' That was not the connection I had expected him to make; but I liked what he said a bit later in our talk: 'To be humane is to be rational.' Detente was 'in our interest' (and in the interest of world peace).

If there was an element of self-interest in Sweden's humanitarian foreign policy, what was the harm of that? Sweden might very well find it militarily advantageous that an invader was forbidden to use cluster bombs; whether or not this judgment was an element in the Swedish proposals (as some of the NATO delegates believed), a ban on cluster bombs would be a plus for humanity.

The Lugano conference was not without its lighter moments.

Proffering an article of mine on fragmentation weapons to an expert on chemical weapons, I said, 'I know it's not your cup of tea.' 'Do you mean T.E.A.?' quipped another expert. (Note: triethyl aluminum (TEA) was the incendiary agent being used in new American flame-throwing rockets. It creates a controlled fireball which burns so intensely that the heat is transferred to people nearby, scorching them even though they are not directly hit.)

'Let me diplomatically ask you to be militarily precise and return in twenty minutes from the coffee break,' said a colonel presiding over a military experts' working group on mines and booby traps.

'We are military men, mission-oriented, so let us decide on the mission and then get on with it, in the limited time available,' an Asian colonel smilingly declared at the start of another working group.

'Conferences like this should be banned on humanitarian grounds,' said a disconsolate Canadian expert, sitting in the bar of his hotel and sipping a beer.

A British proposal for the recording of minefields received considerable support, but there were doubts whether in this day and age it was reasonable to expect that a soldier would be capable of reading a map and recording the location of a mine on it. 'The soldier is not an intellectual,' a French expert explained.

In the interval between the two conferences, the Swedes and the Swiss had done some tests on the wounding effects of small-caliber bullets, and they presented their findings at Lugano. One day there appeared, in the glass display cases in the lobby of the conference center, blocks of pine-scented bath soap, cast in the shape of a woman's thigh, through which various rifle bullets had been shot.[13] The delegates could take their cups of coffee over to the display cases and examine the soap blocks, which clearly showed that certain bullets had left a narrow, through-and-through wound while others made a track that started small but blossomed where a mass of soap the size of a fist had been violently thrust aside as the bullet passed through.

In the conference sessions, many experts voiced caution about such tests (which have been done routinely by developers of military and hunting ammunition for many years). What was the best target material? Did the tests accurately reflect the key factors in wounding? How could anything be concluded when different tests appeared to give different results? One Asian diplomat became so confused that he wondered out loud how the military ever managed to design a weapon at all.

The soap blocks spoke for themselves on at least one basic point – some wounds were much worse than others. To make the point in a more dramatic way, and to show the non-military experts what a test looked like, the Swiss arranged a demonstration at an army testing ground in the Ticinese mountains outside Lugano. On a fine Thursday afternoon, three busloads of government experts set out from the conference center for their scientific and humanitarian investigation. As two buses lost their way, and one had trouble negotiating the hairpin turns and became stuck on a patch of ice, its front end staring down a precipice, there were many jokes about 'unnecessary suffering.'

In the tests, 'wounds' of various sizes were produced in soap-block thighs, ranging from a 7.62mm bullet wound (through-and-through) to a 5.56mm wound (gaping and extensive). Some of the 'experts,' though, had to be told why different rifles and different ammunition rounds were being used in the tests.

Back at the conference, as one expert droned on with his speech, a handwritten note was passed around the American delegation: 'High velocity mouth, small caliber brain.'

Despite the cynicism, by the end of the Lugano conference agreement seemed to be emerging on three proposals. One, by Mexico and Switzerland, was to ban the use of weapons whose main effect was to injure by fragments undetectable by the usual medical methods, such as X-rays. The second, by France, the Netherlands, and the United Kingdom, provided for recording the location of minefields and imposed restrictions on the use of scatterable (or 'remotely delivered') mines. The third, on incendiary weapons, was to prohibit incendiary attacks against civilian areas, and against military objectives within such areas unless suitable precautions were taken. Significantly, this proposal had gained the support of the United States by the end of the meeting.

The 1980 Conventional Weapons Convention

The discussions continued at the Diplomatic Conference on the Reaffirmation and Development of International Humanitarian Law Applicable in Armed Conflicts ('Diplomatic Conference'), held in Geneva, in 1976 and 1977;[14] at a UN preparatory conference in Geneva in 1978 and 1979; and finally at the United Nations Conference on Prohibitions or Restrictions of Use of Certain Conventional Weapons which May Be Deemed to Be Excessively Injurious or to Have Indiscriminate Effects, also held in Geneva, in 1979 and 1980. The outcome was a new UN treaty, the first formal ban on conventional weapons to be adopted by the international community since the 1899 Hague Declaration on dum-dum bullets.

The Convention on Prohibitions or Restrictions on the Use of Certain Conventional Weapons Which May Be Deemed to Be Excessively Injurious or to Have Indiscriminate Effects (usually referred to today as the 'Conventional Weapons Convention') consists of a main text (the Convention proper) with attached Protocols. The bans and restrictions on specific weapons are contained in the protocols; three were adopted in 1980, but the convention allows for the creation of further protocols at a later date.[15]

Any state wishing to become a party to the convention must agree to accept at least two protocols. The convention and protocols are binding among states which become parties to the convention and accept the respective protocols, but the scope of application is potentially wider. During a conflict, a state party is also required to observe the provisions of the convention and protocols toward the ally of another state party and toward national liberation movements, if they themselves agree to accept and apply the convention and the relevant protocols. Under its Article 1, the convention and protocols apply only to international armed conflicts and to a limited class of wars of national liberation,[16] but here, too, the scope is potentially wider: it has been argued that 'it is improbable that governments will feel free to use against their own population, in conflicts not of an international nature or in internal unrest, weapons and combat methods which they have agreed to forgo against an alien enemy.'[17]

Important as the convention is as a framework for antipersonnel weapons bans and restrictions, the limitations of the three protocols become apparent when one compares the texts with actual weapons used in Vietnam and elsewhere, and with the proposals offered by Sweden and other countries in 1974 and 1975. The protocols are limited in that whereas some weapons are banned completely, elsewhere only certain uses are banned; the military importance of the banned and restricted weapons varies; and many important types of weapons are not covered at all.

Protocol I to the convention, stemming from the Mexican and Swiss proposal at Lugano, prohibits the use of 'any weapon the primary effect of which is to injure by fragments which in the human body escape detection by X-rays.' The idea for this protocol (which was not one of the original Swedish proposals) came from allegations that US forces in Vietnam were using bomblets with plastic fragments (Chapter 4). But the Rockeye bomblets dropped on North Vietnam in 1972 would not be banned under the protocols, as injury from splinters of the plastic tail fins is incidental to the 'primary effect' of the warhead with its shaped charge (against armor) and its metal casing (against personnel).

Protocol I, in fact, bans a weapon which does not exist and is not even likely to be developed, given the advantages of metal fragments over plastic ones (they are tougher and denser, and hence have more range and penetrating capability). One commentator has written that Protocol I is a 'medically important provision' which 'is useful ... in that it prevents the future development of such munitions.'[18] Another, more skeptically, has noted that 'Once the proposal was suggested, it received unanimous support because none of the States participating in the [UN] Weapons Conference had such weapons in their inventory nor did they foresee any conceivable use for such weapons in the future.'[19]

Protocol II provides for the recording of the location of minefields. It prohibits the 'indiscriminate use' of land mines, but its provisions on this point do not go much beyond the general prohibition of indiscriminate attacks in Additional Protocol I to the Geneva Conventions, adopted by the Diplomatic Conference in 1977 ('Additional Protocol I of 1977').[20] It also prohibits the use of certain kinds of booby traps and similar devices.

Protocol II imposes special restrictions on 'remotely delivered mines' – mines deployed by such means as artillery or aircraft. The use of such mines is not prohibited, as in the Swedish proposal of 1974, but is subject to safeguards which, however, are weakened by several loopholes. The location of minefields is to be recorded, but this requirement applies only to 'pre-planned minefields,' leaving open the possibility of sowing quantities of mines in the heat of battle without recording their location (Article 7).[21] Remotely delivered mines are not to be used unless their location can be accurately recorded *or* the mines contain an effective neutralizing mechanism. Advance warning must be given of the delivery of remotely delivered mines which may affect the civilian population 'unless circumstances do not permit' (Article 5) – another significant loophole.

As one commentator has noted, the provision for recording the location of preplanned remotely delivered minefields 'appears to require the impossible,' while the requirement to give advance warning 'would seem to be one which would be most often honored in the breach, both for technical reasons and because of the escape clause "unless circumstances do not permit." '[22] On the whole, Protocol II gives the impression of having been written to satisfy the needs of military forces, which may later have to occupy a mined area, rather than to protect civilians.

Protocol III, on incendiary weapons, is more satisfying than the other two. It deals with an important class of weapons, and it contains a restriction which is more clear-cut than those in Protocol II. It goes further than the proposal which emerged from Lugano by prohibiting, in all circumstances, attacks by air-delivered incendiary weapons against 'any military objective located within a concentration of civilians.' Under this formulation, it could no longer be claimed that the World War II firebomb raids against Japanese cities were legal: the American bombers would no longer be allowed to set fire to them on the pretext that they were attacking military objectives within those cities, such as the 'household industries' in Tokyo which were said to be supporting the Japanese war effort (Chapter 4). However, the majority of states participating in the drafting of Protocol III were not willing to go still further and protect soldiers against being burned by banning the use of incendiary weapons altogether, as Sweden and other states had originally proposed.[23]

Despite a series of proposals by Mexico and Sweden, the UN conference did not reach agreement on a new ban on especially injurious small-caliber projectiles. Instead, at its first session in 1979, the conference adopted a resolution inviting governments to carry out further research and appealing to all governments 'to exercise the utmost care in the development of small-calibre weapon systems, so as to avoid an unnecessary escalation of the injurious effects of such systems.' The text of the resolution was included in the Final Act of the conference.[24]

An ICRC legal expert who was involved in the process later wrote that the adoption of the 1980 Convention 'marks the completion of a significant phase in the evolution of international humanitarian law, a phase whose prime purpose has been to provide better legal protection for the civilian population against the effects of hostilities.' The Conventional Weapons Convention and the two Additional Protocols to the Geneva Conventions, adopted in 1977, were (he wrote)

> the result of patient effort and we should welcome their adoption. But progress made in international humanitarian law is never completely satisfactory: there is always the question whether it could not have been taken a step further, whether more lives could have been saved, more suffering avoided. Alongside the advances made, however substantial, there is the shadow of those which have perhaps failed to come into being for lack of perseverance or persuasion.[25]

As embodied in the convention, the nine years' effort to ban the worst of the new antipersonnel weapons had achieved some results. A form of warfare which not so long before had caused immense destruction and suffering – aerial incendiary attacks on cities – was now banned outright. There was an agreement providing some safeguards on the use of land mines, and a ban on non-metallic fragments, unimportant now but possibly helpful in curbing future weapons developments. On the other hand, whole classes of antipersonnel weapons covered in the original Swedish proposals remained untouched by any specific ban. There was nothing on cluster bombs, on flechettes, or on other new fragmentation weapons of enhanced effectiveness. There was no new binding instrument banning modern versions of the dum-dum; the furthest the conference got was to appeal for restraint. Compared to the needs for humanitarian protection shown by the Vietnam war, the achievements of the UN conference were meager.

Grounds for Weapons Bans: Humanitarian Protection versus 'Military Necessity'

What is the point of trying to impose bans on antipersonnel weapons? Is it not a futile exercise, while war itself continues?

The best thing, of course, would be to get rid of wars altogether. Wars should be prevented from breaking out; those that do start should be stopped. Measures should be introduced to promote the peaceful settlement of disputes between nations and peoples. The underlying causes of wars should be addressed. Here is a huge agenda, and one that deserves urgent and sustained effort by governments and individuals. But as it will not be achieved overnight, efforts to limit the suffering caused by war can only be to the good. One of the routes to doing this is to impose legal limits on the weapons available to armies engaged in combat.

The weapons bans achieved thus far are based on two general rules. These rules have evolved over the years and are incorporated in the body of international law relating to armed conflict. Their most modern and authoritative statement is in the Protocols Additional to the Geneva Conventions of 12 August 1949, adopted in 1977 ('Additional Protocols of 1977').

(1) *Prohibition of use of weapons causing 'superfluous injury' or 'unnecessary suffering.'* The notion in international law that certain forms of harm to soldiers are unnecessary or superfluous goes back to the 1868 Declaration of St Petersburg, a document which has been described as 'a cornerstone of the laws of war.'[26] This declaration was an agreement among states parties to renounce the use in war of explosive or incendiary projectiles under 400 grams in weight, a new type of munition which Russia did not want used either by its troops or against them.[27] The reasoning behind the prohibition, as stated in the preambular paragraphs of the declaration, was that 'the only legitimate object which States should endeavor to accomplish during war is to weaken the military forces of the enemy'; that 'for this purpose it is sufficient to disable the greatest possible number of men'; that 'this object would be exceeded by the employment of arms which uselessly aggravate the sufferings of disabled men, or render their death inevitable'; and that 'the employment of such arms would, therefore, be contrary to the laws of humanity.'[28]

From these notions evolved the statement in the Hague Conventions of 1899 and 1907 that the *means* of injuring the enemy are not unlimited, and the prohibition in these two instruments of weapons 'of a nature to cause superfluous injury' (in the 1899 formulation) or 'calculated to cause unnecessary suffering' (in the 1907 formulation).[29] The modern formulation in Additional Protocol I of 1977 incorporates the notion of *methods* as well as means of warfare (see below), and includes both the 1899 and the 1907 formulations. Article 35 of Additional Protocol I states, in part:

1. In any armed conflict, the right of the Parties to the conflict to choose methods or means of warfare is not unlimited.

2. It is prohibited to employ weapons, projectiles and material and methods of warfare of a nature to cause superfluous injury or unnecessary suffering...

(2) *Prohibition of use of indiscriminate weapons.* This prohibition, too, is contained in Additional Protocol I of 1977. Article 51(4) of Additional Protocol I prohibits 'indiscriminate attacks,' including 'those which employ a method or means of combat which cannot be directed at a specific military objective' and 'those which employ a method or means of combat the effects of which cannot be limited as required by this Protocol' and, consequently, 'are of a nature to strike military objectives and civilians or civilian objects without distinction.' (As stated in the ICRC Commentary on the Additional Protocols, 'The term "means of combat" or "means of warfare" ... generally refers to the weapons being used, while the expression "methods of combat" generally refers to the way in which such weapons are used.'[30])

The prohibition on indiscriminate weapons is one of a number of measures intended to protect civilians against the effects of hostilities. As mentioned in Chapter 4, the Hague Regulations of 1907 afforded some protection by prohibiting the attack of undefended settlements, but this rule had failed to keep up with technological developments since then, including bombardment by aircraft and the development of ever more powerful bombs.[31] The Diplomatic Conference for the Establishment of International Conventions for the Protection of Victims of War, convened in 1949, 'did not have the task of revising the Hague Regulations,' and the Geneva Convention Relative to the Protection of Civilian Persons in Time of War (Fourth Geneva Convention) of 12 August 1949, adopted by that conference, for the most part protects civilians (including civilians in occupied territories) only 'against arbitrary and wanton acts of the enemy, leaving aside their protection against dangers arising from certain methods of warfare and the use of certain weapons.'[32]

The fact that the Hague Regulations were not brought up to date 'meant that a serious gap remained' in the codified international humanitarian law of armed conflict.[33] After the need for further development of this law had been repeatedly raised by the ICRC and at the UN General Assembly, the Diplomatic Conference on the Reaffirmation and Development of International Humanitarian Law Applicable in Armed Conflicts was held from 1974 to 1977, leading to the adoption of the two Additional Protocols. Part IV, 'Civilian Population,' is the longest part of Additional Protocol I; and its Section I, 'General Protection against Effects of Hostilities,' 'represents the crowning achievement of the Diplomatic Conference of 1974–1977 and the most significant victory achieved in international humanitarian law since the adoption of the Fourth Geneva Convention in 1949,' according to the ICRC Commentary on the Additional Protocols.[34]

Section I of Part IV comprises Articles 48–67 of Additional Protocol I. Article 48, 'Basic rule,' states:

> In order to ensure respect for and protection of the civilian population and civilian objects, the Parties to the conflict shall at all times distinguish between the civilian population and combatants and between civilian objects and military objectives and accordingly shall direct their operations only against military objectives.[35]

Articles 49 and 50 define the terms 'attacks' and 'civilians.' They provide, among other things, that 'The presence within the civilian population of individuals who do not come within the definition of civilians does not deprive the population of its civilian character' (Article 50(3)).

Article 51, 'Protection of the civilian population,' is the one which contains the prohibition on indiscriminate weapons. Several parts of this article are especially relevant:

2. The civilian population as such, as well as individual civilians, shall not be the object of attack...

4. Indiscriminate attacks are prohibited. Indiscriminate attacks are:

   (a) those which are not directed at a specific military objective;

   (b) those which employ a method or means of combat which cannot be directed at a specific military objective; or

   (c) those which employ a method or means of combat the effects of which cannot be limited as required by this Protocol;

   and consequently, in each such case, are of a nature to strike military objectives and civilians or civilian objects without distinction.

5. Among others, the following types of attacks are to be considered as indiscriminate:

   (a) an attack by bombardment by any methods or means which treats as a single military objective a number of clearly separated and distinct military objectives located in a city, town, village or other area containing a similar concentration of civilians or civilian objects; and

   (b) an attack which may be expected to cause incidental loss of civilian life, injury to civilians, damage to civilian objects, or a combination thereof, which would be excessive in relation to the concrete and direct military advantage anticipated.

Further underlying the protection of soldiers and civilians in armed conflict is the need to be bound by (in the formulation of the Hague Convention No. IV of 1907) 'the usages established among civilized peoples,' 'the laws of humanity,' and 'the dictates of the public conscience.' This limitation is expressed in the so-called 'Martens clause,' named after the nineteenth-century Russian jurist Fedor Martens and incorporated in the Hague Conventions of 1899 and 1907. The modern formulation is in Article 1(2) of Additional Protocol I of 1977: 'In cases not covered by this Protocol or by other international agreements, civilians and combatants remain under the protection and authority of the principles of international law derived from established custom, from the principles of humanity and from the dictates of public conscience.' It has been pointed out that the principle of the Martens clause 'underlines the applicability of international law even in such cases where prohibitions of specific weapons do not appear in existing international conventions.'[36]

Important as these general rules are, their application to particular weapons is far from automatic. As one expert has written, the principles of unnecessary suffering and indiscriminate effects 'are not particularly suited to serve as yardsticks' for determining whether or not the use of a particular weapon is legal.[37] The principles are excellent, but they cannot serve as yardsticks because too much room is left for argument. They are useful as guidelines, but the guidelines must be applied.

As established in Additional Protocol I, one route in applying the rules is national. Article 36 states: 'In the study, development, acquisition or adoption of a new weapon, means or method of warfare, a High Contracting Party is under an obligation to determine whether its employment would, in some or all circumstances, be prohibited by this Protocol or by any other rule of international law applicable to the High Contracting Party.'[38] The other route is international, as shown in the arduous process leading to the adoption of the 1980 Convention.

Efforts to ban or restrict specific weapons usually come up against the notion of 'military necessity.' This notion is basic to international humanitarian law,[39] and implicit in the general rules discussed above. The concept of 'unnecessary suffering' implies that some suffering is necessary, and therefore not illegal.[40] The notion of 'military necessity' also comes into the principle of indiscriminateness. Under Article 51(5)(b) of Additional Protocol I, an attack is indiscriminate if it may be expected to cause 'incidental loss of civilian life, injury to civilians, damage to civilian objects, or a combination thereof' which 'would be excessive in relation to the concrete and direct military advantage anticipated.' The implication is that an attack, or the use of a particular weapon, will not be considered indiscriminate under Article 51(5)(b) if it is judged that the 'concrete and direct military advantage' is so great as to outweigh the incidental damage to civilians. Further complicating the picture is the difficulty of establishing that a weapon is inherently indiscriminate, and hence unlawful. It is usually possible to entertain the argument that at least some uses of a given weapon would be discriminate.[41]

Within the traditional approach of international humanitarian law, it can be considered that the rationale for adopting specific weapons bans is that 'there are some weapons the possession of which does not materially affect the balance of forces in the world, and which are not essential from the military viewpoint, but whose effects are particularly cruel or cause extensive damage without military justification,' to borrow a phrase from one author.[42] If this statement is accepted, it is vital that the weapons excluded on grounds of 'military necessity' from being the subjects of bans or restrictions are those which are 'essential,' not merely desirable. Military need must not be taken to equal 'military necessity.' But progress is difficult, because judgments of military necessity are usually left in the hands of the experts – the armed forces. The relatively meager results of the process leading to the adoption of the 1980 Conventional Weapons Convention can be attributed to the willingness of most participants to defer to their military experts' claims that the weapons under consideration were very useful, not very harmful, or not inherently indiscriminate.

The Role of the Public Conscience

If the results of efforts over the years to ban excessively injurious and indiscriminate weapons have been so slim, are they worth anything at all? How can they be effective?

Rather surprisingly, the historical record shows that at least some weapons bans have managed to stick. Through two world wars and many smaller conflicts, the ban on dum-dum bullets has been largely observed. The ban on poisonous gases and germ warfare, laid down in the Geneva Protocol of 1925, has also been respected – or was largely so until Iraq started using chemical weapons in the 1980s: first against Iranian troops and then against Kurdish settlements in northern Iraq. There was little initial outcry: most other countries supported Iraq's war effort and wanted Iran to lose the war. After Iraq invaded Kuwait in 1990 and its erstwhile supporters turned against it, many commentators voiced regret that these same countries now risked having chemical weapons used against their troops because they had not acted earlier to make it clear that Iraq's use of them was beyond the pale of humanity.

As a weapons ban becomes accepted, the terms of the debate change. The weapon in question becomes known as a prohibited weapon: a dum-dum, for instance, is commonly referred to in journalism as 'the outlawed dum-dum.' When a bullet similar to a dum-dum is used or developed for sale, the debate is not over whether or not dum-dums *per se* should be banned, but whether this particular bullet fits the definition of a dum-dum and is therefore prohibited.

An army contemplating the use of a banned weapon may be deterred by three considerations. First, they themselves may accept that its use is illegal, especially if their government has become a party to a treaty banning its use and this international prohibition has been incorporated in the country's own laws of warfare. Second, they may reason that any short-term advantage gained through its use will be offset if the weapon is used against them. Soldiers hit by dum-dums will be out of action longer than otherwise, and their comrades may be terrified and demoralized. Soldiers gassed may be horribly injured, and an effective defense against chemical warfare poses enormous logistical problems.

The third reason for not using a banned weapon is the risk of international opprobrium. A country which does so undermines the legitimacy of its war effort as well as its own international standing. This country becomes an international outlaw. In the words of the 1907 formulation of the Martens clause, it has departed from the 'usages of civilized peoples,' broken the 'laws of humanity,' and offended the 'dictates of the public conscience.'

For a ban to hold, the 'public conscience' is very important. The public must be reminded that certain weapons are outlawed, and must make its voice heard whenever there is a risk of a ban being broken. Had there been more of a public outcry when Iraq started using chemical weapons against Iran, Iraq's supporters might have been impelled to put pressure on Iraq to stop it.

The public conscience also has an important role in getting a ban adopted in the first place. The Geneva Protocol of 1925 was adopted against a background of public horror over the sufferings of gas victims in World War I. The ban on dum-dums was a reaction to their use by British forces.[43] Public opinion played a crucial role in the adoption of the ban at the Hague Peace Conference of 1899.

As described by the historian Barbara Tuchman, the impetus for the Hague conference came from the Russians, who were anxious to avoid having to rearm in the face of the imminent Austrian adoption of a new field gun. The conference opened in a mood of cynicism and disdain, but peace groups from Europe and America converged on The Hague, eager for results; a flood of leaks, published in the leading Hague newspaper, led the conference to open its meetings to the press; and after the first two weeks, as the head of the British delegation wrote, the delegates 'became interested in spite of themselves.' Out of the conference came the dum-dum ban – a product of the anti-British feeling of the time, and of a sense among the delegates that here, at least, was something they could accomplish.[44]

Of the three protocols agreed on by the UN conference in 1980, it is not surprising that the most important was on the weapons against which there had been the strongest recent outcry: incendiaries. The Vietnam war protests over napalm had their echo in Geneva when the conference adopted Protocol III to the new convention. The protests had been stirred by reports from Vietnam, symbolized by the famous photograph of a Vietnamese girl burned by napalm, running naked toward the camera.

That photograph was evoked by Hans Blix, a member of the Swedish Foreign Ministry, driving force of the Swedish effort for antipersonnel weapons bans and later Foreign Minister, in a speech before the *Ad Hoc* Committee on Conventional Weapons of the Diplomatic Conference in 1974:

> Several speakers have mentioned the picture of the little girl screaming in horror and pain from being hit by incendiary. We have all seen it. We shall certainly coldly and rationally analyze the various factors which argue in favour of a ban on use of incendiaries and the factors which, on the contrary, militate against such a ban. But at the same time I confess that I hope and trust we shall be influenced by that picture.

Anyone can understand the horror of being burned; but in general, the 'dictates of the public conscience' were less well represented in Lucerne and Lugano than at the Hague Peace Conference seventy-five years before. There were no peace groups pounding on the doors; the sessions were not open to the press, and the conferences were bound by their own rules to abstain from discussions of a 'controversial or political nature.' Public opinion was barely represented at all, and the mood of the day was set by the weary ordnance and military experts who had been snatched from their work and made to sit for hours on end, under the tutelage of their foreign offices, listening to dull speeches sprinkled with diplomatic innuendoes whose meaning was obscure at best.

Given the cynicism, given the lack of public pressure, the inertia of governments and the antagonism of armies, it was easy for a British delegate to say in a statement at the end of the Lucerne conference that there had been few 'definitive results,' that there was a 'need for more research'; or for the US delegation at Lugano to report to their Secretary of State that 'with regard to specific weapons categories, United States interests were generally well served by the Lugano discussions.'[45]

The interests of humanity had not been so well served, but delegates and their governments could take comfort in the fact that the status quo had, for the time being, been preserved.

Notes

1. One expert has written: '*International humanitarian law* – also called the *law of armed conflict* and previously known as the *law of war* – is a special branch of law governing situations of armed conflict – in a word, war. International humanitarian law seeks to mitigate the effects of war, first in that it limits the choice of means and methods of conducting military operations, and secondly in that it obliges the belligerents to spare persons who do not or no longer participate in hostile actions' (Gasser, 1993, p. 3; original emphasis).

2. Sweden, Royal Ministry of Foreign Affairs, 1973.

3. On the background to the Lucerne conference, see Blix, 1974; Sandoz, 1981, pp. 4–6; Aubert, 1990, pp. 478–80.

4. These proposals were contained in a working paper submitted by Sweden and the six other countries to the Diplomatic Conference on the Reaffirmation and Development of International Humanitarian Law Applicable in Armed Conflicts (referred to below as the 'Diplomatic Conference') in 1974. The text is taken from Blix, 1974.

5. Although it was not obvious from the expert's presentation, the comparison was between a conventional high explosive artillery shell and an Improved Conventional Munition containing small bomblets which produce small fragments on explosion. The comparison was misleading in that other antipersonnel munitions which were used much more widely in Vietnam produce fragments which are much larger and will therefore cause worse wounds – the 10.5-grain steel balls of the Claymore mine and the 'guava' bomblet, for example, or the 16-grain balls in the 'pineapple' bomblet. The admission that ICMs 'wound more targets' gives rise to the question: should not such an increase in antipersonnel battlefield lethality also be a cause for international concern and scrutiny?

6. Allred, 1967, p. 4.

7. ICRC, 1975, paragraph 96, p. 29.

8. Rule 8 of the Lucerne conference stated: 'Experts shall speak in their personal capacity, and their statements shall not bind in any way the government that appointed them...' The fiction of government 'experts' speaking in their 'personal capacity' is a diplomatic device to facilitate detailed discussions on a matter which has not reached the stage of moving toward formal agreement.

9. As the historian Geoffrey Best has noted, the North Vietnamese took a similar position the same year at the Diplomatic Conference. Their statement to that conference spoke of 'new war conditions which set unarmed or inadequately armed men and under-developed and ill-equipped peoples against imperialism's modern war machine.' International humanitarian law should 'take all possible measures to prevent the use of the war machine of aggression by morally condemning it as a war crime.... In severely condemning the war machine of aggression as criminal, the rules prohibiting means and methods of criminal

combat should be as complete and detailed as possible. Similarly, the inadequate and dangerous concepts of "unnecessary injury", "unnecessary suffering", "due proportion" and "military necessity" should be excluded.' As Best observed, 'So the law of war was proposed to be turned into a positive aid to parties presumed, by this extreme variant of standard marxist–leninist theory, to be incapable of aggressive or inhumanitarian warfare, at the expense of parties presumed by the same lights to be capable of nothing else' (Best, 1983, p. 314).

10. ICRC, 1975, paragraphs 277–8, p. 77.

11. *Ibid.*, paragraph 282, p. 79.

12. The Swedish proposals, revised in light of the discussions at Lucerne, had been presented to the Diplomatic Conference in 1975 as document number CCDH/IV/201, with thirteen co-sponsors (Algeria, Austria, Egypt, Lebanon, Mali, Mauritania, Mexico, Norway, Sudan, Sweden, Switzerland, Venezuela, and Yugoslavia). A further revision of the proposal on incendiary weapons was presented in 1975 as document number RO 610/4b, with twenty-one co-sponsors. The two documents are reproduced in ICRC, 1976, annexes 21–2, pp. 198–207.

13. Soap, because it had the density of flesh and recorded the passage of a bullet; the thigh, because it was the largest mass of muscle in the body; a woman, because she would not suffer from hairs being pulled out when the plaster mould for casting the soap was removed from her leg.

14. The Diplomatic Conference had been preparing the two Additional Protocols to the Geneva Conventions, which it adopted in 1977 (see below). The question of including bans or restrictions on specific weapons had been under discussion in the Conference's *Ad Hoc* Committee on Conventional Weapons (the discussion had moved back and forth between the committee and the Lucerne and Lugano conferences). In the end, no provisions dealing with specific weapons were included in the Protocols, but the Diplomatic Conference passed a resolution recommending the convening of a conference of governments on the subject. That recommendation was taken up at the UN General Assembly in 1977, and the UN Conference, with its preparatory conference, was the result.

15. Under Article 8 of the convention, once the convention comes into force, any state party may propose additional protocols covering other types of weapons. New protocols can be adopted at a new conference, which is to be convened either if a majority of states parties so agree, or upon the request of a single state party if there has been no new conference for the past ten years. The preamble to the convention also cites the possibility that 'the General Assembly of the United Nations and the United Nations Disarmament Commission may decide to examine the question of a possible broadening of the scope of the prohibitions and restrictions contained in this Convention and its annexed Protocols.'

16. Human Rights Watch Arms Project and Physicians for Human Rights, 1993, p. 282 (cited below as *Landmines: A Deadly Legacy*).

17. Sandoz, 1981, p. 16.

18. Aubert, 1990, p. 486.

19. Fenrick, 1990, p. 503.

20. As noted in a detailed critique of Protocol II published in *Landmines: A Deadly Legacy* (pp. 286–91), several important provisions in Article 51(4) of Additional Protocol I of 1977 spelling out what exactly constitutes an indiscrimi-

nate attack are omitted from Protocol II to the 1980 convention, weakening the latter protocol. More generally, the formulation of the prohibition of indiscriminate use of land mines in Protocol II 'ignores the basic problem of indiscriminateness in landmine use: the future harm to civilians that may be caused by mines outliving their military purpose. The requirement [in the protocol] that combatants weigh expected harm to civilians against anticipated military advantage fails in two respects. First, it imposes on field commanders the impossible duty of predicting future consequences of a particular use of mines. Second, it ignores the essential fact of mine warfare: time delay.'

21. Article 7 of Protocol II merely enjoins the parties to a conflict to 'endeavour' to record the location of mines and minefields which are not preplanned.

22. Levie, 1986, vol. 1, p. 75.

23. As Sandoz has written (1981, pp. 13–14), 'there is no provision [in Protocol III] to protect combatants against incendiary weapons. This is because emphasis was placed on the indiscriminate nature of these weapons and on the danger they present for civilians, rather than on their cruelty, an aspect which would have justified restriction of their use against combatants also.' He noted that 'several delegates [at the UN conference] regretted that no agreement could be reached after all on protecting combatants.'

24. The text of the resolution is reproduced in Sandoz, 1981, p. 33.

25. *Ibid.*, pp. 16, 17.

26. SIPRI, 1978, p. 212.

27. According to Roberts and Guelff (1982, p. 29), the prohibition in the Declaration of St Petersburg

> followed the development of a bullet which exploded upon contact with a hard surface. In 1863 the bullet was introduced into the Imperial Russian Army to be used for blowing up ammunition wagons. In 1864 the Imperial War Minister considered it to be improper to use such a bullet against troops and its use was therefore strictly controlled. However, in 1867 a modification of the bullet was developed which enabled it to explode on contact with even a soft surface. Moreover, unlike the previous projectile, the new bullet shattered upon explosion. Understanding that such a bullet posed a greater danger to troops, the Imperial War Minister did not want it used either by the Imperial Russian Army or the armies of other states. The Imperial War Minister proposed to Tsar Alexander II that the use of all explosive bullets, or at least the bullet developed in 1867, should be renounced. Tsar Alexander II invited states to attend an International Military Commission in St. Petersburg to consider the matter.

The result was the Declaration of St Petersburg.

28. The text of the Declaration of St Petersburg is reproduced in Roberts and Guelff, 1982, pp. 30–31.

29. Article 22 of the Regulations Respecting the Laws and Customs of War on Land, annexed to the Hague Convention No. IV of 1907 and known as the Hague Regulations of 1907, states: 'The right of belligerents to adopt means of injuring the enemy is not unlimited.' Article 23 states, in part: 'In addition to the prohibitions provided by special Conventions, it is especially forbidden.... (e) To

employ arms, projectiles, or material calculated to cause unnecessary suffering...'

30. ICRC, 1987, paragraph 1957.

31. As Hans-Peter Gasser has written (1993, p. 61):

> Until the 20th century, war usually meant a confrontation between two armies seeking to settle an issue in battle. Consequently, military operations were largely restricted to the armed forces opposing each other or to the place under siege. Destruction occurred within the range of the weapons then available, *i.e.*, small arms and artillery. The concept of the battlefield contains the idea of geographic limitation. Civilians in the area were often able to move away or flee (or even watch the fighting from the surrounding hills)...
>
> The advent of the airplane fundamentally altered the nature of warfare and brought in its wake a vast potential for destruction to the civilian population. Long-range missiles have taken this process even further. Bomb and missile attacks on strategic targets carry destruction far behind the front line, into the heart of a country, where they can strike at cities, towns, roads and railways, cultivated land and above all, at the population that is not involved in the hostilities.

32. ICRC, 1987, paragraphs 1829, 1817.

33. *Ibid.*, paragraph 1830.

34. *Ibid.*, paragraph 1816.

35. The ICRC Commentary on the Additional Protocols (paragraph 1872) states: 'In general the word "respect" implies the concept of sparing the persons and objects concerned, and not attacking them, while the word "protection" implies an act of positive aid and support.' The Commentary notes (paragraph 1863) that the basic rule of protection and distinction was already implicitly recognized in the statement in the Declaration of St Petersburg (1868) that 'the only legitimate object which States should endeavor to accomplish during war is to weaken the military forces of the enemy.'

36. ICRC, 1973, p. 11.

37. Kalshoven, 1990, p. 517.

38. According to the ICRC Commentary on the Additional Protocols (paragraph 1482), Article 36 implies the obligation of states parties 'to establish internal procedures with a view to elucidating the problem of illegality...'

39. 'The law of armed conflict is a compromise based on a balance between military necessity, on the one hand, and the requirements of humanity, on the other. It is customarily expressed in the form of prohibitions which take military necessity into account. Military necessity means the necessity for measures which are essential to attain the goals of war, and which are lawful in accordance with the laws and customs of war' (ICRC, 1987, paragraph 1389). See also Doswald-Beck and Vité, 1993, pp. 95–101.

40. Yves Sandoz has suggested that the notion of cruelty may be 'preferable to that of utility ... because the latter opens the door to all abuses.' The cruelty of a weapon could be recognized 'without regard to the circumstances surrounding its eventual use' (Sandoz, 1975, pp. 19–20). In other words, the cruelty and – hence – illegality of a weapon would be recognized as something absolute, not something to be weighed against what is militarily 'necessary.'

The notion of cruelty would also allow for a philosophical link to international human rights law, where the right not to be subjected to cruel, inhuman, or degrading treatment is recognized as a right which may not be derogated from under any circumstances, including war or other public emergency which threatens the life of the nation (International Covenant on Civil and Political Rights, Articles 4, 7). International humanitarian law might have a more progressive character than at present if it were recognized that one of its aims is to protect basic human rights (including the right to life and the right not to be subjected to cruel, inhuman or degrading treatment), which are absolute, rather than simply to mitigate the sufferings of war in so far as military demands will allow (cf. Doswald-Beck and Vité, 1993).

41. Cf. ICRC, 1987, paragraphs 1958, 1965.

42. The passage quoted is from Sandoz, 1981, p. 7.

43. Dum-Dum was an arsenal near Calcutta which the British colonial authorities commissioned to design the bullet which came to bear its name (SIPRI, 1978, p. 14).

44. Tuchman, 1966, pp. 236–7, 256–62; Best, 1983, pp. 139–40; Sellier and Kneubuehl, 1994, pp. 180–83.

45. US Department of State, 1976.

CHAPTER 7

THE FUTURE OF
ANTIPERSONNEL WEAPONS:
CONTROL OR CHAOS?

As chairman of the Foreign Operations Subcommittee of the United States Senate, I have seen the terrible toll of antipersonnel land mines on innocent civilians. Hundreds of thousands – perhaps millions – of people, many of them children, have lost their lives, their legs and arms, or their eyesight from stepping on land mines. These insidious weapons, sometimes designed to look like toys to lure unsuspecting children, are strewn indiscriminately in fields, along jungle paths, and on main travel routes. From Cambodia to Nicaragua, tens of millions of land mines have rendered whole areas uninhabitable long after the conflicts end and the causes of war are forgotten.

US Senator Patrick J. Leahy[1]

Concerned by the toll of land mine injuries around the world, six organizations issued a call in October 1992 for an international ban on the use, production, stockpiling, and transfer of antipersonnel mines.[2] Twelve years after the adoption of the Conventional Weapons Convention and seventeen years after the end of the US–Indochina war, antipersonnel weapons were back on the international agenda. What had happened in the intervening years?

The Proliferation of Antipersonnel Technologies

A nation develops a weapon in the hope of gaining a military advantage. It keeps the knowledge and ideas to itself at first, or shares them only with its closest allies. But once a weapon is used, or sold to other countries, the secret is lost. The advantage is diffused as more nations acquire the weapon or make use of the surrounding technologies. The developer's original purpose is defeated, and the overall result is an increase in the efficiency and destructiveness of warfare worldwide.

The great American achievement in antipersonnel weaponry in the 1950s and 1960s was to increase many times over the number of wounding fragments delivered to a given area. Two technologies were principally responsible: fragmentation, typified by the hand grenade; and the technology of deploying many small munitions over a wide area, typified by the cluster bomb. Singly or in combination, these two technologies yielded many new munitions of different sorts which were used for the first time in Vietnam. The subsequent proliferation of the technologies can be illustrated by reference to these two typical weapons, the hand grenade and the cluster bomb.

As described in Chapter 2, the M26 fragmentation grenade was one of the first of the new munitions. Its coil of notched steel wire yielded over a thousand small fragments on explosion, giving an effective casualty radius of 15 meters. Other improvements over the old 'pineapple' grenade included a more powerful explosive, a lighter weight, and a more lethal geometrical distribution of fragments. Other possible shapes and sizes of grenades and other methods of fragmentation had also been considered by the US Army in the original studies done in the early 1950s.[3]

These lessons were not lost on arms manufacturers in other countries. When Jane's military publishing house brought out its first edition of *Jane's Infantry Weapons* in 1974, the volume included 120 pages on grenades; while the Stockholm International Peace Research Institute (SIPRI) study *Anti-personnel Weapons*, published three years later, had a table of hand and rifle grenades running on for five pages. Of the seventy-three grenade models listed in the SIPRI study, only four were manufactured in the United States. Many of the models in the SIPRI list were old cast-iron types or rifle grenades, but the list showed that by 1978 some ten countries in addition to the United States were producing modern fragmentation hand grenades. These new grenades had various shapes (spherical, egg-shaped, tomato-shaped, barrel-shaped), sizes (down to a Dutch 'mini-grenade' the size of a golf ball), fragmentation devices (internally serrated casings, notched wire, steel balls, metal fragments embedded in plastic cases), and numbers of fragments (with such large quantities as 2,100 steel balls and fragments in the Dutch EMZ grenade, 3,500 steel balls in the Austrian HdGr 69, and 5,900 2mm steel balls in the West German DM-51 grenade). Even America's erstwhile enemy, Vietnam, had absorbed the lessons of controlled fragmentation and produced a hand grenade with steel balls embedded in an aluminum casing.[4]

The proliferation of cluster bomb technologies was slower but no less dramatic. The 1978 SIPRI study listed only five models of high explosive cluster bombs in production or under development in three countries outside the United States (France, the Federal Republic of Germany, and the United Kingdom) as against some thirty-two US models.[5] In contrast, the 1994 edition of *Jane's Air-Launched Weapons* lists some sixty-four high explosive cluster bombs in production or under development in fourteen countries, of which only nine are US models. Included are such novelties as the German MW-1, an aircraft-mounted sideways-ejection dispenser from which the pattern of bomblet dispersal can be selected in flight, resulting in the deployment of 4,536 armor-piercing bomblets over an area which can be varied from 55 to 500 meters in width and 200 to 2,500 meters in length, and with other types of bomblets and mines also available; the British JP 233 airfield attack weapon, dispensing thirty runway-cratering bomblets interspersed with 215 shaped charge/fragmentation bomblets with random delay fuzes, intended to impede runway repairs; and the Italian Skyshark series, under development, comprising a choice of three dispensers – one free-fall, one rocket-powered, and one, turbojet-powered, able to fly 250 kilometers from the attack aircraft before releasing the bomblets carried within it. In contrast to the earlier proliferation of hand grenades, which was mostly to NATO countries, cluster bomb producers and developers listed in *Jane's* include not only Western (France, Germany, Italy, Spain, UK, USA) and former Warsaw Pact (Poland, Russia) countries, but other emerging or established arms-producing countries: Chile, China, Iraq, Israel, South Africa, and the former Yugoslavia.

New Weapons Used in New Wars

Even before the end of the US–Indochina war, the new weapons were starting to be used elsewhere. Cluster bombs supplied to Israel were dropped on Damascus in the October war of 1973,[6] and flechette-filled Beehive projectiles and rocket warheads supplied to Israel were used against Egypt in the same war, according to a participant in the Lugano conference in 1974 (Chapter 6). Modern antipersonnel weapons have been used in various conflicts since then, and today's news reports contain routine references to 'cluster bombs' being dropped, although usually without sufficient details to indicate the models used or the probable effects. Two such conflicts deserve special mention here: the war involving Soviet forces in Afghanistan (1979–89) and the Gulf war of 1991.

In December 1979, Soviet troops entered Afghanistan, ousting the government and ushering in the tragedy of an unending civil war. Like the Americans in Vietnam, the Soviet forces controlled the towns, facing rural guerrillas who received support from the other superpower.[7] Like the Americans in Vietnam, the Soviet forces conducted massive bombardments of the countryside, killing and injuring civilians, driving families from their homes, creating millions of refugees who fled to neighboring countries,[8] and destroying crops and livestock.

Jeri Laber and Barnett R. Rubin, who interviewed refugees in the mid-1980s, wrote: 'Every time we asked an Afghan villager why he or she came to Pakistan, the answer began with the words *shurawi bombard* (Soviets bomb).' In their book *'A Nation Is Dying'* they quoted refugees and other eyewitnesses who described the bombing of villages, killing and wounding of civilians, and destruction of plants and livestock. Among the weapons cited in these accounts were fragmentation bombs, incendiaries, air-dropped mines, and manually emplaced mines and booby traps.[9]

Like Vietnam, Afghanistan served as a proving ground for new weaponry; and the details which reached the West showed how quickly the new antipersonnel technologies had spread to the other side. Among the new Soviet weapons were:

- A 30mm automatic grenade launcher, modelled after the 40mm automatic grenade launchers which the United States introduced in Vietnam. It is an infantry weapon for ground attack, firing a fragmentation grenade filled with one of the more powerful high explosives.[10]

- Cluster warheads for the BM-27 surface-to-surface multiple rocket system.[11]

- The AK-74 (not to be confused with the AK-47), an automatic rifle with a caliber of 5.45mm, slightly smaller than the American M16. The description provided by *Jane's Infantry Weapons 1982–83* (pages 191–2) gives the strong impression that the bullet has been designed with the deliberate intention of inflicting the worst possible wounds. It is long and thin, and the core is hollow at the tip. These two factors lower the stability of the bullet, making it much more prone to tumble soon after hitting the body. 'It is undoubtedly a clever way of extracting the maximum target effects from a small calibre bullet,' *Jane's* commented.[12]

Most damaging to civilians of the new Soviet weapons was the PFM-1, a small plastic antipersonnel mine modeled closely after the Dragontooth mine used in Vietnam. Huge numbers of these mines were dropped across the countryside from Soviet aircraft. Today Afghanistan is considered the most heavily mined country in the world.[13]

In the Gulf war of 1991, most of the fighting was away from populated areas. The use of precision-guided munitions reduced the risk of civilian casualties, although normal life was badly disrupted by the destruction of bridges, telephone centers, oil production and distribution, and electric power plants, affecting such vital areas of life as water supplies, sewage treatment, medical care, and agricultural production.[14] Cluster weapons were used in great numbers: William M. Arkin, Director of Military Research of Greenpeace International, has estimated that a minimum of 24,000,000 bomblets and mines were dropped from artillery, rockets, and aerial dispensers.[15] (As the Allied forces gained control of the air very quickly, the Iraqi Air Force was not able to use its cluster bombs.)

Some new cluster weapons were used: the British JP 233 airfield attack weapon, described earlier in this chapter; and cluster warheads for the Tomahawk, a ship-launched cruise missile for ground attack that was used for the first time in the Gulf war.[16] The Gulf war also saw the use of Vietnam-era weapons such as Rockeye II, the antitank bomb with an antipersonnel 'fringe benefit' which was used in the bombing of North Vietnam in 1972 (Chapter 4). Huge stocks of Rockeyes were on hand when the war began, and over 20,000 Rockeyes were reportedly dropped, deploying some 5,000,000 bomblets across the battlefield.[17] Rockeye bomblets were the most prevalent form of unexploded ordnance in Kuwait after the war, according to an official of a company engaged in clearing mines there.[18]

The most devastating of the new weapons was the Multiple Launch Rocket System (MLRS), a US weapon used for the first time in the Gulf war. Adopting the Soviet tradition of a multiple surface-to-surface rocket, this twelve-tube launcher fires one rocket from each tube. The aiming is controlled by a computer and the launcher is mounted on a tracked vehicle, enabling it to be driven away quickly after firing to elude enemy replying fire.

In the version used in the Gulf war, each of the twelve rockets has a warhead containing 644 bomblets, giving a total of 7,728 bomblets deployed when the rockets are fired together. The bomblet has a shaped charge, and is designed to be effective against light armor, materiel, and personnel; its destructive power is similar to that of a hand grenade. A salvo of twelve rockets is said to deploy bomblets over an area of twenty-three hectares at midrange, and almost twice that area at the maximum range of over thirty kilometers.[19]

With its long range and wide area coverage, the MLRS carries an obvious risk of indiscriminate effects. Its targets in the Gulf war may have been military targets in the desert (MLRS targets in the war were reported to include troops, artillery, armor, air-defense systems, combat engineering equipment, and command centers), but it is easy to envision other wars where civilians would be nearby. Accuracy of delivery could be a problem: in other wars the MLRS might well be used in situations where no visual observation or other on-the-spot target designation was possible, or where the weapon's computer would not work accurately.

The introduction of the MLRS was accompanied by reports of its supposedly terrifying effects on soldiers of the opposing force. After the war, a US military affairs magazine reported that according to captured Iraqi soldiers, a volley of bomblet-filled MLRS rockets directed against Iraqi artillery 'shut down the operations' of the artillery, 'partially because of the destruction it caused and partially because of its devastating psychological effects.'[20]

A New Humanitarian Response: The Landmines Campaign

G.Z. is a 20-year-old peasant farmer and tradesman from Zavala (Inhambane). In October 1992, G.Z. went into his field to cut grass. While cutting the grass his sickle hit a land mine which exploded. He was helped by friends who evacuated him by tractor to the rural hospital in Zavala. After one week there, he was transferred to the hospital in Chicuque, where he underwent surgery and remained in the hospital for a month. He has lost both hands and one eye and is undergoing eye surgery in Chicuque.
                From the Human Rights Watch report *Landmines in Mozambique*[21]

In 1979, when we discovered the size of the problem, there were about 10,000 Cambodian amputees. After 10 years of hard work, energy and devotion by over 120 volunteers on both sides of the conflict, nearly 15,000 are walking again. The problem is that – today – there are 30,000 amputees! And the figures are growing at just such an incredible rate in almost half of the countries we are working in: and I will only mention a few – Laos, Kurdistan, Mozambique, Ethiopia, Somalia or, even closer to home, former Yugoslavia.
                Statement by Handicap International, a French voluntary
                organization fitting artificial limbs to mine victims[22]

Eighty-five million, and possibly over one hundred million, unexploded land mines are believed to lie scattered in over sixty countries. Some are air-delivered mines, like those which first saw service in Vietnam; others are cheap hand-emplaced mines, many varieties of which are now readily available to armies and guerrilla forces from government arms plants and private manufacturers around the world. Most of these mines have long outlived any legitimate military purpose and are lying on or under the ground, ready to detonate when disturbed by a farmer, a passer-by, an animal, or someone trying to clear them.

Many of the mines are made of plastic and are very hard to detect. Many are camouflaged. Some have mechanisms which render them harmless or destroy them after a certain period of time; others do not, and will remain dangerous for years to come. Land mine explosions continue to kill and injure; families suffer great hardships through losing their productive members; large areas of land are rendered inaccessible; refugees are prevented from returning to their homes; precious resources are expended on mine clearance, medical treatment, and rehabilitation.

The problem grows worse each day as the rate of minelaying outpaces the rate at which mines can be cleared.

The problem of unexploded mines is an eloquent testimony to the failure of the efforts in the 1970s to adopt new bans on especially injurious and indiscriminate weapons. As described in Chapter 6, in 1974 Sweden and six other countries had proposed an outright ban on the aerial emplacement of antipersonnel mines. In the ensuing discussions, military considerations won the day, and the resulting Protocol II to the Conventional Weapons Convention is full of loopholes.

The war in Afghanistan is one example. As a major military power, the Soviet Union had taken part in the discussions, and was fully aware of the contents of the 1980 convention and its protocols, which it ratified in 1982. Had the Soviet Union, with its PFM-1 mines, been sympathetic to the humanitarian aims of the Swedish proposal; had it even respected the provisions on record-keeping, self-neutralizing devices, and warnings to civilians which, as a party to the convention, it was legally bound to do, the problem of unexploded mines in Afghanistan would be much less severe than it is today. But through lack of control and lack of publicity, the Soviet Army felt free to act without fear of effective sanctions or public censure, as have government and opposition forces in many other conflicts since 1980.

Confronting the ever-developing nightmare is the Landmines Campaign. It is a new campaign, and a campaign of a new kind. It arose not from the traditional arms control and disarmament movements, but from groups concerned with issues such as human rights and overseas medical assistance. Its six founding members are Handicap International; the US organizations Human Rights Watch, Vietnam Veterans of America Foundation, and Physicians for Human Rights (the latter with its special knowledge of medical aspects of human rights); the German organization Medico International; and the Mines Advisory Group, a nonprofit organization in Great Britain providing technical expertise on mine clearance.

In contrast to the disdain with which the Vietnam war protestors were treated, the Landmines Campaign has been able to attract public sympathy and favorable treatment of its cause by the news media through its forthright portrayal of the sufferings of mine victims.[23] Benefiting from a maturity of leadership which is the result of years of experience by many nongovernmental organizations since the Vietnam war, the campaign has displayed abilities and achieved results which would have astonished the anti-napalm and anti-cluster bomb campaigners of the 1960s and 1970s:

- An ability to conduct field research quickly and efficiently, and to publish the results. Individual experts and teams comprising doctors and explosive ordnance disposal specialists have visited various countries to survey the extent and effects of unexploded land mines, and the problems of mine clearance and medical rehabilitation. Reports have been published on El Salvador, Nicaragua, Cambodia, Iraqi Kurdistan, Somaliland, Angola, and Mozambique.[24]

- The ability and resources to compile essential information and make it available rapidly to activists. Thus the book *Landmines: A Deadly Legacy* was prepared by the Arms Project of Human Rights Watch and Physicians for Human Rights in a matter of months. This 510-page report includes case studies on seven of the worst-affected countries; chapters on the medical and social consequences, on mine clearance, and on attempts to control land mines in different countries; and a detailed chapter on the international law governing land mines, with an analysis of the weaknesses of Protocol II to the Conventional Weapons Convention. The report also has a chapter on the global trade in antipersonnel mines, with a list of mines reportedly produced by government factories or private firms in forty-six countries, and drawings of the most common models.

- Access to national decision-makers and an ability to persuade them to act quickly and decisively. One of the most remarkable achievements of the campaign was the adoption by the US Congress in 1992 of legislation imposing a moratorium on the sale, transfer, or export of antipersonnel mines from the United States to other countries.[25] Similar comprehensive moratoria on the export of antipersonnel mines have since been imposed by Argentina, Belgium, Canada, the Czech Republic, France, Germany, Greece, Israel, Italy, Poland, the Slovak Republic, South Africa, Spain, and Sweden; and limited moratoria have been imposed by the Netherlands, Switzerland, and the United Kingdom.

- An ability to get results at the United Nations. At its 48th session in 1993, the UN General Assembly adopted a resolution welcoming the establishment of a coordinated UN mine clearance program and asking the UN Secretary-General to explore the feasibility of setting up a voluntary fund for such activities as mine clearance training. A second General Assembly resolution called on states 'to agree to a moratorium on the export of antipersonnel land mines that pose grave dangers to civilian populations,' and urged states 'to implement such a moratorium.' A third resolution dealt with the organization of the review conference of the Conventional Weapons Convention (see below). Yet another resolution, concerning children in armed conflict, called for a study to produce recommendations on ways and means of protecting children against antipersonnel mines.[26] The resolutions on mine clearance, on a moratorium on exports, and on the protection of children were all adopted without a vote – a sign of a high degree of agreement among UN members.

One of the most original contributions of the Landmines Campaign has been in the very boldness of its demands. In calling for a ban on exports, the campaign is tackling an area of human activity – arms sales – in which, except with major weapons deemed to have strategic implications, where governments are likely to impose strict controls, the pursuit of profits has normally been the guiding force. The accompanying demand for a complete ban on use neatly undercuts the traditional logic of such discussions, where the outcome has normally been thought of as the result of a balancing exercise between humanitarian considerations and military needs.

Applied to antipersonnel mines, that logic would dictate that where the military need is clear and the risk to civilians small – as, for example, when hand-emplaced mines, clearly marked, recorded, detectable, and fitted with self-destruct or self-neutralizing mechanisms, are placed around a military encampment to guard against intrusion – then 'military necessity' would prevail and such munitions or such uses of them would be allowed, whatever bans might be placed on other mines or other uses. But the campaign calls for a total ban. It does so on two grounds: first, that the adverse effects on society are so great as to outweigh any possible military needs; and second, that antipersonnel mines must be stigmatized altogether, so that any use of them will be unacceptable to public opinion and the community of nations. Stigmatization, in other words, is an important technique of control, and for a weapon to be stigmatized, the ban must be total.

Aryeh Neier, former executive director of Human Rights Watch, has stated that 'the arguments against a ban collapse in the face of the extraordinary cost that mines represent for the countries where they are used.' On the need for the ban to be total, Neier has drawn an analogy to torture, a practice which the community of nations, under successive international human rights instruments adopted since World War II, has declared to be totally outlawed:

> There are always arguments that torture should be legitimate in certain circumstances, but we can all readily understand that if we were to permit torture even in those special circumstances the stigma would disappear. Torturers would be, in effect, licensed. It is the same with mine manufacture.[27]

New Moves for International Bans: The 1995
Review Conference of the Conventional Weapons Convention

Responding to the pressure from the Landmines Campaign, and especially from Handicap International in France, the French government in 1993 formally requested the UN Secretary-General to convene a conference for the purpose of reviewing the Conventional Weapons Convention. For the first time since the adoption of the convention in 1980, there would be an opportunity to strengthen Protocol II on land mines by amending it, to amend other parts of the convention and other protocols, or to adopt restrictions and bans on other types of weapons.[28]

The review conference, due to be held in Geneva in September–October 1995, has been preceded by official preparatory meetings of a 'Group of Governmental Experts' in 1994 and 1995. At its first session, the group reached a tacit understanding that in contrast to the Lucerne and Lugano meetings and the UN conference in 1979–80, non-governmental organizations would not be permitted to attend its meetings as observers. This outrageous decision (which was opposed by many governments) meant that the organizations which had done most to raise the issue of mines and to relieve the sufferings of mine victims would have no opportunity to hear what the governmental representatives were saying, and so be able to press their concerns effectively. Apart from the International Committee of the Red Cross, which was allowed to attend, the 'conscience of humanity' was, in effect, excluded from the meetings. Matters were not improved by the decision taken at the first session that the decisions of the Group of Governmental Experts would be by consensus, meaning that any proposal on the organization of the conference could be blocked by a single state party to the convention.

In preparing for the conference, as in the 1970s, a leading role has been taken by the ICRC. With its expert knowledge of the laws of armed conflict and its experience of the medical treatment of war victims, the ICRC has been in a unique position to convene meetings of experts in such fields as weapons design, wound treatment, international law, and explosive ordnance disposal. Expert meetings have been held on land mines (in 1993 and 1994), laser weapons (between 1989 and 1991), and other weapons which might be the subject of bans or restrictions (in 1994). The ICRC has also prepared documentation and proposals for consideration by the review conference.

In addition to land mines, topics raised by the ICRC have included the following.

Laser weapons: warfare by blinding

A laser ('Light Amplification by Stimulated Emission of Radiation') 'can be thought of as a funnel that absorbs energy from a large spectrum and compresses it into a narrow one for a very short amount of time. The very high concentration of energy involved enables it to be pinpointed, thereby concentrating damage in a restricted area.'[29] It can damage hard and soft materials, including human tissues, and is especially harmful to the eye, where it can easily cause permanent blindness. The eye focuses the laser beam onto a small point on the retina. The effect magnifies the brightness of the laser beam by a factor of up to half a million. As two experts have written, this effect 'can be further multiplied by any magnifying or light-collecting optics placed in front of the eye,' such as the binoculars which a soldier might be using to survey an enemy position.[30]

Laser devices are available for various military uses, such as rangefinding and target designation. Even these devices are dangerous to the eyes, and there have been accidents. Developmental work has also been done on lasers designed to destroy optical sensors (sensors simulating human eyesight which are mounted on tanks or other military equipment or positions). From there it is but a short step to a laser deliberately intended to dazzle or blind. At least one country, the United Kingdom, is reported to have fitted its warships with laser guns intended to dazzle the pilots of attacking aircraft.[31]

Between 1989 and 1991 the ICRC convened four experts' meetings, attended by specialists in laser technology, ophthalmology, military medicine and psychiatry, and international humanitarian law. As summarized in the ICRC reports, the meetings found that:

- Lasers can be very small and very cheap. Clip-on devices that can now be fitted to rifles for training purposes could easily be made non-eye-safe. Laser rangefinders could be misused to blind intentionally. And 'As the energy and wave length of the laser necessary to destroy sensors is similar to those necessary to damage eyes, laser systems said to be designed for anti-sensor purposes could also be used for antipersonnel purposes.'[32]

- It is not easy to produce a laser which will dazzle but not blind. For dazzling systems to be effective over long ranges, it is inevitable that at shorter ranges eye damage will result. The exact range for dazzling as against permanent blindness is unpredictable, as, in battlefield conditions, factors such as smoke, dust, and humidity will cause variations. Most infrared wave lengths cannot produce temporary effects (dazzling or flash blindness) but only permanent effects.[33]

- It is difficult to protect soldiers by means of special goggles. Goggles 'would only screen out a limited range of known wave lengths, whereas lasers can operate over a wide range of wave lengths.'[34]

- Blinding was characterized by the experts as an especially severe form of disability, permanent and incurable, often causing severe long-term depression, and placing a heavy burden on the victim's family and on a country's medical and social services. It was estimated that if blinding as a method of warfare became a common practice, serious damage to the eye might account for between 25 and 50 per cent of all casualties.[35]

At the final ICRC expert meeting, attended by officials from twenty-two countries, there was 'a division of opinion' as to whether the use of blinding weapons is illegal under existing law, which prohibits the use of weapons of a nature to cause superfluous injury or unnecessary suffering, as set forth in Article 35 of Additional Protocol II to the Geneva Conventions (Chapter 6).[36] But: 'The majority of participants thought that whatever the assessment of the present lawfulness of such use, it should be subject to legal regulation because there are important policy reasons for prohibiting blinding as a method of warfare. Many thought that such a prohibition ought to be introduced simply because blinding weapons are horrific and therefore totally unacceptable.'[37]

In August 1994, at the third session of the Group of Governmental Experts to prepare the review conference, draft texts for a new protocol banning the use of blinding lasers were offered by Sweden and the ICRC. A somewhat weaker text emerged from the fourth session of the Group of Governmental Experts in January 1995.[38] As of the time of writing of this book, the chances of its success at the review conference were uncertain.

Fuel-air explosives and other wide-area blast weapons

A fuel-air explosive (FAE) is a cloud of gas or an aerosol cloud of small particles or vapor droplets which spreads over a target and is then detonated, as in an explosion from gasoline fumes or a gas leak.[39] Because of the spreading of the cloud, the blast covers a much wider area than that produced by the same weight of high explosive.[40]

Fuel-air explosives can be used to clear minefields and to attack 'soft targets' such as aircraft, antennas, and troops. Not only will a fuel-air explosive kill anyone within the area of the blast, chiefly by rupturing the lungs, but the cloud envelops the target area, and the blast will kill soldiers sheltering in foxholes and trenches.[41] The capacity of fuel-air explosives to get behind defensive barriers makes cover from bombardment virtually impossible for combatants and civilians alike.[42]

Fuel-air explosives were first used in Vietnam,[43] as was a much larger blast weapon, a 15,000-lb bomb nicknamed the 'daisy cutter' because it explodes just above the ground.[44] In the 1991 Gulf war, US fuel-air explosives were used to clear minefields, and reportedly also to attack Iraqi troops in bunkers and defensive fortifications.[45]

Besides the United States, Russia has a fuel-air explosive bomb, twice the size of the original US bomb, and China displayed a fuel-air explosive bomb at the 1991 Paris Air Show.[46] Iraq, too, was able to develop a fuel-air explosive bomb; one of the sources available to it was a 300-page Honeywell report which the company sold to a Swiss corporation in violation of its own restrictions on the export of weapons technology.[47] Future developments are likely to improve the functioning of fuel-air explosives, and make them more powerful.[48]

At the Lugano conference in 1976, Sweden proposed banning the antipersonnel use of fuel-air explosives, while Switzerland proposed prohibiting the use of fuel-air explosives altogether. Later in the year, at the Diplomatic Conference (Chapter 6), the two countries joined forces and presented a revised proposal banning the antipersonnel use of fuel-air explosives which sought to take account of the criticisms levelled against their earlier proposals. With language borrowed from the 1868 Declaration of St Petersburg, an explanatory note stated: 'The effects of use of FAEs against personnel would be far in excess of what is needed to place a soldier *hors de combat* and would in a large number of cases render death inevitable.'[49] In response, the United States in 1977 produced experimental findings purportedly showing that fuel-air explosives were no worse than high explosive weapons.[50]

In 1979 Sweden and Switzerland, now joined by Mexico, submitted a similar proposal at the UN conference. No action was taken on it, and no such prohibition was included in a protocol to the Conventional Weapons Convention.

In 1990 two ICRC staff members drew attention to the problem of fuel-air explosives in an article in the *International Review of the Red Cross*.[51] But governments have shown little interest, and there is little chance of the review conference taking any action.

Cluster weapons

As described earlier in this chapter, cluster technologies have proliferated since the 1960s and are now available to the armed forces of many countries. There has been some interest among organizations participating in the Landmines Campaign in the problem of unexploded bomblets or 'submunitions' from cluster weapons, which is akin to the problem of unexploded land mines, but on the wider issue of the indiscriminate effects of cluster weapons there seems little chance that the review conference will take action. One difficulty in doing so would be that of drawing a line between cluster weapons and uses of cluster weapons which are inevitably indiscriminate or are highly likely to be so, and those at the other extreme where the target is of clear military value and there is little risk of indiscriminate effects.[52] Looming behind this technical difficulty is the political difficulty of persuading military forces even to contemplate renouncing a weapon which they have determined to be useful and in which they have invested.

'Future weapons'

Apart from lasers, other possible 'future weapons' raised in the ICRC discussions have included 'directed energy weapons' such as high-power microwaves and infrasound devices; 'non-lethal' weapons involving chemicals; and the possible use of biotechnology and genetic engineering for the development of weapons of mass extermination. In its expert meetings, the ICRC has endeavored to obtain information about the effects of such technologies, and about any likely weapons developments based on them. There are as yet no reports that any of these technologies has been turned into weapons, but warnings are being voiced about the need to monitor and control developments.[53]

Strengthening the convention

In a February 1994 report for the review conference, the ICRC pointed to a number of problems in the Conventional Weapons Convention. One is 'the fact that most damage inflicted by weapons, frequently as a result of indiscriminate use, occurs during internal armed conflicts,' to which the convention formally does not apply (Chapter 6). Another is '[t]he total lack of implementation mechanisms.'

Among the possible measures for implementation of the convention suggested in the ICRC report are the establishment of procedures for the compulsory adjudication of complaints that the convention has been violated, possibly through the creation of a special court for the convention; the creation of a supervisory body to which states parties would report and which would collect information from other sources; attaching criminal sanctions to individual violations of the rules contained in the protocols; incorporating the provisions of the convention into national laws and regulations; providing armed forces with appropriate training; and requiring armed forces to have legal advisers at different levels to give guidance on matters relating to the use of weapons.

Another suggestion in the ICRC report is to extend the application of the convention to non-international armed conflicts, either by amending it or through other means by which states parties could formally accept such extension if they so wished.

The ICRC also suggested that the procedure for review of the convention 'ought to be used regularly. Such reviews could evaluate the effectiveness of the provisions of the Convention and also take timely preventive measures in relation to new developments, whether entirely new weapons or new designs of existing weapons, that are likely to create problems.'[54]

A further problem regarding the Conventional Weapons Convention is the low number of states parties. By January 1995 only 42 states had ratified or acceded to the convention, as against 135 states parties to Additional Protocol I to the Geneva Conventions of 1949, 125 states parties to Additional Protocol II and 185 states parties to the Geneva Conventions themselves. It is to be hoped that the interest raised by the review conference will lead many more states to become parties to the 1980 convention.[55]

Bringing the 1899 Dum-Dum Ban up to Date

In the realm of rifle bullets, curiously, the outlook for restraint is more positive than on some other antipersonnel weapons. In 1974, Sweden and six other countries had proposed banning the use of small-caliber projectiles which are 'so designed or have such velocity that they are apt to deform or tumble on or following entry into a human body or to create shock-waves which damage tissue outside their trajectories or to produce secondary projectiles.' The proposal, fiercely criticized, did not lead to the development of a protocol on the subject, but the UN conference in 1979 adopted a resolution appealing for restraint in the development of small-caliber weapon systems 'so as to avoid an unnecessary escalation of the injurious effects of such systems,' and inviting governments to carry out further research (Chapter 6).

That research had already begun. In 1975 Sweden convened an international, interdisciplinary symposium on wound ballistics. Further symposia were held in 1977, 1978, 1981, 1985, and 1988. Many papers were presented by military and medical experts from different countries and many topics were discussed, including not only the physical process of wounding but complex physiological effects, the surgical treatment of injuries, and techniques of testing and observation, with a special focus on bullet wounding. A body of knowledge was being built up, freely available in the open literature and reflecting the approaches of different national research traditions.

At an ICRC expert meeting in May–June 1994, the Swiss ballistic scientist Beat P. Kneubuehl presented experimental findings on the wounding effects of different military rifle bullets. Drawing from a recently published textbook on wound ballistics which he had written with the German professor of forensic medicine Karl G. Sellier,[56] Kneubuehl was in a position to present a comprehensive and convincing account of the process of bullet wounding and the design parameters producing different levels of injury.

It has long been known that bullets can tumble inside the body and that tumbling is a cause of severe wounding, as, in moments when a bullet is moving through the body with a wide angle of incidence rather than nose-on, the area of the bullet pushing against the tissues is relatively large, and the transfer of energy to the tissues is correspondingly great. According to Sellier and Kneubuehl, a bullet which is fully enclosed in a metal jacket, as are virtually all military rifle bullets today, will start to turn around a lateral axis at some distance after entering the body. Once it starts to turn, the rate of turning increases rapidly; the angle of incidence reaches 90 degrees and the bullet continues turning until it is traveling nearly tail first. After that, it can partly turn several more times before entering the last phase, when it will again be traveling tail first. Depending on its construction, a full-metal-jacketed bullet can deform or break up because of the stresses placed on it during turning, but deformation or breakup of a full-metal-jacketed bullet is a byproduct of turning and not an independent process, although once it happens, the deformation or breakup adds to the wounding effect because of the increase in the surface area of bullet material pressing against the tissues.[57]

The tumbling of a bullet is thus the critical mechanism resulting in severe injury, and the likelihood of causing a severe wound will depend on how far a bullet penetrates the body before tumbling. According to Sellier and Kneubuehl, the tendency of a bullet to tumble early on entering the body is dependent on the angle of incidence on impact, the shape of the bullet nose, and the gyroscopic stability of the bullet.[58] Gyroscopic stability, in turn, is dependent on such factors as the rate of spin, the moments of inertia, and the geometry of the bullet. In general, the greater the gyroscopic stability of a bullet (for example, because of a higher spin rate), the further it will go in the body before starting to tumble; and the shorter a bullet is in relation to its diameter, the less likely it is to tumble.

It is consistent with these findings to suppose that an ammunition designer who is intent on inflicting the greatest possible damage will want to have the bullet turn as soon as possible, thus achieving the same effect (rapid transfer of the bullet's kinetic energy) as with the outlawed dum-dum bullet. Conversely, a designer wishing to avoid severe wounds will want the bullet to travel as far as possible before turning: a soldier hit in the arm or leg will be out of action temporarily, but is unlikely to suffer permanent injury or to die.

The possibility of applying the findings of wound ballistics to reduce rather than increase the level of injury is not merely a theoretical one. In 1981, the North Atlantic Treaty Organization announced its decision to adopt a second standard caliber for small arms, alongside the previous standard caliber of 7.62mm. The second caliber selected was 5.56mm, the same as that of the US M16 rifle, but a Belgian round, the SS 109, was adopted rather than the M16 round as a basis for standardization of ammunition for NATO rifles.

In a presentation to the fourth International Symposium on Wound Ballistics in 1982, a representative of the Belgian *Fabrique Nationale*, manufacturer of the SS 109, said that the new bullet had a 'high coefficient of essential stability' and a high rate of spin imparted by a rifling twist of one turn in 7 inches, as compared with the M16 twist of one turn in 12 inches. He made it clear that the SS 109 design program had been heavily influenced by the 1979 resolution of the UN conference appealing for restraint in the development of small-caliber weapon systems.[59] Several participants at the ICRC expert meeting in 1994 recalled, with satisfaction, that the 1979 resolution had had an effect.

Two months later, at the meeting of the Group of Governmental Experts, Switzerland presented a proposal for a new protocol to the Conventional Weapons Convention. The Swiss draft Protocol on Small-Caliber Weapon Systems reads:

1. It is prohibited to use arms and ammunition with a caliber of less than 12.7 millimeters which from a shooting distance of at least 25 meters release more than 20 joules of energy per centimeter during the first 15 centimeters of their trajectory within the human body.

2. The States Parties commit themselves to intensifying their cooperation in order to establish an internationally recognized experimental method by which the effect of small-caliber projectiles in the human body can be precisely assessed.

The Swiss draft Protocol has several advantages over previous texts. Unlike the 1899 Hague Declaration, which refers only to 'bullets,' the term 'small-caliber weapon systems' encompasses both ammunition and the weapons firing it, an acknowledgment that design features of a weapon, such as the rifling twist, may be responsible for wound effects.[60] Also unlike the Hague Declaration and the texts proposed in the 1970s, the Swiss draft refers only to the effects of small-caliber weapon systems, not to the ways in which these effects are produced, thus avoiding the arguments raised in previous discussions over what mechanisms are actually responsible for the effects produced, and ensuring that the ban will cover any future weapons producing similar effects through other mechanisms. The effect of a small-caliber projectile is specified in terms of energy deposit, a physical process which can be measured by a simple procedure such as measuring the size of the cavity formed in a block of soap at different distances of penetration.[61] Finally, the missile effects described in the Swiss draft correspond to the critical features of the wounding process as shown in experimental tests and explained in wound ballistics theory.[62]

The formulation of the Swiss proposal and the numbers used in it would have the effect of prohibiting the use of small-caliber weapon systems which cause worse wounds than a 5.56mm rifle firing an SS 109 bullet. This ammunition round, which is accepted as a NATO standard, would be allowed, as would older, still widespread systems such as the NATO 7.62mm rifle system and the Russian AK-47, but anything worse would not be allowed.

Such a proposal should be immensely attractive to major armies of the world, as it would prevent small-caliber weapons worse than what they themselves now use, being used against their soldiers. But the proposal had received little backing at the time of writing of this book, and it looked unlikely to be accepted by the review conference. Once again, it seemed that an opportunity to mitigate the sufferings of war would be lost.

The Future of Antipersonnel Weapons

There is an urgent need in the world today for public examination of the weapons of antipersonnel warfare. These arms are devised in the name of the public, for its protection. The public must consider whether they can be justified in the name of humanity.

Antipersonnel weapons may be characterized by efficiency, lethality, safety,[63] reliability, adaptability, rugged construction, or low manufacturing cost, but the ethical quality which characterizes them can be summed up in the word 'cruelty.' To take a science devoted to healing and apply it to discover how to inflict worse wounds cannot be considered an act of kindness. Yet the quality of cruelty is seldom mentioned.

'Men are greedy, men are vicious, men are cruel,' said the verisimilar colonel who made his appearance at the beginning of this book. Yet a society cannot be based on cruelty. Cruelty is ascribed to one's opponents, while nobility characterizes one's own war effort, and morality and good citizenship are supposed to permeate interpersonal relations in one's country.

Avoiding the contradiction, the weapon is mentally distanced from its effects. The flier or the artilleryman launching a cluster munition does not see the people hit by the fragments of an antipersonnel bomblet. The minelayer does not meet the farmer or the child who will fall victim years later to the mine which he has emplaced. The ordnance engineer does not know who will be affected by the products of his art.

A weapons designer is not, first and foremost, a killer; he is a statistician, a metallurgist, an engineer. He is trained for his profession and he thinks in its terms.

Enter the world of the munitions designer. It is filled with 'lethal area estimates' and 'kill probabilities,' 'effective casualty radius' and 'expected damage to a circular target area.' There are 'sensitivity studies' and 'compatibility tests' – not a form of marriage counselling, but a procedure for making sure that a given bomb can be used with a given airplane.

Cruelty is disapproved of morally, and certain forms of cruelty are crimes, punished by law. But when war intervenes, a new logic takes over. To set fire to a person or to put out a person's eyes would be serious crimes in normal circumstances, but in war these methods of attack are claimed to be justified on grounds of 'military necessity.'

Imperfect and limited as it is, international humanitarian law is the best conceptual and legal system devised to date to limit the sufferings inflicted in war. This law needs to be applied and developed.

The campaign against land mines is the most encouraging recent development for tackling the antipersonnel effects of modern warfare and trying to roll back the new technological capacity for inflicting widespread harm on civilians. The campaign needs to be supported as widely as possible.

These matters are too important to be left to the specialists. Ordinary citizens must learn how wars are conducted, become aware of the basic concepts of international humanitarian law, and find ways of acting to restrict the damage being inflicted daily across the globe.[64] Without this involvement, the development and use of antipersonnel technology will continue to grow.

One day, during the Lucerne conference, I lunched in a popular restaurant with a weapons designer from a European country. He suggested that I try the *steak tartare*; it was especially good *feurig*, he said – mixed with a dash of brandy. He was most enthusiastic about this excellent dish. 'I do not think that you will get such good beef in my country,' he exclaimed.

After generous helpings of apple pie and coffee, we pushed our plates aside and settled down to a discussion of methods of lethal area calculation.

Until lethal area calculations become a matter of outrage, until governments are pressed to adopt strict limits for the prohibition of weapons causing superfluous injury or having indiscriminate effects, until there is a truly effective worldwide citizens' movement concerned about wars and the conduct of warfare, the growth in suffering inflicted in armed conflicts will continue.

Notes

1. Human Rights Watch Arms Project and Physicians for Human Rights, 1993, p. xi (cited below as *Landmines: A Deadly Legacy*).

2. *Ibid.*, Appendix 1, pp. 361–2.

3. The 1952 study cited in Chapter 2 considered spherical and barrel-shaped grenades, and notched wire, steel balls, and preformed rectangular parallelepipeds as sources of fragments. The confidential results of this study were immediately shared with America's British and Canadian allies, as shown by the distribution list at the end of the report (Dunn and Sterne, 1952).

4. *Jane's Infantry Weapons 1975*; SIPRI, 1978, Table 5.1, pp. 127–31.

5. SIPRI, 1978, Tables 5.12 and 5.13, pp. 152–8.

6. Dale S. De Haan, counsel to the US Senate Subcommittee on Refugees and Escapees, was sent to the Middle East on a fact-finding mission shortly after the war and returned with strong reservations about the use of US antipersonnel weapons in the Middle East, according to the newspaper columnist Nick Thimmesch:

> 'I saw what happened in Syria because of them,' he told me. 'These weapons should be banned from use in populated areas. Cluster bombs were used in Damascus and it was horrible. There were some 2,000 casualties.' (Nick Thimmesch, 'War's Double Standard', *Philadelphia Bulletin*, 20 December 1973)

7. Shortly after a peace agreement providing for the withdrawal of Soviet forces was signed in 1988, a *New York Times* journalist reported: 'With help from China and many Moslem nations, the United States led a huge international operation to arm the Afghan guerrillas with the weapons they needed to drive the Soviet army from their country.' The operation was 'one of the biggest ever mounted by the Central Intelligence Agency,' costing more than $2 billion over eight years, he wrote. His report was based on interviews with members of Congress, US government officials, and intelligence agencies (Robert Pear, 'How US Armed the Afghans,' *International Herald Tribune*, 19 April 1988).

8. By 1987 an estimated five million or more refugees had taken shelter in Pakistan and Iran, representing one-third of the country's prewar population (Laber and Rubin, 1988, p. xii).

9. *Ibid.*, pp. 10–17, 42–8.

10. Urban, 1988, p. 212. In an early account, *Jane's Infantry Weapons 1980–81* (pp. 53–5, published in 1980) commented:

We see this grenade launcher as a latter-day support machine gun and we see it being deployed and used in much the same way as were the old Maxim machine guns in the First and Second World Wars. The difference is that there is probably no need to use the grenade launcher in pairs, as was always the case with the machine guns, and it also seems that the crew for the launcher is less than it was for the machine guns. In other words, it is a more efficient and more cost-effective weapon. Certainly it is better to put down a beaten zone of high explosive projectiles, however small, than it is to put down the same beaten zone with lead bullets.

According to *Jane's Infantry Weapons 1988–89*, the 30mm grenade used with the AGS-17 launcher is filled with RDX/WX 94/6, and a diagram reproduced in *Jane's* indicates that steel balls embedded in the casing serve as the fragmentation material. *Jane's* reported that there is also a helicopter-mounted version of the launcher.

11. Urban, 1988, p. 212. Unlike the USA, the Soviet Union and its Warsaw Pact allies had long had multiple rocket launchers as a standard weapon in their arsenals. According to *Jane's Weapon Systems 1987–88* (p. 124), the BM-27 version is a truck-mounted, 16-tube, 220mm multiple rocket system which was introduced into the Soviet Army in 1977. *Jane's* reported: 'The rockets can be fitted with a variety of warheads including chemical, high explosive and bomblet (minelet, fragmentation and incendiary).' According to Urban, Soviet forces also used cluster warheads for the FROG-7 battlefield support missile in Afghanistan.

12. Recent test firings conducted by the Swiss ballistic scientist Beat P. Kneubuehl confirm the wounding capacity of the AK-74 bullet. According to Kneubuehl's figures, the bullet begins rapidly transferring energy to the tissues much sooner after entering the body than the SS 109 5.56mm NATO bullet. By the time it penetrates 15 centimeters into the test medium, the AK-74 bullet has deposited 700 joules of energy, while the SS 109 bullet penetrates 20 centimeters before depositing the same amount. This means that the AK-74 bullet is much more likely than the NATO bullet to cause a severe wound (ICRC, 1994b, pp. 36–7; see also Fackler *et al.*, 1984).

13. *Landmines: A Deadly Legacy*, pp. 145, 298–9.

14. Arkin *et. al.*, 1991, pp. 19, 28–9, 55–60.

15. William M. Arkin, 'Military Technology and the Banning of Land Mines,' presentation at the first NGO Conference on Landmines, London, 24–26 May 1993.

16. According to the Greenpeace study of the Gulf war, the following cluster bombs were also used: the British BL 755 (see Chapter 6); the French Belouga, a 305-kg free-fall cluster bomb dispensing 151 1.3-kg fragmentation or antitank bomblets; and US cluster bombs – the CBU-52 (SUU-30 dispenser with BLU-61 2.2-lb fragmentation bomblets), CBU-58 (SUU-30 with BLU-63 fragmentation bomblets, successor to the CBU-24), CBU-71 (SUU-30 with BLU-86 fragmentation bomblets), CBU-78 scatterable mine system, and CBU-87 1,000-lb combined effects munition (SUU-65 Tactical Munitions Dispenser with 202 BLU-97 fragmentation/antitank/incendiary bomblets, originally developed by Honeywell Inc. for the US Air Force according to *Jane's Air-Launched Weapons*) (Arkin *et al.*,

1991, Appendix A). Allied forces also used bomblet-filled artillery shells.

17. Arkin *et al.*, 1991, Appendix A.

18. *Landmines: A Deadly Legacy*, p. 53. According to information presented at the ICRC Symposium on Anti-personnel Mines (Montreux, 21–23 April 1993), Rockeye bomblets dropped in Kuwait had several different fuzing systems which could not be distinguished externally, and the only safe method of disposal was *in situ* demolition, an expensive and destructive procedure (ICRC, 1993b, p. 134).

19. *Jane's Weapon Systems 1987–88*, pp. 128–9.

20. '"Steel Rain" Shut Down Iraqi Artillery,' *Armed Forces Journal International*, May 1991, p. 37. During the war, a British army spokesman described the use of the MLRS against Iraqi artillery and said that the allies were attacking Iraq's 'will to resist' as much as their weaponry (William Branigin, 'Iraqi Losses "Horrendous," Official Says,' *Washington Post*, 20 February 1991). From a humanitarian perspective, it is doubtful that the inherent damage to civilian life posed by the deployment of a volley of 7,700 bomblets can be justified by the hope of frightening the enemy.

21. Human Rights Watch Arms Project and Human Rights Watch/Africa, 1994, p. 47.

22. Statement at the first international NGO Conference on Landmines, London, 24 May 1993.

23. Assessments of the campaign and a chronology of its accomplishments are given in the Report of Proceedings of the Second NGO Conference on Landmines (Geneva, 9–11 May 1994), issued by Vietnam Veterans of America Foundation, 1994, pp. 1–18.

24. Americas Watch, *Land Mines in El Salvador and Nicaragua: The Civilian Victims*, New York, Americas Watch, 1986; Asia Watch and Physicians for Human Rights, *Land Mines in Cambodia: The Coward's War*, published by Human Rights Watch and Physicians for Human Rights, 1991; Middle East Watch, *Hidden Death: Land Mines and Civilian Casualties in Iraqi Kurdistan; October 1992*, New York, Middle East Watch, 1992; Physicians for Human Rights, *Hidden Enemies: Land Mines in Northern Somalia*, Boston, Physicians for Human Rights, 1992; Africa Watch, *Land Mines in Angola*, New York, Human Rights Watch, 1993; Human Rights Watch Arms Project and Human Rights Watch/Africa, 1994.

25. For the texts of the 1992 one-year US moratorium and its three-year extension adopted in 1993, see *Landmines: A Deadly Legacy*, Appendices 7 and 8.

26. Respectively, resolution 48/7; part K of resolution 48/75; and resolutions 48/79 and 48/157. Follow-up resolutions were adopted by the General Assembly in 1994 (resolutions 49/215, part D of resolution 49/75, and resolutions 49/79 and 49/209).

27. Ryle, 1993, p. 135.

28. The French initiative was in accordance with Article 8 of the convention, which provides for the convening of conferences at the request of states parties for the purpose of reviewing, amending, or adding protocols to the convention. Any amendments to the convention or to its protocols may be adopted only by states which are parties to the convention or are bound by the respective protocols, but all states may attend as observers and may participate fully in any decision to adopt new protocols.

29. ICRC, 1993a, p. 23.

30. Bengt Anderberg and Myron L. Wolbarsht, 'Blinding Lasers: The Nastiest Weapon?', *Military Technology*, March 1990 (reprinted in ICRC, 1993a, p. 161).

31. Fermin Gallego and Mark Daly, 'Laser Weapon in Royal Navy Service,' *Jane's Defence Weekly*, 13 January 1990 (reprinted in ICRC, *ibid.*, pp. 170–71).

32. ICRC, 1994a, p. 151.

33. ICRC, 1993a, pp. 99, 109.

34. ICRC, 1994a, p. 151.

35. *Ibid.*, pp. 152–3.

36. In September 1988 the Judge Advocate General of the US Army, the Army's highest legal officer, issued a Memorandum of Law which concluded that the use of a laser as an antipersonnel weapon 'would not cause unnecessary suffering when compared to other wounding mechanisms to which a soldier might be exposed on the modern battlefield, and hence would not violate any international law obligation of the United States. Accordingly, the use of anti-personnel laser weapons is lawful.' The ruling pointed out that soldiers also suffer eye wounds from bomb fragments and battlefield debris, and that 'Unlike lasers, however, injury from each of these mechanisms frequently results in death; therefore antipersonnel laser injury is more humane than injury caused by comparable weapons.' It stated that the extent of actual injury from lasers is subject to a 'myriad of factors,' and maintained that 'potential laser injuries can be minimized with the utilization of appropriate protective equipment and defensive actions.' (ICRC, 1993a, pp. 367–71).

This bizarre assemblage of facts follows the same logic as that which was behind US attempts to demolish the Swedish proposals at the Lucerne and Lugano conferences in the 1970s: if a weapon can be shown to be no more harmful than others already in use, then the claim that it is indiscriminate or causes unnecessary suffering is refuted. A better approach would be to endeavor to advance the laws of war as far as possible in the direction of reducing the suffering inflicted on soldiers and civilians.

37. ICRC, 1994a, p. 153.

38. The Swedish proposed draft text read: 'It is prohibited to use laser beams as an antipersonnel method of warfare, with the intention or expected result of seriously damaging the eyesight of persons.' The ICRC text read:

1. Blinding as a method of warfare is prohibited.
2. Laser weapons may not be used against the eyesight of persons.

The ICRC text was broader than the Swedish, as it prohibited blinding by any means, and forbade the use of lasers to dazzle as well as to blind. The weaker text which emerged from the January 1995 meeting had the support of twenty-five countries, but its first paragraph, forbidding the use of blinding lasers against the eyesight of persons 'as a method of warfare,' was opposed by several major military powers.

39. SIPRI, 1978, p. 171.

40. A Honeywell expert has reported that 227 kilograms of a typical fuel-air explosive fuel has a lethal radius of 30 meters within which the destruction of a hypothetical soft target such as troops, vehicles, unreinforced buildings or

antennas is assured, as against a lethal radius of 12 meters for a 227-kg charge of TNT. The area of assured destruction by this amount of fuel-air explosive fuel is thus six times greater than that for a comparable charge of a normal high explosive (Lavoie, 1989, pp. 66–8).

41. A study by the US Central Intelligence Agency reported that 'Before ignition, the aerosol or fuel-air mixture ... will enter any space not totally sealed, creep into houses, seep into ventilation systems, be drawn into the air intakes of engines, and settle in any depression the terrain offers.' The study also stated: 'The effect of an FAE explosion within confined spaces is immense. Those near the ignition point are obliterated. Those at the fringe are likely to suffer many internal, and thus invisible, injuries, including burst eardrums and crushed inner ear organs, severe concussions, ruptured lungs and internal organs, and possibly blindness' (US Central Intelligence Agency, 'Conventional Weapons Producing Chemical-Warfare-Agent-Like Injuries,' *ca.* 1991).

42. Doswald-Beck and Cauderay, 1990, p. 570.

43. The fuel-air explosive bomb used in Vietnam, the CBU-55/B, is still in US service. It was described in a 1971 Navy manual as 'a free-fall weapon delivered by helicopters and slow-speed, fixed-wing aircraft to clear helicopter landing zones of mines, booby traps, foliage, and enemy personnel' (US Navy, 1971, p. 1-1). The CBU-55/B is a cluster weapon comprising three BLU-73/B bombs filled with ethylene oxide. The three bombs burst open just before reaching the ground, forming an aerosol cloud, which is then ignited.

44. The BLU-82 'daisy cutter' contains some 5,715 kilograms of a special dense blasting agent in the form of a gelled aqueous slurry, and is fuzed to explode just above ground level. The energy yield is about twice that of TNT, and the concussive blast is said to be greater than that of the smallest nuclear devices. The radius of 100 per cent mortality for plant and animal life is said to be 65 meters about the point of explosion, and the zone of death and injury is said to extend to nearly 400 meters. Several hundred BLU-82s are thought to have been dropped between 1970 and 1972 in the US–Indochina war. Its main purpose was to produce helicopter landing zones in jungles, but use against suspected enemy troop concentrations was also reported (SIPRI, 1978, p. 171).

45. Arkin *et al.*, 1991, Appendix A, p. A-3.

46. *Jane's Air-Launched Weapons*, 1992.

47. 'Honeywell Admits it Erred in Selling a Bomb Report,' *Los Angeles Times* report reprinted in the *International Herald Tribune*, 18 February 1991. A Honeywell internal investigation into the sale concluded that the report did not contain any information which could have contributed to the Iraqi capability of making fuel-air explosives (*ibid.*).

48. Lavoie, 1989; 'FAE Development: Disturbing Trends,' *Jane's Defence Weekly*, 21 February 1987, pp. 280–82.

49. Document No. CDDH/IV/215, reproduced in Switzerland, Federal Political Department, 1978, vol. 16, p. 619 (cited below as *Official Records of the CDDH*). The 1977 version of the proposal was in document No. CDDH/IV/GT/5 (*ibid.*, p. 622).

50. A US representative, speaking at the *Ad Hoc* Committee on Conventional Weapons in 1977, stated (in the words of the summary record): 'The blast effect

of FAE [fuel-air explosive], in the lethal area, caused rupture of the lung tissue with subsequent release of air bubbles into the blood circulation. Those air bubbles, or air emboli, travelled rapidly to the heart and brain blood vessels, blocking the blood supply, and death ensued in a matter of minutes.' He presented this information to refute the Swedish statement that 'death often ensues first after prolonged suffering and great agony of the victims.' He also said: 'In the United States animal studies of the sub-lethal lung, ear and eye effects had been considered as wounds, and the ratio of killed to wounded was 0.16. That compared favorably with the Vietnam killed-to-wounded ratios of random-fragmentation and improved-fragmentation munitions, which were 0.25 and 0.16 respectively' (Summary records of the 36th to 42nd meetings of the *Ad Hoc* Committee on Conventional Weapons, 19 April to 24 May 1977, paragraphs 6–11, reproduced in *Official Records of the CDDH*).

51. Doswald-Beck and Cauderay, 1990, pp. 569–71.

52. In a paper presented to the ICRC expert meeting held in May–June 1994, I suggested four approaches short of a total ban which would merit consideration by the review conference: banning the use of fragmentation and possibly other types of cluster munitions, as well as attacks with multiple cluster munitions where the area coverage is above a certain strict limit; requiring that all submunitions be fitted with self-destruct or self-neutralizing mechanisms with a view to lowering the incidence of unexploded submunitions; setting a maximum permitted delay time for submunitions fitted with delay fuzes (any submunition with a delay time in excess of the limit would be considered a mine and would be subject to such controls on mines as are provided in Protocol II to the 1980 Convention or may be subsequently adopted); and banning types of attack with cluster munitions where there is a high risk of civilian casualties. (One way of doing this would be to adopt a formula, similar to that contained in Article 2(2) of Protocol III to the 1980 Convention, forbidding the use of cluster munitions against a military objective located within a concentration of civilians.)

Support for the second idea could be found in an Australian government 'non-paper' reproduced in the report of the expert meeting (ICRC, 1994b, pp. 64–70). The paper pointed out that when cluster munitions are used for immediate effect, it is undesirable for any significant number of unexploded submunitions to be left on the ground, as 'a force which bombards ground by any means may seek to manoeuvre on or occupy that ground at some time afterwards.' A self-destruct feature is desirable to cut down on unexploded submunitions. As for longer-term ground denial, unless specially designed area denial submunitions were used for this purpose, 'the unpredictability of the submunition fuze failure rate would lead to an unpredictable number of UXOs [unexploded ordnance], and hence to an unreliable denial effect. This would argue against the retention of simple non-self-destruct cluster munitions as a ground denial weapon.'

53. ICRC, 1994a, p. 158; ICRC, 1994b, pp. 89–119; SIPRI, 1978, Chapter 8.

54. ICRC, 1994a, pp. 129, 130, 146.

55. See *International Review of the Red Cross*, no. 302, September–October 1994, pp. 451, 458–63, for lists of states parties as of September 1994.

56. Sellier and Kneubuehl, 1994.

57. A full-metal-jacketed bullet striking the body at less than about 600 meters per second remains intact despite tumbling, but at impact velocities above 600 meters per second it deforms as a result of stresses during tumbling. The bullet is squeezed, mainly at the base; bits of lead are squeezed out of the base, forming separate fragments, and the bullet is flattened. When the impact velocity is increased to a certain threshold, the bullet separates into two parts of approximately equal size, in addition to the fragments from the core. At still higher impact velocities, more fragments are produced (*ibid.*, pp. 174–7).

58. *Ibid.*, p. 138.

59. De Veth, 1982.

60. The use of this broader term also encompasses non-bullet-like shapes such as flechettes.

61. The authors of the draft have not tried to specify a standard test procedure, perhaps out of a sense that such an attempt could excite controversy among the different national schools of wound ballistics, some of which use gelatin as a flesh simulant while others use soap. The advantage of soap is that the passage of the missile through it leaves a permanent record of the temporary cavity, whose dimensions can then be easily measured. Soap is inexpensive and readily available to agencies wishing to conduct tests in different countries.

62. The stipulation that the missile should deposit no more than a certain amount of energy per centimeter during a certain length of penetration into the body corresponds to what Sellier and Kneubuehl have called the 'narrow channel' – the wound track created in the first phase of the passage of the projectile while it is still traveling nose-on and has not yet started to tumble.

63. 'Every man working here has what amounts to a compulsive dedication to the preservation of human life and property,' a supervisor at Aberdeen Proving Ground told the Army publication *Army Research and Development Newsmagazine* (February 1965). The men with a 'compulsive dedication' to the 'preservation of human life and property' were munitions assemblers who worked in shifts around the clock, 'in rooms as starkly clean as surgical wards,' in the words of the magazine, loading and unloading ammunition for testing. No one spoke: the workers believed that 'silence is a true adjunct to safety.' Their safety record was said to be excellent.

64. One hopeful initiative along these lines is called War Witness International. This proposed organization would conduct on-site investigations of the conduct of armed conflicts; publish reports on its findings with a view to opposing violations of international humanitarian law and human rights law; and conduct educational programs, particularly regarding the promotion of international humanitarian law and ratification of the relevant treaties. At present the organization is seeking funds to begin several pilot projects in different parts of the world.

In the words of a declaration issued by a working group meeting in Bochum, Germany, in March 1993 which called for the creation of the organization, 'concerned individuals must organize themselves to monitor armed conflicts systematically and to mobilize pressure to stop the violation of the rules and principles of humanitarian law which regulate the conduct of armed conflicts.' These efforts, the declaration stated, would 'add the voice of public opinion' to the existing work of the ICRC, the UN and other organizations.

BIBLIOGRAPHY

Allred, J.M. (1967) *Parametric Investigation of End-Projecting Fragmentation and Flechette Warheads*, US Air Force Armament Laboratory technical report AFATL-TR-67-175.

Arkin, William M., Damian Durrant, and Marianne Cherni (1991) *On Impact: Modern Warfare and the Environment: A Case Study of the Gulf War*, Washington, Greenpeace.

Aubert, Maurice (1990) 'The International Committee of the Red Cross and the Problem of Excessively Injurious or Indiscriminate Weapons,' *International Review of the Red Cross*, no. 279, November–December, pp. 477–97.

Baxter, Gordon (1967) *13/13; Vietnam: Search and Destroy*, Cleveland, OH, World Publishing Company.

Benner, Robert L. (1968) *Recent Advances in High Fragmenting Steels*, US Army Picatinny Arsenal technical report 3833.

Bergerud, Eric M. (1991) *The Dynamics of Defeat: The Vietnam War in Hau Nghia Province*, Boulder, CO, Westview.

—— (1993) *Red Thunder, Tropical Lightning: The World of a Combat Division in Vietnam*, Boulder, CO, Westview.

Best, Geoffrey (1983) *Humanity in Warfare: The Modern History of the International Law of Armed Conflicts*, paperback edition with postscript, London, University Paperback.

Beyer, James C., ed. (1962) *Medical Department, United States Army: Wound Ballistics*, Washington, Department of the Army.

Black, A.N., B.D. Burns, and Solly Zuckerman (1941) 'An Experimental Study of the Wounding Mechanism of High-Velocity Missiles,' *British Medical Journal*, 20 December 1941, pp. 872–4.

Blix, Hans (1974) 'Current Efforts to Prohibit the Use of Certain Conventional Weapons,' *Instant Research on Peace and Violence*, Tampere, vol. 4, no. 1, pp. 21–30.

Bradlee, Benjamin C. (1975) *Conversations with Kennedy*, New York, Norton; paperback edition, Pocket Books, 1976.

Branfman, Fredric R., ed. (1972) *Voices from the Plain of Jars: Life under an Air War*, New York, Harper Colophon Books.

Brophy, Leo P., Wyndham D. Miles, and Rexmond C. Cochrane (1959) *United States Army in World War II; The Technical Services; The Chemical Warfare Service:*

From Laboratory to Field, Washington, Department of the Army.

Browning, Frank and Dorothy Forman, eds (1972) *The Wasted Nations: Report of the International Commission of Enquiry into United States Crimes in Indochina, June 20–25, 1971*, New York, Harper & Row.

Cable, Larry (1991) *Unholy Grail: The US and the Wars in Vietnam, 1965–8*, London and New York, Routledge.

Callender, George R. and Ralph W. French (1935) 'Studies in the Mechanism of Wound Production by Rifle Bullets,' *Military Surgeon*, vol. 77, no. 4, October, pp. 177–201.

Chase, Martin (1973) 'Long Range Planning for 40mm. Ammunition,' in US Army Munitions Command, 1973, pp. L-1 to L-31.

Crossman, Jim (1966) 'Grenades, Now and Then,' *Ordnance*, July–August.

Davidson, Phillip B. (1988) *Vietnam at War; The History: 1946–1975*, London, Sidgwick & Jackson.

DeMarco, R.J. (1990) *Design and Development History of US Aircraft Bombs*, China Lake, CA, US Naval Weapons Center.

De Veth, C. (1982) 'Development of the New Second NATO Calibre: The "5.56" with the SS 109 Projectile,' in T. Seeman, ed., *Wound Ballistics: Fourth International Symposium, Acta Chirurgica Scandinavica*, Stockholm, Supplementum 508, pp. 129–34.

Dellinger, David (1967) 'North Vietnam: Eyewitness Report,' *Liberation*, December 1966, pp. 3–15.

Democratic Republic of Vietnam, Commission for Investigation on the American Imperialists' War Crimes in Vietnam (1966) *American Crimes in Vietnam*, Hanoi.

Democratic Republic of Vietnam, Ministry of Foreign Affairs (1964) *US 'Special War' in South Viet Nam*, Hanoi, Ministry of Foreign Affairs, Press and Information Department.

Dickson, Paul (1976) *The Electronic Battlefield*, Bloomington, IN, Indiana University Press.

Dimond, Francis C., Jr, and Norman M. Rich (1967) 'M-16 Rifle Wounds in Vietnam,' *Journal of Trauma*, vol. 7, no. 3, pp. 619–25.

Doswald-Beck, Louise and Gérald Cauderay (1990) 'The Development of New Anti-personnel Weapons,' *International Review of the Red Cross*, no. 279, November–December, pp. 565–77.

Doswald-Beck, Louise and Sylvain Vité (1993) 'International Humanitarian Law and Human Rights Law,' *International Review of the Red Cross*, no. 293, March–April, pp. 94–119.

Duffet, John, ed. (1968) *Against the Crime of Silence: Proceedings of the Russell International War Crimes Tribunal; Stockholm–Copenhagen*, New York, Bertrand Russell Peace Foundation, O'Hare Books.

Dunn, Dennis J., Jr, and Theodore E. Sterne (1952) *Hand Grenades for Rapid Incapacitation*, US Army Ballistic Research Laboratories report R-806.

Dunn, Eldon L. (1959) *Some Results of a Study of the Effectiveness of Cluster Weapons against Tanks*, US Naval Ordnance Test Station technical publication TP 2352.

Ellsberg, Daniel (1972) *Papers on the War*, New York, Simon & Schuster.

Fackler, Martin L., John S. Surinchak, John A. Malinowski, and Robert E. Bowen (1984) 'Wounding Potential of the Russian AK-74 Assault Rifle,' *Journal of*

Trauma, vol. 24, no. 3, pp. 263–6.

Fenrick, W.J. (1990) 'The Conventional Weapons Convention: A Modest but Useful Treaty,' *International Review of the Red Cross*, no. 279, November–December, pp. 498–509.

Fieser, Louis F., George C. Harris, E.B. Hershberg, Morley Morgana, Frederick C. Novello, and Stearns T. Putnam (1946) 'Napalm,' *Industrial and Engineering Chemistry*, vol. 38, no. 8, August, pp. 768–73.

French, Ralph W. and George R. Callender (1962) 'Ballistic Characteristics of Wounding Agents,' in James C. Beyer, ed., 1962, pp. 91–141.

Gasser, Hans-Peter (1993) *International Humanitarian Law*, Geneva, Henry Dunant Institute and Haupt. (Separate print from Hans Haug, *Humanity for All: The International Red Cross and Red Crescent Movement*, Geneva, Haupt.)

Green, C. McL., H.C. Thomson, and P.C. Roots (1955) *United States Army in World War II; The Technical Services; The Ordnance Department: Planning Munitions for War*, Washington, Department of the Army.

Guilmartin, John, Jr, and Michael O'Leary (1988) *The Illustrated History of the Vietnam War*, New York, Bantam.

Hammerman, Gay M., Brian Bader, Trevor N. Dupuy, and Charles R. Smith (1985) *Human Impact of Technological Innovation on the Battlefield*, Historical Evaluation and Research Organization, report 114, Fairfax, VA.

Harvey, E. Newton, J. Howard McMillen, Elmer G. Butler, and William O. Puckett (1962) 'Mechanism of Wounding,' in James C. Beyer, ed., 1962, pp. 143–235.

Harvey, Frank (1967) *Air War – Vietnam*, New York, Bantam.

Hay, John H. (1974) *Vietnam Studies: Tactical and Materiel Innovations*, Washington, Department of the Army.

Heflin, W.A., ed. (1956) *The United States Air Force Dictionary*, Air University Press.

Hexner, Peter E. (1970) 'Fuzes – Brains of Munitions,' *Defense Industry Bulletin*, June, pp. 35–7.

Hitchman, Norman A. (1952) *Operational Requirements for an Infantry Hand Weapon*, Johns Hopkins University, Operations Research Office, technical memorandum ORO-T-160. Chevy Chase, MD.

Horsley, Victor (1894) 'The Destructive Effects of Projectiles,' *Proceedings of the Royal Institution of Great Britain*, vol. 14, pp. 228–38.

Human Rights Watch Arms Project and Human Rights Watch/Africa (1994) *Landmines in Mozambique*, New York, Human Rights Watch.

Human Rights Watch Arms Project and Physicians for Human Rights (1993) *Landmines: A Deadly Legacy*, New York, Human Rights Watch.

International Committee of the Red Cross (ICRC) (1973) *Weapons that May Cause Unnecessary Suffering or Have Indiscriminate Effects: Report of the Work of Experts*, Geneva, ICRC.

———— (1975) *Conference of Government Experts on the Use of Certain Conventional Weapons (Lucerne, 24 September–18 October 1974); Report*, Geneva, ICRC.

———— (1976) *Conference of Government Experts on the Use of Certain Conventional Weapons (Second Session – Lugano, 28 January–26 February 1976); Report*, Geneva, ICRC.

———— (1987) *Commentary on the Additional Protocols of 8 June 1977 to the Geneva Conventions of 12 August 1949*, Geneva, ICRC and Nijhoff.

———— (1993a) *Blinding Weapons: Reports of the Meetings of Experts Convened by the International Committee of the Red Cross on Battlefield Laser Weapons: 1989–1991*, Geneva, ICRC.

———— (1993b) *Symposium on Anti-personnel Mines: Montreux 21–23 April 1993*, Geneva, ICRC.

———— (1994a) 'Report of the International Committee of the Red Cross for the Review Conference of the 1980 United Nations Convention on Prohibitions or Restrictions on the Use of Certain Conventional Weapons...; February 1994,' *International Review of the Red Cross*, no. 299, March–April, pp. 123–82.

———— (1994b) *Expert Meeting on Certain Weapon Systems and on Implementation Mechanisms in International Law: Geneva 30 May–1 June 1994; Report*, Geneva, ICRC.

Jane's Air-Launched Weapons, Duncan Lennox and Arthur Rees, eds, Coulsdon, Surrey, UK, Jane's Information Group, 1992 with updates.

Jane's Infantry Weapons 1975 (1975) F. Hobart, ed., London, Jane's Yearbooks, 1974.

Kahin, George McTurnan (1986) *Intervention: How America Became Involved in Vietnam*, New York, Knopf; paperback edition, New York, Anchor, 1987.

Kahin, George McTurnan and John W. Lewis (1969) *The United States in Vietnam*, revised edition, New York, Delta.

Kalshoven, Frits (1990) 'The Conventional Weapons Convention: Underlying Legal Principles,' *International Review of the Red Cross*, no. 279, November–December, pp. 510–20.

Kanegis, Arthur, Michael T. Klare, Fay Knopp, Marilyn McNabb, Eric Prokosch, Chris Robinson and Martha Westover (1970) *Weapons for Counterinsurgency: Chemical/Biological, Anti-personnel, Incendiary*, Philadelphia, American Friends Service Committee, National Action/Research on the Military Industrial Complex.

Katterhenry, Glenn E. (1957) *90mm. Canister Ammunition. Final progress report 8*, Report by Whirlpool Corporation prepared for US Army Frankford Arsenal.

Kearns, Doris (1976) *Lyndon Johnson and the American Dream*, New York, Harper & Row; paperback edition, New York, Signet, 1977.

Keith, Arthur and Hugh M. Rigby (1899) 'Modern Military Bullets: A Study of their Destructive Effects,' *Lancet*, 2 December, pp. 1499–1507.

Klare, Michael T. (1972) *War without End: America's Planning for the Next Vietnams*, New York, Knopf.

Kleber, Brooks E. and Dale Birdsell (1966) *United States Army in World War II: The Technical Services; The Chemical Warfare Service: Chemicals in Combat*, Washington, US Army.

Krauss, Max (1957) 'Studies in Wound Ballistics: Temporary Cavity Effects in Soft Tissues,' *Military Medicine*, vol. 121, no. 4, October, pp. 221–31.

Krepinevich, Andrew F., Jr. (1986) *The Army and Vietnam*, Baltimore, MD, Johns Hopkins University Press.

Krepon, Michael (1974) 'Weapons Potentially Inhumane: The Case of Cluster Bombs,' *Foreign Affairs*, vol. 52, no. 3, April, pp. 595–611.

Laber, Jeri and Barnett R. Rubin (1988) *'A Nation Is Dying': Afghanistan under the Soviets, 1979–87*, Evanston, IL, Northeastern University Press.

Lavoie, Louis (1989) 'Fuel-Air Explosives, Weapons, and Effects,' *Military Technology*, no. 9, pp. 64–70.

Levie, Howard S. (1986) *The Code of International Armed Conflict*, New York, Oceana.

Limqueco, Peter and Peter Weiss, eds (1971) *Prevent the Crime of Silence: Reports from the Sessions of the International War Crimes Tribunal Founded by Bertrand Russell...* London, Allen Lane.

Littauer, Raphael and Norman Uphoff, eds; Air War Study Group, Cornell University (1972) *The Air War in Indochina*, revised edition, Boston, MA, Beacon.

McMillen, J. Howard and J.R. Gregg (1945) *The Energy, Mass and Velocity Which Is Required of Small Missiles in Order to Produce a Casualty*, National Research Council, Division of Medical Sciences, acting for the Committee on Medical Research, Office of Scientific Research and Development, Missile Casualties Report no. 12, Washington.

Magis, S.F. (1967) *Material Selection for Naturally Fragmenting Munitions*, US Naval Weapons Laboratory technical memorandum T-13/67.

Marolda, Edward J. and Oscar P. Fitzgerald (1986) *The United States Navy and the Vietnam Conflict*, vol. II, *From Military Assistance to Combat: 1959–1965*, Washington, US Navy, Naval Historical Center.

Ott, David E. (1975) *Vietnam Studies: Field Artillery 1954–1973*, Washington, Department of the Army.

Painter, Harry W. (1974) 'Picatinny Arsenal in Research and Development,' *Army Research and Development News Magazine*, January–February, pp. 16–19.

Parks, W. Hays (1982) 'Rolling Thunder and the Law of War,' *Air University Review*, 1982, pp. 2–23.

—— (1990) 'Air War and the Law of War,' *Air Force Law Review*, Maxwell Air Base, Alabama, vol. 32, no. 1, pp. 1–225.

Pepke, Donn R. (1970) 'Economy of Force in the Central Highlands,' *Military Review*, vol. 50, no. 11, November, pp. 32–43.

Perry-Robinson, Julian (1983) 'Quasinuclear Weapons,' in William Gutteridge and Trevor Taylor, eds, *The Dangers of New Weapon Systems*, London, Macmillan.

Pike, Douglas (1966) *Viet Cong: The Organization and Techniques of the National Liberation Front*, Cambridge, MA, MIT Press.

—— (1986) *PAVN: People's Army of Vietnam*, Novato, CA, Presidio Press.

Prokosch, Eric (1972) *The Simple Art of Murder: Antipersonnel Weapons and their Developers*, Philadelphia, American Friends Service Committee, National Action/Research on the Military Industrial Complex.

Rees, David (1964) *Korea: The Limited War*, London, Macmillan.

Ridgway, Matthew B. (1967) *The Korean War*, Garden City, NY, Doubleday.

Riffaud, Madeleine (1967) *Au Nord Viet-Nam (écrit sous les bombes)*, Paris, Julliard.

Riffin, Paul V. (1972) *High Fragmentation Steels for Artillery and Tank Munitions*, US Army Materials and Mechanics Research Center report SP-72-17.

Roberts, Adam, and Richard Guelff, eds (1982) *Documents on the Laws of War*, Oxford, Clarendon.

Rogers, Bernard William (1974) *Vietnam Studies; Cedar Falls-Junction City: A Turning Point*, Washington, Department of the Army.

Ryle, John (1993) 'The Invisible Enemy,' *New Yorker*, 29 November, pp. 120–35.

Sale, Kirkpatrick (1973) *SDS*, New York, Random House.

Salisbury, Harrison (1967) *Behind the Lines – Hanoi*, New York, Bantam.

Sandoz, Yves (1975) *Des armes interdites en droit de la guerre*, Geneva, Imprimerie Grounauer.

—— (1981) 'Prohibitions or Restrictions on the Use of Certain Conventional Weapons,' *International Review of the Red Cross*, no. 220, January–February, pp. 3–33.

Science in War (1940) London, Penguin.

Sellier, Karl G. and Beat P. Kneubuehl (1994) *Wound Ballistics and the Scientific Background*, Amsterdam, Elsevier.

Stockholm International Peace Research Institute (SIPRI) (1972) *Napalm and Incendiary Weapons: SIPRI interim report*, Stockholm, SIPRI.

—— (1973) *The Problem of Chemical and Biological Warfare*, vol. 3, *CB Weapons Today*, Stockholm, Almqvist & Wiksell.

—— (1975) *Incendiary Weapons*, Stockholm, Almqvist & Wiksell.

—— (1976) *Ecological Consequences of the Second Indochina War*, Stockholm, Almqvist & Wiksell.

—— (1978) *Anti-personnel Weapons*, London, Taylor & Francis.

—— (1985) *Explosive Remnants of War: Mitigating the Environmental Effects*, London, Taylor & Francis.

Stone, I.F. (1952) *The Hidden History of the Korean War*, New York, Monthly Review Press.

Swearington, Chief Warrant Officer (1969) *Staff Study on Pernicious Characteristics of US Explosive Ordnance*, Washington, US Marine Corps.

Sweden, Royal Ministry of Foreign Affairs (1973) *Conventional Weapons; Their Deployment and Effects from Humanitarian Aspect: A Swedish Working Group Study*, Stockholm.

Switzerland, Federal Political Department (1978) *Official Records of the Diplomatic Conference on the Reaffirmation and Development of International Humanitarian Law Applicable in Armed Conflicts: Geneva (1974–1977)*, Bern.

Thompson, Reginald (1951) *Cry Korea*, London, Macdonald.

Tilford, Earl H., Jr (1993) *Crosswinds: The Air Force's Setup in Vietnam*, College Station, Texas, Texas A & M University Press.

Tompkins, J.S. (1966) *The Weapons of World War III: The Long Road Back from the Bomb*, New York, Doubleday.

Truckenmiller, W.C. (1964) 'Developing Cast Shell,' *Ordnance*, March–April, pp. 554–6.

Tuchman, Barbara (1966) *The Proud Tower: A Portrait of the World Before the War, 1890–1914*, New York, Macmillan.

UK Air Ministry (1963) *The Origins and Development of Operational Research in the Royal Air Force*, Air Publication 3368, London, Her Majesty's Stationery Office.

UN Secretary-General (1973) *Napalm and Other Incendiary Weapons and All Aspects of their Possible Use*, Report of the Secretary-General, Document no. A/8803/Rev.1, New York, United Nations.

US Air Force (1970) *Tactical Air Force Operations: Operational Concept for Ground Sensor Technology*, Air Force manual AFM 2-9, Washington.

—— (1972) *Aerospace Operational Doctrine: Tactical Air Operations – Employment* of *Air Delivered Target Activated Munitions (ADTAMs)*, Air Force manual AFM 2-10, Washington.

US Air Force Special Air Warfare Center (1965) *Final Report of Operation Test and Evaluation: CBU-14/B Dispenser and Bomb, Aircraft*, technical documentary report SAWC-TDR-65-15.

——— (1968) *Operational Test and Evaluation of the CBU-25/A Munition*, report TAC-TR-66-61.

US Air Force Tactical Air Command (1963) *Operational Test and Evaluation; CBU-2/A*, report TAC-TR-61-40.

US Air Force Test Unit, Vietnam (1965) *Final Report; Evaluation of the CBU-2/A and CBU-14/A Munitions*.

US Army (1956) *The Law of Land Warfare*, field manual FM 27-10, Washington.

——— (1966a) *Bombs and Bomb Components*, technical manual TM 9-1325-200, Washington.

——— (1966b) *Individual Weapons and Marksmanship*, Reserve Officers' Training Corps manual ROTCM 145-30, Washington.

——— (1966c) *Antipersonnel Mine M18A1 and M18 (Claymore)*, field manual FM 23-23, Washington.

——— (1967a) *Artillery Ammunition*, technical manual TM 9-1300-203, Washington, 1967, with subsequent changes.

——— (1967b) *Military Explosives*, technical manual TM 9-1300-204, Washington.

——— (1967c) *Handling, Maintenance, Storage, and Inspection (Including Repair Parts and Special Tool Lists); Dispenser and Bomb, Aircraft: CBU-1A/A, CBU-2/A, CBU-2A/A, CBU-2B/A, CBU-2C/A, CBU-3/A, CBU-3A/A, CBU-8A/A, CBU-9/A, CBU-9A/A, CBU-12/A, CBU-12A/A, and CBU-26/A*, technical manual TM 9-1325-202-50/1, Washington, 1967 with changes to 1971.

——— (1968) *Canister, Mine, CDU-4/B, CBU-5/B, CBU-10/B and CBU-14/B*, technical manual TM 9-1345-204-50, Washington.

——— (1969) *Landmine Warfare (Scatterable Mines)*, field manual FM 20-32A, Washington.

——— (1970) *Adapter, Cluster Bomb: ADU-253/B, ADU-253A/B, ADU-253B/B, ADU-256/B, ADU-256A/B, ADU-256B/B, ADU-272A/B, ADU-272B/B, ADU-285A/B, and ADU-285B/B, and Bomb Cluster, Fragmentation: CDU-22/B*, technical manual TM 9-1325-207-50, Washington.

——— (1971) *Grenades, Hand and Rifle*, technical manual TM 9-1330-200, Washington.

——— (1972a) *40mm. Grenade Launchers M203 and M79*, field manual FM 23-31, Washington.

——— (1972b) *Dictionary of United States Army Terms*, army regulation AR 310-25. Washington.

——— (1978) *Field Artillery Target Analysis and Weapons Employment: Nonnuclear*, field manual FM 6-141-1, Washington.

US Army Armament Command (1974) *Laboratory Posture Report: Fiscal Year 1974*, Rock Island, IL.

US Army Materiel Command (1963) *Research and Development of Materiel; Engineering Design Handbook; Elements of Armament Engineering: part 2, Ballistics*. Army Materiel Command pamphlet AMCP 706-107, Washington.

——— (1969) *Arsenal for the Brave: A History of the United States Army Materiel Command 1962–1968*, Washington.

US Army Munitions Command (1973) *Brochure of Mortar Ammunition Manufacturers Conference: 28–29 March 1973*, Dover, NJ.

US Army Ordnance Corps (1960) *Ordnance Engineering Design Handbook; Elements of Armament Engineering: Part 3, Weapon Systems and Components*, Ordnance Corps pamphlet ORDP 20-108, Washington.

US Department of Defense (1971) *The Senator Gravel Edition; The Pentagon Papers; The Defense Department History of United States Decisionmaking on Vietnam*, Boston, MA, Beacon, vols 1–4.

US Department of State (1976) *Report of the United States Delegation to the Second Session of the Conference of Government Experts on the Use of Certain Conventional Weapons; Lugano, Switzerland; January 28–February 26, 1976*, Washington.

US Military Academy (1968) *Ordnance Engineering*; vol. 2, *Ballistics; Book 2, Exterior Ballistics and Terminal Ballistics*, textbook for 1968–9, West Point, NY.

US Navy (1971) *Unpacking, Inspection and Maintenance Instructions with Repair Parts List; Intermediate; Fuel-Air Explosive Bomb Cluster CBU-55/B*, technical manual NAVAIR 11-5A-26, China Lake, CA, Naval Weapons Center.

——— (1972a) *Antitank Bomb Cluster Mk 20 Mods 2 and 3 and Antipersonnel/ Antimateriel Bomb Cluster CBU-59/B*, technical manual NAVAIR 11-5A-3, Washington.

——— (1972b) *Description, Safety, Service, and Handling Instructions (Intermediate); Airborne Rockets*, technical manual NAVAIR 11-85-5, revision 1, Washington.

Urban, Mark (1988) *War in Afghanistan*, London, Macmillan.

Vien Phuong (1970) *The Inventor of Twig-Triggered Mines: A Narrative*, Giai Phong Publishing House, South Vietnam.

Weigley, Russell F. (1967) *History of the United States Army*, New York, Macmillan.

Weymouth, F.A. (1952) *The Effect of Metallurgical Properties of Steel upon Fragmentation Characteristics of Shell*, US Army Ballistic Research Laboratories memorandum report 585.

Wilson, Louis B. (1921) 'Disperson of Bullet Energy in Relation to Wound Effects,' *Military Surgeon*, vol. 49, no. 3, September, pp. 241–51.

Woodruff, Charles E. (1898) 'The Causes of the Explosive Effect of Modern Small-Calibre Bullets,' *New York Medical Journal*, vol. 67, 30 April, pp. 593–601.

Zuckerman, Solly (1940) 'Wounds from Bomb Fragments,' *British Medical Journal*, 27 July, pp. 131–2.

——— (1966) *Scientists and War: The Impact of Science on Military and Civil Affairs*, London, Hamish Hamilton.

CONVERSION TABLE

Metric and Non-Metric Measures
Used in this Book

1 inch = 25.4 millimeters

1 foot = 0.3048 meters

1 mile = 1.6 kilometers

1 ft/sec = 0.3048 m/sec

1 square foot = 0.0929 square meter

1 ounce = 28.35 grams

1 grain = 0.0648 gram

1 millimeter = 0.03937 inches

1 meter = 3.281 feet

1 kilometer = 0.6214 mile

1 m/sec = 3.281 ft/sec

1 square meter = 10.76 square feet

1 gram = 0.03527 ounce

1 gram = 15.43 grains

5.56mm = .223 caliber

7.62mm = .30 caliber

Source: Sellier and Kneubuehl, 1994, sections 8.2, Conversion Tables; 8.4, Caliber Designations.

INDEX

AAI Corporation, 44–7, 57
Aberdeen Proving Ground, 149, 201
accidents, study of, 25
Additional Protocols (1977) to the
    Geneva Convention, xiii, xiv
Additional Protocol I (1977) to the
    Geneva Convention, xii, 161, 164,
    165, 166, 167, 190
Additional Protocol II (1977) to the
    Geneva Convention, 162, 187, 190
aerial delivery of mines, 7, 56, 81, 105,
    107–11, 115, 162
Aerojet-General Corporation, 75, 134
Afghanistan, 178–9, 195
    mining of, 179
Agenda for Peace, xii
air bursts, 72, 88
Air Delivered Target Activated
    Munitions (ADTAMs), 111
air raids, effects of, 15
aircraft, 91
    B-52 bomber, 97, 105, 152
    B-57 bomber, 105
    C-123 cargo plane, 105
    costs of, 62
    effect on war, 174
    F-4 Phantom, 96
    F-105 Thunderchief, 84, 96
    use of, 57, 58
Albion Malleable Iron Company, 41, 63
Alexander II, Tsar, 173
aluminum, used for firebombs, 133
Aluminum Company of America, 133
American Friends Service Committee,
    140, 143
American Ordnance Association, 63
ammunition, artillery, 4, 36, 69, 77,

105–7, 169, 181
    76mm, 79
    105mm, 67, 69, 76, 105
    105mm, Beehive, 70, 71, 79
    152mm, Beehive, 71
    155mm, 79, 105
    8-inch, 105
Anderson, Major, 108, 124
Andrews, Mr, 59
Angola, 183
antiaircraft artillery, 24, 96, 106, 118
    in Vietnam war, 92
antipersonnel weapons, 1, 10, 25, 56,
    71, 72, 81, 88, 90, 92, 98, 104, 112,
    132, 142, 143, 154, 156, 161, 163,
    186
    design of, 6, 9, 30–52
    future of, 176–201
    large area, 83, 85
    proliferation of, 176–8
    proposed banning of, 148–7, 163,
    170
    restrictions on, 161
antipersonnel/antimateriel bombs
    (APAM), 102
antitank weapons, 59, 78, 81, 101–2,
    180
antiwar movement, 7, 56, 84, 126,
    127–9, 134, 138, 169
area bombardment, 112
area denial, 108, 123, 154
area Denial Artillery Munition
    (ADAM), 108, 154
area of coverage, 68, 99, 151
Argentina, 183
Arkin, William M., 179
armed reconnaissance, 96, 118

arms manufacturers, 7, 49, 184
    campaigning against, 126–47
artillery
    airborne, 59
    cluster shells for, 105
    in Vietnam, 61–3
    incentives for use of, 62
    high explosive, 68, 70
    massive use of, 63
    see also ammunition, artillery
Association of Military Surgeons (US),
    14
atomic bomb, 124
Australia, 200
Austria, 169, 177
automated production of fuzes, 103
Avco Corporation, 75, 134, 135
Avroc ammunition, 75

bacteriological warfare, banning of, 6
Baldridge, Malcolm, 135
ballistics, underwater, 22
banning of weapons, 3
Barr, Irwin R., 44–7, 57, 68, 157
battle casualty surveys, 22–5
battles
    Bougainville Island, 24, 42, 48
    Cassino, 24
    New Guinea, 82
    Solferino, xii
Baxter, Gordon, 57
Beehive munitions, 4, 56, 67–71, 76,
    80, 112, 134, 151, 155, 178
Belgium, 183
Bergerud, Eric M., 80
Berlin Wall crisis, 45, 81
Bethlehem Steel Company, 64
Beyer, Major James C., 17, 25, 29
Bigeye munition, 115
Binger, James H., 138, 139, 140, 141,
    142, 143, 144
biological weapons, 8, 115, 117
biotechnology, use in weapons, 189
Black, A.N., 16
blinding weapons, xiv, 8, 187, 198
Blix, Hans, 170
BLU series bombs, 105, 116
    BLU-3 'pineapple,' 87, 92, 98–101,
        104, 105, 114, 119, 120, 122,
        171
    BLU-17, 104
    BLU-24 'orange,' 52, 105, 122

BLU-26 'guava,' 83, 84, 85, 104,
    116, 119, 137
BLU-61, 102, 196
BLU-63, 196
BLU-73, 199
BLU-82 'daisy cutter,' 188, 199
BLU-86, 196
BLU-97, 196
body armor, 23, 24, 26, 55
body counts, of US in Vietnam, 55
bomber crews, casualties among, 24
bombing
    'pinpoint,' 113
    'precision,' 88
    damage in N. Africa, 23
    of North Vietnam, 54, 94, 100, 112,
        118, 125, 138, 180
    figures for, 96, 105
    policy, 118
    saturation, 2
    theory of, 94
bomblets, 2, 3, 82, 112, 154, 171;
    see also BLU series
bombs, high explosive, 2, 3, 15, 62, 89,
    91, 112, 154
bone, damage to, 19
booby traps, 39, 114, 158
Boutros-Ghali, Boutros, xii
bow and arrow, use of, 6
Branfman, Fredric R., 100, 142
Brasket, Denis, 142, 146
Briteye bomb, 115
British Army, 153, 154
    Medical Service, 23
Browning, John, 45
buffaloes, killed in target practice,
    55
bullets, 18, 76
    5.56mm, 76
    7.62mm, 77
    advances in, 11
    AK-47, wounding capacity of, 196
    design of, 179
    effects on tissue, 12
    explosive, 173
    fired in crucifix pattern, 43
    full-metal-jacketed, 191, 201
    gyroscopic stability of, 191
    lighter, 44, 60–1
    M193, 76
    movement in air, 14
    multiple, 46

pointed, 27
rifle, 156, 190, 191
SS 109, 192, 193, 196
standard, 44
wounding by, 156; *see also* tumbling
of projectiles
Burns, B.D., 16, 25, 33
BZ psychochemical, 75

caliber
of small arms, 192
reduction in, 44, 77
small, 3, 159
see also small-caliber weapons
systems
Callender, Colonel George, 13, 14, 17,
23–4, 25, 152
Cambodia, 149, 176, 183
invasion of, 141
mines in, ix, x
Canada, 156, 159, 183
cancer research, 144
canisters, 67–71, 151
capillaries, damage to, 19
carelessness, as cause of wounding, 25
cartridges
40mm, 142
M1, 78
M381, 75
M386, 75
M406, 74, 75
M441, 75
XM398, 74
XM463, 74
XM576E1, 75
Case Institute of Technology, 107
cast metals, 40
casualty survey unit, 23
catapults, censure of, xiii
cavities, liquid-filled, damage to, 14
cavitation, 12, 16, 18, 152, 156
cavity
permanent, 18–20
temporary, 18–20, 21
Central Office for South Vietnam
(COSVN), 55
centrifugal movement of flesh in
response to bullet, 12
Chapelier, Georges, 100
chemical warfare, 79, 169
chemical weapons, xiii, 4, 74, 82, 105,
115, 133, 158, 168, 189

defoliants, 55
Chesarek, General F.J., 58, 59, 67
children
as victims
of cluster bombs, 93
of mines, xiv, 194
of napalm burns, 128
killing of, 138
to be protected against
antipersonnel mines, 184
Chile, 178
China, 31, 40, 48, 52, 53, 112, 178,
188, 195
civil disobedience, 138
civilians, 180
and mines, 162
as casualties, ix, xiii, 2, 7, 92, 98,
102, 109, 113, 119, 137, 151,
162, 176, 178, 179, 184, 197
as targets, 6
attacks on, 94, 95, 117, 126, 143
definition of, 166
effects of mines on, 8
killing of, 1, 3, 5, 8, 31, 55, 88–9,
91
protection of, 112, 163, 166
war against, 93–8
Clergy and Laity Concerned
organization (CALC), 142, 143, 144
cluster bombs, 2, 7, 56, 73, 77, 81–125,
135, 136, 151, 157, 163, 177, 178,
195
BL 755, 154
CBU-1, 105
CBU-2, 99, 120
CBU-14, 99, 104, 120
CBU-22, 104
CBU-24 'guava,' 84, 85, 87, 91, 97,
98, 109, 124, 151, 196
demand for, 86
CBU-24/29, 86
CBU-25, 104, 122
CBU-42 Wide Area Antipersonnel
Mine (WAAPM), 110
CBU-52, 196
CBU-55 fuel-air explosive bomb,
199
CBU-58, 97, 119, 196
CBU-59, 102, 121
CBU-71, 196
CBU-72, 105
CBU-78, 196

CBU-87, 196
implications of, 111
in Vietnam, 83–7
operation of, 102–4
production of, 7
proposed banning of, 7, 149, 200
requests to use, 97
wide area, 8
COINTELPRO, 146
Colt Company, 77
communism, fight against, 54
Conference of Government Experts on
Weapons that May Cause
Unnecesary Suffering or Have
Indiscriminate Effects, *see*
Conference of Government Experts
on the Use of Certain Conventional
Weapons
Conference of Government Experts on
the Use of Certain Conventional
Weapons
First session (Lucerne, 1974), 148,
149–55
Second session (Lugano, 1976),
155–60
Conference on Missile Casualties, 17,
23–4
Convention on Prohibitions or
Restrictions on the Use of Certain
Conventional Weapons which May
be Deemed to be Excessively
Injurious or to have Indiscriminate
Effects (Conventional Weapons
Convention) (1980), xi, xiv, 6, 7, 9,
160, 167, 168, 176, 190, 192
Conference (1980), 160–3, 170
Review Conference (1995), 185–90
Protocol I, 161
Protocol II, 161, 182, 183, 185
strengthening of, 189–90
conventional munitions, 8, 81, 115, 143
corporate responsibility, 7
Corporate War Crimes Investigation,
142
costs of munitions, 102, 133, 137
Council for Corporate Review, 141
counterinsurgency, weapons for, 53–80
cracks in shells, analysis of, 65
cruelty, 150, 174, 175, 193, 194
Crummey, John D., 132, 133
CS gas, 57
Czech Republic, 183

dagger, use of, 6
'daisy-cutter bomb', *see* BLU series
bombs
Davidov, Marv, 138, 141, 143, 144, 145
de Puy, Brigadier General William C.,
53
de-mining, ix, 8
death
immediate causes of, 23, 24
rapidity of, 43
Defense Communications Planning
Group, 124
defensive fire, 42
defoliation, 55, 73, 74
deforming projectiles, 152; proposed
banning of, 149
delayed explosion devices, 2, 81
Dellinger, David, 87, 103, 113
Demilitarized Zone, Vietnam, 109
Deneye aerial mine dispenser, 106, 115
design of weapons, 6, 7, 9, 11
Dickson, Paul, 108
Diplomatic Conference for the
Establishment of International
Conventions for the Protection of
Victims of War (1949), 165; *see also*
Geneva Conventions
Diplomatic Conference on the
Reaffirmation and Development of
International Humanitarian Law
Applicable to Armed Conflicts
(1974–77), 165
directed energy weapons, 189
dispensers of bomblets, 82, 87, 99, 102,
104–5, 134, 178
Hayes, 105, 122, 152
MW-1, 178
SUU-7, 99, 104
SUU-13, 108, 123
SUU-14, 104, 121
SUU-30, 85, 117, 196
SUU-38, 108
SUU-41, 108
SUU-65, 196
distance of penetration, 21
Dow Chemical Company, 131
recruiting interviews disrupted, 131
drag, in ballistics, 21
dud ordnance, figures for, 114
dum-dum bullets, 13
banning of, 6, 47, 160, 163, 168,
169, 170, 192

origin of name, 175
Dunant, Henry, xii
duplex cartridges, 43

effective casualty radius, 38, 57, 194
Egypt, 149, 155, 178
Eisenhower, Dwight D., 90
El Salvador, 183
electronic battlefield, 108, 109, 110,
    111, 122, 123, 124
    effects on citizens, 110
energy
    loss, of projectiles, 21, 29
        rapidity of, 15, 22
    optimum, 34
    see also kinetic energy
ENSURE program, 75
ethics, raising of questions, 17
Ethiopia, 181
Evans, General, 84, 86, 114
explosions
    premature, 63
    process of, 65
explosives, 6, 38, 40, 57, 71, 177
    C4, 50
    Composition B, 37, 38, 50, 57, 78,
        116
    cyclotol, 116
    fuel-air, 187-8, 198, 199, 200
    H-6, 114
    lead azide, 122
    RDX, 38, 50, 116, 122
        brisance of, 49
    TNT, 38, 50, 78, 116

Fabrique Nationale, 192
fatal or severe wounding, 33-4
Federal Bureau of Investigation (FBI),
    138, 146
Fireye firebomb, 106, 115
Fisher, Professor Roger, 108
flak suppression, 84, 92, 151
flechettes, 4, 44-7, 68, 69, 71, 76, 79,
    80, 132, 133, 145, 150, 155, 156,
    157, 163, 178, 201
    altering tips of, 47
    cruelty of, 113
    filling rocket warheads with, 59
    non-announcement of new shell,
        132
    proposed banning of, 149
    rifle delivery, 4

tumbling tendency of, 46, 152,
    157
    wounds from, 157
flesh simulants, 28
    gelatin, 10, 13, 16, 18, 21, 22, 25,
        27, 66
    modelling clay, 13
    soap, 13, 27, 159, 172, 193
    water, 10, 18, 21, 22, 28, 29
    see also wound ballistics test
        materials
Flood, Mr, 58, 59, 60, 67
FMC Corporation, 132, 133, 134
Ford Motor Company, 74
forests, destruction of, 55
fractures, indirect, 19
fragmentation, 87, 134, 154
    controlled, 37-8, 39, 49, 56-7, 82,
        85
    definition of, 33
    natural, 39-41, 58-60, 63-6
    of ICMs, 106
    of warhead, 58
        pre 38-9, 38
    tests, 64
    theory of, 66
fragmentation munitions, 88, 94, 137,
    142, 158
    accidental detonation of, 25, 29
    proposed banning of, 200
fragments, 6, 18, 56, 71, 73, 87, 112,
    120, 156, 176, 195
    deployment of, 56
    distribution area of, 25
    effect of, 3
    non-metallic, ban on, 6, 163
    non-spherical, 18
    size, 10, 27, 30, 35, 36, 37, 39, 40,
        55, 57, 66, 74, 150, 177
        reduction of, 34
    spherical, 16
    undetected by X-rays, 161
    velocities of, 15, 36, 39, 51, 64
    weight of, 50
    wounding by, 15
France, 53, 140, 159, 160, 177, 178,
    183, 197
    Army, 94
free fire zones, 55, 62, 73
French, Ralph, 13, 14, 152
Friends World Committee for
    Consultation, 149

fuel-air explosives, 8, 105, 187–8, 198, 199, 200
Fulbright, Senator, 89
fuzes, x, 58, 71–3, 76, 102–4, 134, 137, 199
  design of, 139
  delay, 145
  dual action, 102, 103
  failure rate of, 200
  impact, 71
  M216, 104
  M219, 103
  mechanical time, 67, 68, 71, 80, 103, 117
  proximity, 59, 71, 103
    costs of, 72
    M517, 137
  random delay, 178
    M218, 103

gangrene, 14
gas warfare, 115, 169
General Time Corporation, 133, 134
General Tire and Rubber Company, 134
Genetic engineering, 189
Geneva Convention (1864), xi
Geneva Conventions (1949), 165, 166
Geneva Protocol (1925), 6, 168, 169
genocide, 94, 137
germ warfare, banning of, 168
Germany, 82, 177, 178, 182, 183
  bombardment of Britain, 15
  incendiary bombs used against, 115
Gladeye dispenser, 115, 120
Goldsworthy, Major General, 83, 86
Goldwater, Senator Barry, 108, 109
grape munitions, 134
Greece, 183
Greenpeace International, 180, 196
Gregg, J.R., 33, 35, 36, 49
grenade launchers, 196
  30mm, 179
  40mm, 179
  AGS-17, 196
  M79, 57, 74
grenades, 75, 106, 114, 117
  30mm, 196
  40mm, 56, 57, 61, 74, 112, 125
    helicopter launched, 72
  DM-51, 177
  EMZ, 177

for helicopters, 75
  hand, 35, 85, 143, 177
    design of, 36
    effect of weight, 49
    M26, 37, 50, 51, 56, 74, 116, 177
    Mk II, 37, 38, 50, 177
    new generation of, 37
  HdGr 69, 177
  M36, 122
  M39, 122
  M40, 152
  M43, 122
  rifle, 177
Group of Governmental Experts, 185, 187
'guava' bombs, 87, 92, 100, 103, 105, 109, 134, 135, 152; see also BLU series bombs, cluster bombs
guerrillas, 54, 69, 81, 95, 99, 178, 195
  tactics for, 7
  tunnels used by, 55
Gulf war, 178, 179–81
  figures for munitions consumed in, 180, 196

Hague Convention (1899), xii, 164, 167
Hague Convention (1907), xii, 95, 164, 167
Hague Declaration (1899), 6, 47, 160, 192
Hague Peace Conference (1899), 169, 170
Hague Regulations (1907), 6, 43, 165, 173
hand weapons, 41
  Colt pistol, 45
Handicap International, 181, 182, 185
harassing fire, 73
harassment and interdiction fire, 55, 78, 112
Harvard University, 126
Harvey, E. Newton, 17
Harvey, Frank, 100
Hayes dispenser, 105, 122, 152
Hayes International Corporation, 105, 122
head, human, damage to, 19, 28
helicopters
  AH-1G, 76
  as weapon platforms, 56, 59, 60, 100

use of, 54, 57, 58
vulnerability of, 74
Henderson, Dr Oliver, 130, 139
Hexner, Lieutenant Colonel Peter E., 71
Hiroshima, bombing of, 32, 116
hit probability, 46
Ho Chi Minh, 53
Ho Chi Minh trail, 109, 110, 113
Honeywell Inc., 85, 94, 103, 121, 122, 136, 137, 141, 145, 188, 196, 199
    management's view of Vietnam war, 136
    Ordnance Division, 139
Honeywell Project, 137, 139, 140, 142
Hopkins, Captain James E.T., 25, 48
Horsley, Professor, 12, 13
Human Rights Watch, 182, 183, 184
human-sea troop charges, 39, 51, 55, 68, 69
humanitarian protection, 163–8
humanitarianism, 4, 11; see also law, international humanitarian
Humphrey, Hubert H., 135
hydrodynamics, 12

Improved Conventional Munitions (ICMs), 105–7, 153, 171
incapacitation
    criterion
        5-second, 36, 38, 49
        30-second, 36
        5-minute, 36
    immediate, 36
    probability of, 150
    rapid, 37
incendiary munitions, 82, 102, 115, 126, 133, 134, 158, 170, 173
    air-delivered, 162, 163
    proposed restrictions on, 6, 150, 160
indiscriminate weapons, 150;
    prohibition of, 6, 165–8
infantry, 61
    overrunning of positions, 42, 69
infection of wounds, see wounds, infection
inhumanity of weapons, 3
injuries, typology of, 23
Institute for Defense Analyses, 109
integrated political and military struggle, 53

interdiction fire, 73
International Committee of the Red Cross (ICRC), xi, xiv, 148, 163, 165, 166, 174, 185, 186, 187, 188, 189, 190, 191, 192, 200, 201
    Symposium on Anti-personnel Mines, 197
International Covenant on Civil and Political Rights, 175
International Harvester Company, 68, 79
International Symposium on Wound Ballistics, 192
International War Crimes Tribunal, 93, 95, 117
intestines, damage to, 19
Iran, 169, 195
Iraq, 168, 178, 181, 188, 197
    invasion of Kuwait, 168
    use of chemical weapons, 169
iron
    cast, 37, 39–41, 52, 58, 64, 177
        strained production capacity, 66
    ductile, 63
    gray, 40
    nodular graphite, 104
    pearlitic malleable, 40, 41, 58, 63, 64
iron foundries, 78, 79
Israel, 178, 183
Italy, 178, 183

Japan, 53, 68, 116, 126
    incendiary devices used against, 82, 162
jargon of arms industry, 5
JASON Division, 109, 123–4
Jews, killing of, xiii
Johns Hopkins University, 41, 60
Johnson, Admiral, 97
Johnson, Lyndon B., 53, 91, 119, 135
jungle warfare, 55, 56, 57, 68, 75, 104, 121, 134, 199
    casualties in, 25

Kaylor, Robert, 70
Keith, Arthur, 12
Kennedy, John F., 45, 60, 79, 81
Kenney, Brigadier General George, 82
Kent, R.H., 17
Khmer Rouge, 145
kill probability, 42, 43, 48, 194

killing zones, 39
kinetic energy, 20, 21, 33, 44, 191
Klare, Michael T., 77
Kneubuehl, Beat P., 191, 196
Korea, ruined by liberation, 32
Krepinevich, Andrew F., 62
Krepon, Michael, 97, 118, 119
Kurdistan, 181, 183
Kurds, 168

Laber, Jeri, 179
land, made unusable by land mines, 7,
    181
Landmines Campaign, 181–4, 188
Laos, 100, 120, 141, 145, 149, 181
    bombing of, 119
        figures for, 122
laser rangefinders, 186
laser weapons, xiv, 8, 185, 186–7, 198
    proposed banning of, 187
law
    international, 5, 98, 148–75, 198
        applicability of, 167
    international humanitarian, xi, xii,
        xiii, 163, 167, 168, 171, 194
    of war, 1, 5, 91, 95, 98, 169, 198
Le Thuy village, 120
lead balls, 27, 67
leaflet bombs, 85, 137
League of Nations, Covenant of, xii
Leahy, Patrick J., 176
lethal area, 2, 3, 195
lethality, 2, 23, 33, 39, 59, 67, 69, 98,
    106, 112, 119, 122, 134, 142, 193,
    194
lines of communication, 96, 118, 123
Lipscomb, Mr, 114

MacArthur, General Douglas, 30
machine guns, 31, 82, 196
    .30, 45
    .50, 45
    and infantry attacks, 51
machine warfare, 31, 32, 48, 55, 100
MacLeod, Norman A., 50, 51
magnesium bombs, 115, 116
magnus lift, 85
Mahon, Mr, 86
Manhattan Project, 124
manufacturing defects in munitions,
    114
marksmanship, improving of, 42

Martens, Fedor, 167
Martens clause, 167, 169
Martin Company, 45
Martin, Joseph I., 24
massive firepower
    characteristic of US troop
        movements, 30
    use of, 48, 112, 153
mathematics of wounding, 20–2
Matt, Mr, 58, 59, 67
McMillen, J. Howard, 33, 35, 36, 48, 49
McNamara, Robert S., 79, 94, 109, 120
McNaughton, John T., 108
Meacham, Stewart, 140
mean projected area, 25
Medical Laboratories Army Chemical
    Center, 35
medical science, and design of
    weapons, 11
Medico International, 182
Mexico, 149, 160, 162, 188
Mildren, General Frank T., 73
military necessity, xiv, 163–8, 184
Miller, Senator, 97
minefields
    anvil, 111
    clearing of, 187
    interdiction, 111
    location of, 160
    marking of, 155
    obstacle, 111
    recording of, 159, 161, 162
    retrograde, 111
mines, 114, 163
    aerial, 56, 81, 105, 107–11, 115, 162
        proposed ban on, 182
    antipersonnel, 2, 51, 107, 110, 150
        call to ban, ix, 4, 6, 8, 176
        moratorium on export from US,
            8, 183
        plastic, 7
        repeating, 134
    bamboo, 155
    campaign against, 181–4, 194;
        see also Landmines Campaign
    Claymore, 38–9, 51, 56, 85, 171
        development of, 50
        M18, 39
        M18A1, 39, 50
    directional, 155
    Dragontooth, 108, 111, 114, 122,
        179

as antipersonnel weapon, 108
gravel, 107, 109, 114, 123
    XM41E1, 111, 123
    XM65, 123
ground emplacement of, 111
indiscriminate use of, 173
laying of, 7, 8
made of plastic, 181
PFM-1, 179, 182
rehabilitation of victims, 8
scatterable, 110–11, 122, 123
    restrictions on use of, 160
self-destruct mechanism, 200
spider, 108
teabag, 107
training in clearance of, 183
unexploded, 183, 189
Wide Area Antipersonnel
    (WAAPM), 110, 124
Mines Advisory Group, 182
Ministry of Home Security (UK), 15,
    16
Minnesota, arms production in, 136
missiles, 174
characteristics of, 10, 11
Lance, 119
    bomblet warhead, 145
Tomahawk, warheads, 180
Misteye dispenser, 115
Mondale, Walter, 135
mortar shells
    60mm, 79
    81mm, 56, 79
mortars, 40
    60mm, 41, 52, 57
    design of, 40
Mozambique, 181, 183
Multiple Launch Rocket System
    (MLRS), 180
multiple rocket launchers, 196
munitions, homemade, 113, 114
munitions, various
    ADU-253 cluster adapter, 120
    JP 233 munition, 178, 180
    M117 bomb, 84
    WDU-4/A warhead, 76
muscle
    as target, 18
    damage to, 19
Mustin, Admiral Lloyd M., 98

Nagasaki, bombing of, 32, 116

Nam Dinh city, 88
Namchonjon, town, destroyed, 31
napalm, 62, 74, 77, 82, 98, 118, 127,
    151, 156, 157, 170
    bombs, 116
    campaign against, 131, 182
    cruelty of, 113
    'exclusively military' nature of, 130
    production of, 7
    wounds from, 127
National Center for Scientific Research
    (France), 93
National Liberation Front of South
    Vietnam, 54, 69, 113
    forces, 54, 67, 70, 73, 100, 114, 128
needle gun, 157
Neier, Aryeh, 184
nerve gas, 133
nerves, damage to, 19
Netherlands, 160, 177, 183
New York Workshop in Nonviolence,
    131, 132
Ngo Dinh Diem, 53, 54
    assassination of, 54
Nicaragua, 176, 183
nongovernmental organizations, ix, 185
    experience of, 182
North Atlantic Treaty Organization
    (NATO), 7, 36, 61, 149, 151, 192,
    193
North Vietnamese Commission for
    Investigation of the American
    Imperialists' War Crimes in
    Vietnam, 87
Norway, 149
notched steel wire, 37, 38, 57, 154,
    177, 195
Notley, Danny T., 142
nuclear weapons, xii, xiii, 8, 32, 116

O'Donnell, Major General Emmett,
    32
Olin company, 46
operations
    Cedar Falls, 74
    Flaming Dart I, 120
    Igloo White, 109, 110, 112
    Junction City, 70, 141
    Rolling Thunder, 83, 95, 96, 100,
        112, 118, 119, 120, 125
Operations Research Office (ORO), 41,
    60

organs, vital, damage to, 10, 14, 16, 19, 21, 33

pacifists, soldiers as, 5
Padeye bomb, 105
Palmer, Major Allan, 24
Paris Peace Agreement, 144
Parks, W. Hays, 118, 119
Pathet Lao, 100
Patton, George S., 48
Pentagon, 90, 100, 132
Pentagon Papers, 94, 95, 108, 109
Pepke, Major General Donn R., 110
Petersen, Joergen E., 92
photography of wounding, 16, 17, 18
Phu Xa village, 89, 90, 91
Phy Ly city, 88
Physicians for Human Rights, 182, 183
physics
    application of, 10
        to wounding, 22
Pillsbury, Charles A., 141, 142
'pin-point' bombing, 88
pine-board test, fallibility of, 79
'pineapple' bomb, see BLU-3
'pineapple' grenade, see grenade, hand, Mk II
Plain of Jars, 100, 119
plastics, use of
    in fragmentation bombs, 102, 108
    in mines, 7, 181
    in munitions, 161
poison gases, banning of, 6
poisoned weapons, xiii
    banning of, 6, 43
Poland, 178, 183
polystyrene, used in Napalm B, 127, 129, 130, 131
Pomona College, 131
pop-up munitions, 103, 105
Princeton Group, see Wound Ballistics Research Group
projects
    Agile, 77
    Balance, 41
    Doan Brook, 107, 116
    electronic battlefield, 108, 109, 110, 111, 122, 123, 124
    Salvo, 43, 45, 46
projected area, 21
projectiles, shape of, 15

Provisional Revolutionary Government of Vietnam, 149, 158
Proxmire, Senator William, 109, 110
psychological effect of munitions, 2, 43, 44, 46, 94
public conscience, role of, 7, 168–71

radar, use of, 71
radiological warfare, 117
Ragano, Colonel Frank P., 59
rapid incapacitation criteria, 35–7
recoil, 43, 44, 68, 70, 79
reconnaissance by fire, 100, 120
Redwood City Committee Against Napalm, 127–9
relief workers, and delayed exploding bombs, 89
Religious Society of Friends, 140, 149
Research and Experiments Department (UK), 15, 16
retardation of missile, 21
    by skin, 22
    coefficient, 21, 29
Rhodes, Mr, 83
Ridgway, Matthew B., 48
Riffaud, Madeleine, 87, 89
rifles, 68
    .22, 45
    5.45mm, 179
    5.56mm, 77, 192, 193
    57mm, 79
    7.62mm, 44, 192, 193
    90mm, 70
    AK-47, 152, 193
    AK-74, 3, 179
    AR-15, 74, 60, 61; see also rifles, M16
    Browning automatic, 45
    development of, 6
    flechette, 4, 44
    M1, 44
    M14, 44, 60
    M16, 60–1, 119, 152, 153, 179, 192
    ORO study, 41–4
    ranges of, 42
    reduction in caliber contested by US, 77
    uncertain accuracy of, 47
Rigby, Hugh, 12–13
rigor mortis, 14
RKO TV chain, 134

rocket assisted projectiles (RAP)
  105mm, 64
  155mm, 64
  M548, 78
rockets, 57
  2.75-inch, 52, 58–60, 63, 72, 76,
    112, 120, 134
    flechette filled, 155
  air-to-air, 58
  air-to-ground, 59, 61, 72
  consumption of, 59
  'Mighty Mouse', 58
  price of, 59
  warheads, 56, 178, 179
  Zuni, 72, 120
Rockeye cluster bomb, 101–2, 105, 116,
  121, 161
  I, 81
  II, 102, 104, 121, 180
rotation of projectile, 21
  effect of, 15, 16
Rubin, Barnett R., 179
Rusk, Dean, 93
Russell, Bertrand, 93
Russia, 178, 188
Rybeck, Bo, 157

Sadeye dispenser, 2, 81, 83, 85, 115,
  120, 137
Salisbury, Harrison, 89, 90, 91
Sarin gas, 115
Scovill Manufacturing Company, 135
search and destroy operations, 54
'Selected Ammunition,' 106
self-destruct feature for mines, 200
Sellier, Karl G., 191
Senate Committee on Armed Services,
  110
Seoul, recapture of, 31
Sharp, Admiral Ulysses G., 96, 97
shells
  105mm M44, 63, 122
  155mm M449, 122
    M692/M731, 123
  8-inch M404, 122
  artillery, 41, 56, 105
    flechette-filled, 47
    launching stresses of, 40
  high explosive, 106, 122
  inspection of, 40
  M453, 122
  mortar, 81mm, 63

shrapnel, 67
Shinn, Admiral, 101
shotgun rounds, 75
shrapnel, manufacture discontinued, 68
signaling cartridges, 57
Sikes, Mr, 101, 114
skin, damage to, 127
Skyshark series, 178
Slovak Republic, 183
small caliber weapons systems, 163
  proposed protocol, 190, 192, 193
smoke munitions, 59, 105
Snakeye munition, 81, 115
snipers, reaction to, 61
Somalia, 181, 183
South Africa, 178, 183
South Vietnam People's Liberation
  Armed Forces, 113
Spain, 178, 183
spark shadowgraphy, 16, 18, 28
Special Purpose Individual Weapon
  (SPIW), 45, 46, 157
spin added to bombs, 117
spin angular deceleration of fuzes, 139
Springfield Armory, 46
squeezebore ammunition, 43
St Petersburg Declaration, 164, 173,
  174, 188
Stanford University, 127
steel, 39, 41, 56
  AISI 06, 64
  AISI 1340, 79
  AISI 52100, 64, 78
  fragmentation of, 66
  HF-1, 64
  high boron alloy, 78
  high fragmentation, 63–6, 78, 79
  PR-2, 64
steel balls, 16, 18, 22, 28, 34, 39, 40,
  50, 51, 83, 85, 87, 89, 90, 91, 98,
  99, 116, 117, 119, 171, 177, 195
  as shrapnel, 2
  effect on body, 2
  penetration of, 21
  threshold energy of, 34
Stevens, Robert T., 32
Sting Ray munition, 79
Stockholm International Peace
  Research Institute (SIPRI), 73, 75,
  105, 106–7, 149, 177
Students for a Democratic Society
  (SDS), 131

Sudan, 149
Sullivan, William H., 120
superfluous injury, 6, 150, 164, 195
Superior Steel Ball Company, 85
surface-to-surface rockets, 179, 180
SUU series, *see* dispensers
Sweden, 7, 140, 156, 162, 182, 183,
    187, 188, 190, 198
    arms manufacture in, ix, 4
    attitudes to, 149–55
    humanitarianism in, 158
    interest in disarmament, 148
    military budget of, 158
    outrage over Vietnam war, 148
Switzerland, 149, 160, 183, 188, 192,
    193

Tactical Air Command, 136
tank guns, 64
    90mm, 70, 79
tanks, M48 Patton, 70
targets, 1, 3, 96, 126
    area, 153, 154, 156
    distribution of, 69, 150
    economic, 93
    exhaustion of, 112
    human, 42
    lack of, in Korea, 32
    lack of, in South Vietnam, 55
    military, 93
    of opportunity, 96, 118
    personnel, 137
    point, 52, 96, 153, 154
    political, 93
    psychosocial, 93
    types of, 72
    wide area, 96
Taylor, General Maxwell D., 81
Thimmesch, Nick, 195
Thompson, Reginald, 30, 31, 55
Tilford, Earl H., 96
tissues
    brain, damage to, 20
    human, damage to, 2, 4, 8, 10, 11,
        12, 13, 14, 16, 19, 20, 23, 61,
        150, 153, 186, 191
    water content of, 28
Tokyo, firebombing of, 116
Tompkins, John S., 39, 111
torture, 184
traumatic shock, secondary, 14
triethyl aluminum (TEA), 158

tripwires, 122
    used with mines, 39, 124
Truckenmiller, William C., 41, 63
Tuchman, Barbara, 169
tumbling of projectiles, 4, 8, 46, 47,
    52, 60, 61, 150, 151, 152, 179, 191,
    201
    flechettes, 152, 157
    proposed banning of, 149, 190

Union of Soviet Socialist Republics
    (USSR), 3, 119, 149, 178, 182, 196
    preparations to destroy, 81
United Kingdom (UK), 23, 33, 82, 90,
    116, 140, 149, 152, 155, 159, 160,
    170, 177, 178, 182, 183, 186
    research in, 15–17
United Nations (UN), 40, 183, 184
    landing in Korea, 30, 31
UN Disarmament Commission, 172
UN General Assembly, 165, 172;
    moratorium on traffic in
    antipersonnel mines, ix
underground shelters, in Vietnam,
    101
unexploded ordnance, 7, 8, 56, 98, 110,
    114, 180, 181, 183, 188, 200
    clearing of CBU-24 bomblets, 119
United Aircraft Corporation, 127
United States of America, 2, 4, 6, 7,
    23, 33, 36, 54, 149, 160, 170, 176,
    177, 179, 188
    accused of war crimes in Vietnam,
        93
    admission of Laos bombing, 101
    as weapons pioneers, 3
    bombing of North Vietnam, 83
    deliberate attacks on civilians in
        Vietnam, 89, 90
    refusal to join weapons working
        group, 148
    research into wound ballistics, 13
    Vietnamese hatred of, 55
    withdrawal from Indochina, 7,
        144–5
US Air Force, 3, 58, 81, 83, 85, 86, 94,
    104, 107, 108, 110, 111, 114, 123,
    130, 151
    Armament Laboratory, 84, 103
    Test Unit, 99
US Army, 10, 16, 22, 24, 25, 41, 42,
    43, 44, 53, 58, 68, 71, 81, 82, 105,

106, 138, 145, 177, 198
1st Cavalry Division, 62
25th Infantry Division, 70, 78, 80
4th Infantry Division, 110
Ballistic Research Laboratories
    (BRL), 35, 36, 37, 50, 65
Harry Diamond Laboratories, 71
Materials and Mechanics Research
    Center, 64
Materiel Command, 67, 107
Medical Corps, 17, 24, 35
Medical Department, 14
Ordnance Special Weapons-
    Ammunitions Command, 41
Project for Selected Ammunition,
    30, 116, 107
Surgeon General, 24, 26
US Far Eastern Air Force Bomber
    Command, 32
US Information Service, 90
US Marine Corps, 113
US Navy, 64, 81, 83, 101, 120, 138
    Ordnance Test Station (NOTS),
        115, 120
    Weapons Laboratory, 64
United Technology Center, 127
universities, protest movement in,
    141
unnecessary suffering, 6, 164, 172
Ut Duc, 113

velocity, 20, 30, 37, 60, 76, 152, 153
    bullet's loss of, 14
    impact, 29
    importance of, in wounding, 15, 16,
        27
    of flechettes, 151
Vietcong, see National Liberation Front
    of South Vietnam
Vietminh, 53
Vietnam Veterans of America
    Foundation, x, 182
Vietnam, North, 113, 149, 155, 171
    proposal to seal off from South,
        108
    see also bombing, of North
        Vietnam
Vietnam, South, 149
Vigier, Dr Jean-Pierre, 93
Vogt, General John W., 110
vulnerable projection area, 48
vulnerable regions, 49

war
    as irrational, 5
    definition of, 174
    elimination of, xii, 5
    law of, 172
    nature of, 7
wars
    Afghanistan, 3, 182
    Arab–Israeli, 4
    Cold, xii
    Gulf, 179–81, 188, 196
    Korean, x, 6, 7, 27, 30–52, 55, 68,
        81, 107, 111, 112, 153
    Laos, 110
    Spanish–American, 22
    Vietnam, x, 2, 3, 4, 7, 41, 44, 52,
        53–80, 81–125, 135, 148, 153,
        155, 157, 161, 163, 177, 178,
        179, 181, 188
        papal view of, 134
        vigils during, 129, 130
    World War I, ix, xiii, 22, 82, 169,
        196
    World War II, ix, xiii, 6, 10, 15–17,
        23, 33–4, 42, 44, 53, 68, 71, 72,
        79, 82, 96, 107, 126, 153, 154,
        162, 184
    World War III, 111
war crimes, 96, 141, 143
    responsibility for, 95, 139
War Witness International, 201
weapons bans, grounds for, 163–8
Westing, Professor Arthur H., 73
Weteye bomb, 115
Whirlpool Corporation, 68–9, 79
white phosphorus, 59, 62, 74, 76
Wide Area Antipersonnel Mine
    (WAAPM), 108, 124–5
Wilson, Louis B., 13, 14
women
    burned by napalm, 128
    casualties of cluster bombs, 93
    killing of, 138
Woodhill Country Club, protest at,
    142
Woodruff, Charles, 12, 13
wound ballistics, 55, 65, 152, 190
    as science, 6, 10–29
    importance of, in defense, 26
Wound Ballistics Research Group (US)
    (Princeton Group), 17–22, 26, 28,
    29, 33–4

wound ballistics test materials
    animals, 25
        anesthetized, 16
        carcasses, 13, 14
    bodily tissues, 22
    cadavers, 14
    cats, 28
        anesthetized, 18, 22
    cattle bladders, 13
    dogs, anesthetized, 18
    frogs' hearts, 28
    goats, 156
        anesthetized, 14
        not anesthetized, 49
    pigs, anesthetized, 14
    tomato cans, 13
    see also flesh simulants
wounding
    and ballistic tests, 159
    fatal or severe, 33–4, 36
    mathematics of, 20–2
    multiple, 151
wounds, 6, 67, 89
    5.56mm bullet, 159
    7.62mm bullet, 159
    caused by fragments, 150
    caused by rotating fragments, 15
    close-range, 77
    description of, 24
    effects of posture, 24
    entrance, 24, 25, 61

    exit, 24, 25, 61
    explosive, 6, 152
        study of, 11–15
    from M16 rifle, 152
    of flechettes, 46, 157
    from napalm, 127
    from small-caliber bullets, 159
    infection of, 2, 13
    narrow channel, 201
    paralyzing, 36, 38
    poisoning of, 76
    study of, 14, 22, 33
    treatment of victims, xiii, 26

X-rays
    in detecting shrapnel, 89, 109
    of target damage, 14
    of wounds, 24
    of wounding process, 18
    unable to detect plastic fragments,
        102

Y Ngo village, 88
Yarborough, Dr, 144
Yen Vuc village, 88
Yugoslavia, 149, 178, 181

zirconium, 121
    used as bomb liner, 102
Zuckerman, Lord (Solly), 15, 17, 23,
    24, 25, 28, 33, 44